COLUMBIA RIVER GORGE HIST~~ORY~~

VOLU

TAHLKIE BOOKS
Box 355, Skamania Rt.
Stevenson, Washington 98648

Other Books Published
TAHMAHNAW – The Bridge of the Gods
COLUMBIA RIVER GORGE HISTORY Volume One

TAHLKIE (Chinook Indian Jargon word for 'yesterday')
Cover Drawing of the first locomotive in the
Pacific Northwest by Dr. Albert W. Attwell.

COLUMBIA RIVER GORGE HISTORY

*   *   *   *   *

VOLUME ONE . . . starts with the early history of this area, the discovery of the great river of the first explorers, native Indians, fur traders, settlers, boat building and transportation around the Cascades.

*   *   *   *   *   *

This second book — VOLUME TWO — continues the history of the area into the 1900's. Little has been written of this area although it played an important part when the first settlers arrived. Building portages around the rapids as the Indians might say in Chinook Jargon words, "Oohut wake siah kopa tumwate." Path around the cascades.

This volume will try to show how the early pioneers gradually developed the gorge area, improving the portages and transportation through this area. Their Indian neighbors, white men settlers taking Indians wives, the primitive county government, wagon road building, steamboats and finally railroads. Because of limited space, many names and stories of early pioneers must be left out for future volumes.

THE COLUMBIA RIVER

The Great River of the West as it was called before the first white explorers ever touched its shores, received many various names: The Ouragon, The Ourigan, The Origon, The Oregon, River of Aguilar, River de los Estrecha, River St. Roc, River Thegayo, Enseneda de Heceta, and The Columbia River after Captain Gray's ship the "Columbia".

Much has been written of the first white explorers on reaching the Columbia River--Captain Gray, Lieutenant W.R. Broughton, Lewis & Clark and David Thompson, but little has been written of the red-haired white man whom the early explorers found living here with the Indians when they first arrived.

Broughton was the first white explorer to leave any record of the Columbia, upriver from its mouth. On receiving word of Captain Gray's discovery of the river and Great Britain's desire to claim the new discovery, Lt. Broughton on Oct. 30, 1792, sailed over the bar on a moonlit night and entered the Great River of the West. With His Majesty's Ship "Chatham" safely anchored, a cutter was launched bearing Lt. Broughton and his sailor-men and they cruised up the river as far as the Washougaly River, planting British flags along the way and sighting Mt Hood and naming it for an English Admiral.

Broughton found the Indians hospitable, and a surprise in meeting a white man with red hair living with the Indians at Neer-chee-ki-oo village. The red-haired white man was chief of these Indians and his name was Soto. Chief Soto ordered his braves to bring fresh salmon and prepare a feast for Broughton and his tars on what is now known as Lady Island and owned by the Crown-Zellerback paper company. Broughton named this island Johnson Island after another Englishman--how much nicer if he had called it Soto Island.

Thirteen years later Lewis & Clark briefly mention meeting Soto with his friendly attitude. Gabriel Franchere, one of Astor's fur traders who came to the mouth of the Columbia River in 1811, tells in his narrative of a trip up the river in May, shortly after his arrival.

"Just below the Cascades, we found here an old blind man, who gave us a cordial reception. Our guide said that he was a white man, and that his name was Soto. We learned from the mouth of the man himself, that he was the son of a Spaniard who with a crew had been ship wrecked at the mouth of the river; part of the crew including Soto had gotten ashore but all were massacred by the Clatsops, with the exception of four who were spared. The men married native women but soon became disgusted with savage life and left hoping to reach a settlement of Spanish people towards the south. Soto never heard of his father or the other men since. He was quite young at the time so was left with the Indians."

Chief Soto lived his later years near Beacon Rock and at Cascade Locks. It is not known where or when he died. Had he lived a little longer, more history might have been left for us by him.

The white men were now coming to stay in the Columbia River Valley. Ways of life of the Indian were to change with the encroachment of the paleface.

ANCIENT CIVILIZATION COULD NOT SURVIVE

Some accepted scientists believe that early man on this continent learned their first lessons in culture in the valley of the Columbia. Enough of their remains have been unearthed to indicate that these early people were hunters living on fish, game, roots and berries; that they made mats, wove cloth from the hair of the mountain goat, wore sandals instead of moccasins, smoked pipes, wore ornaments of claws and sea-shells, used ear and lip plugs like the African Negroes, painted their bodies, wore leather headdresses and used spears and bows and arrows. They cremated their dead, used a cuneiform "writing" and built pit houses like those now found in the Mayan cities.

In fact, Hugh Matier contends that the Egyptians may have descended or learned cultures from the Columbia River early inhabitants. They flattened the heads of their children as the Columbians did for centuries before them. They practiced slavery and human sacrifice, cremation and carving in stone in the same pattern as the early Chinooks had done centuries before.

"The valley of the Columbia, in brief, may well have been the cradle of culture for two continents, if recent evidence is confirmed in subsequent study."

How much of this ancient civilization survived after the earth trembled, the Cascade Mountains smoked and lava flowed to cover the hardwood forests of eastern Washington and Oregon and leave a fertile ash on the valley floors can only be estimated. Yet there seems ample support for the claim that a healthy and intelligent remnant survived from which stemmed the Chinookan Indian linguistic group. These were the "canoe" Indians who ranged from the Columbia River's mouth to the foothills dividing their hunting grounds from the haughty Klickitat and Yakima nations who traveled and warred on the backs of ponies.

While under the reigning wing of the tyee big Chinookan chief, the Columbia River Indians separated into many small nations and were variously named, much as Americans are divided into counties and states. Many had their own language but all used the universal Chinookan 'jargon language' between the nations The aggregate of these small nations of Indians formed a great nation long before the covered wagons rumbled over the prairies and crawled through the mountain passes to finally rest their oxen on the Columbia River Valley.

Once these Indians numbered upwards of 80,000, until smallpox and measles all but wiped out the race. It has been said that the white traders brought these plagues, but much evidence shows that smallpox could have been contracted from slaves taken by the Chinooks on their forays north up the coast towards Cape Flattery. For the early English explorer, Captain Vancouver, found the Clallam Indians pock-marked and at a low ebb of health, and there were Indians of the early days who told of the Ozette tribe being wiped out with smallpox before the white man arrived.

The Columbia River Indians built cedar shake homes, well roofed against the wet climate. Some of these homes could be considered apartment houses, sixty feet wide and several hundred feet long. Many families lived in these houses only separated by flimsy walls.

The first white settlers had Indians as neighbors. Most of these local Indians were friendly and good neighbors to live near. One of the early pioneers tells us of his Indian playmates, and the older Indians of the Cascades.

CASCADE INDIANS

(As told by James Fremont (Monty) Attwell, the first male white child born in Hood River County. His mother always called her four boys by the middle name. Charles Edwin was Eddy, Cassius Marcellus was Celly, James Fremont was Fremont (Monty) and John Wilbur was Wilbur.)

"I was born at Cascades (now Cascade Locks) on Jan. 5, 1855. My father, Roger G. Attwell, took out a donation land claim there in 1853.

"Three hundred Indians remained living on the claim; they were there when he filed on the claim of 320 acres, so were welcome to remain. As a boy, my playmates were Indian children. The older Indians almost considered me another Indian boy. I was often invited into their homes. Adult Indians loved their children and allowed them to do as they pleased from the time they could walk until they were teenagers. Swim, run and play, with little work and no school. The girls had no dishes to do or tables to set.

"These Indians were known as 'flat heads'. No sooner than the child is born, whether male or female, its head is put under a press or mold of boards in order to flatten it, from the eyebrows backward to the crown, while the baby's bones are still soft. The board is hinged behind the baby's head and tied down over its forehead with the necessary pressure to cause the forehead to be flattened, causing the head to be formed into a wedge shape, and the more acute the angle, the greater the beauty. The flatness of the head is considered the distinguishing mark of being born free. All slaves were forbidden to bear this aristocratic distinction.

"Their dress invariably consisted of a loose garment, made of the skins of wood-rats or deer hide neatly sewed for winter wear; nothing but a Gee string when hunting or fishing in warmer weather. While hunting they would never wear coat, leggings or moccasins, nothing to brush against the brush, leaving the noise of a swish to frighten the hunted.

"The Indian hunter wore few things except maybe a decoy hat, sometimes a bird or animal. One time on a hunting trip after ducks, I was creeping through the high ferns with my shotgun, a double barreled 10 gauge, trying to get close enough for a shot at some ducks on a small lake. When I reached fair range, I raised the gun to my shoulder taking aim when another duck raised up between me and the lake. If I had pulled the trigger at that instant, I would have blown the top of the Indian's head off. He was wearing a duck decoy hat and was creeping up on the ducks with his bow and arrows. I lowered my gun and left the ducks to the Indian.

"The Indian women, besides a skin blanket, wore a petticoat suspended from the waist down to the knee; this is made of the inner rind of the cedar bark and hangs loosely down in strings, and keeps flapping and twisting about with every motion of the body, giving them a waddle or cuck walk. It never screened nature from prying eyes, yet it was remarkably convenient on many occasions.

6

"They sit around the fire to eat and when through, just set the dishes on the dirt floor, where they are washed with a dog's tongue. They didn't have many iron pots at this time, so they would take a wooden bowl or a water tight woven basket (opekwan) and fill it half full of water and then place a piece of salmon in the water. They would have stones laying in the fire keeping hot; they would pick a red hot (hyas waum) stone from the fire with wooden tongs and drop the stone into the water, which started boiling instantly. After a few minutes the stone would be removed and another hyas waum stone dropped into the water to continue the cooking. Sometimes a herb or a wapatoe was added with the meat and then the ashes and smoke on the stones helped flavor the stew. It always tasted very good. The salmon's head was always cooked, making excellent soup.

"Smoke was always thick from the open fires with no chimneys but they did not seem to mind. Meat was hanging from the ceiling being smoked and cured. The Indian women would cook their meals around these fires and often be singing while doing it. They were always busy, cutting up the meat, tanning the hides, making baskets or bead work.

"The medicine man or woman was more important to them than medicines. They could not run to the drugstore for something to relieve a stomach ache, or a pill to cure a cold. The medicine man would be called with his or her magic movements to corner the evil spirit and snatch it from the patient's body and drown it in a pan of water, or quickly throw it into the fire nearby. The patient should then soon recover...however, if he or she should die, then it might be serious for the medicine person. The deceased victim's relatives might execute the doctor

7

right there; it was a perilous profession. However, in a healthy camp the medicine man or woman lived 'high on the hog'.

"Something the white woman never learned, was the exercise movement over a log that would bring the menstruation period on in a few minutes, thus controlling pregnancy.

"White man has copied some of their nature remedies like 'Chittum Bark' (cascara sagrada), a purgative medicine obtained from the bark of an American tree.

"One of their treatments for many ills did not work well for measles and smallpox. Hazel brush bows were cut and used to form a small igloo shaped hut and this framework was covered with skins and blankets. Then stones were heated as hot as could be handled and placed inside the hut, then the patient was put into the hut with the hot stones and must remain inside until half cooked with sweat oozing from every pore. If unable to walk they might be carried, but if able to go on their own, come from the hot Turkish sweathouse and plunge or be plunged into ice cold water. This either cured or killed the patient. With smallpox, measles and a few other infections, it was sure death.

"In a way these people were the richest people in North America. Not rich in gold and silver If they had been able to dig these metals from the mountains as the White man did, the Indians would have thought of them as another ornament, like bear claws, eagle's talons or sea shells. Wealth to them was something to wear or eat.

"The Columbia River abounded in fish which was their favorite food In a few months the families could get enough food to last them all year. They smoked and dried the salmon, picked and dried berries, acorns and different roots. The balance of their time was given to art, war, ceremonies and feasting.

"The Indian man was known by the White man as a 'buck', the Indian himself often called himself a Siwash, happy if you called him a 'skookum siwash', they always called Indian Agent Wilbur, 'siwash tyee' (Indian boss). The 'buck's' wife or wives were called squaw or squaws, much as the whites called their adult females woman or women. In Jargon they were called 'Klootch-man", or sometimes 'Siwash klootchman' to separate them from a paleface 'klootchman'.

"The Flatheads did have a few slaves; Chief Chen o wuth had two female slaves which he had purchased from other tribes. The Cascade Flatheads did not have many slaves. These Indians did not rove over the country like the Snake and Cayuse warriors did. The Snakes in large bands would occasionally foray into Southeastern Oregon and over power and capture fishing or hunting parties of Klamaths, Watwashes or Modocs, killing the men and taking the young women and children captives and selling some of them to other tribes. And truly they were slaves, owned body and soul by their masters. The slaves were required to do all the hardest work. The buck would go to the rapids with his dip net and spear and catch a few salmon or sturgeon and leave them there when he came home, then his squaws would go down to the river and get the salmon and carry them home and prepare them. The buck would go into the mountains and kill a deer and then come home and send his squaws into the mountains to bring it home.

"An Indian boy of fifteen is considered a man; he is expected to hunt, fish and go to war. He must start saving values to buy a wife, which might take him several years. A wife must be bought from the father. The beautiful young girls brought the best price. Often an older buck would have more to offer so he would out bid the younger buck for a beautiful wife and the young buck might end up with a not so pretty wife and old enough to be his mother. A good provider might buy several wives, often sisters, as they could ge' along better under the same roof.

"The Indians kept no writt ﹒ history but did pass stories down through generation after generation. Stories like TAHMAHNAW, The Bridge of the Gods, the mountain bridge across the Columbia River. 'When the earth was young, this great mountain blocked the river's passage to the ocean and salmon could not go up it to spawn and feed the Indians, so the big tyee salmon of all the salmon ordered all the salmon to pick up a rock in their mouth and swim against the mountain; each time they did this a small piece of rock was broken from the mountain. Millions of piercing blows finally wore a passage under the mountain and the river poured through enlarging the hole, joining the backwater of the ocean. Salmon then swam under the mountain and was food for the Indians along the river. The Indians could also go under this mountain bridge in their canoes and their papa's papa walked across the mountain bridge.'

"They also had a story of the origin of the Indians. 'Long, long ago, when the sun was young and no bigger than a star, there was an island far off in the middle of the Pacific Ocean. This island was inhabited by people much lighter in color than they, and this island was ruled by a tall, strong, light colored woman called Socomalt. She was a good woman but had problems with some of the people being wicked. Their conduct so enraged her that she had all the wicked ones driven to one end of the island and then cut off this portion of the island where they were and sent it adrift into the waves and the wind. They floated away into the ocean, and being too wicked to work, soon starved and all died but one man and one woman. These two were not so wicked or lazy so they made a canoe and left the sinking island, paddling for days and nights until finding this land.

'"This man and woman were light skinned like their forefathers but they suffered so much from the exposure to the sun and the spray of the salt water on their naked bodies while on their search for the new land that they became brown skinned and have retained that color ever since. From this man and woman all the Indians of America have their origin; and as punishment for their wickedness, they were condemned by Socomalt to poverty and nakedness and to be called Siwashes.'

"My father and mother always spoke well of Chief Chen o wuth and always told of how wrongly he was put to death by Col. Steptoe. At the time, the Yakima and Klikitat Indians attacked the North Bank Cascades, Colonel Steptoe, with very poor judgement, upon learning from his scouts that the warring Indians were having a feast and celebration on beef they were cooking over open fires. Instead of having his troops surround the warriors, he ordered the bugle blown; at the sound of the bugle the warriors vanished into the brush like deer and not a single enemy was captured or seen again. Lt. Sheridan captured a few older local Indians whom the settlers had always found friendly; one of these was Chief Chen o wuth. The army officers, using their own method to prove guilt, and needing scapegoats after allowing the real enemy to escape, hung a few friendly local Indians.

"The Indians loved to gamble and play games. They did not need to worry over paying taxes, the value of stocks and bonds, or how the elected officials were doing in Washington, D.C. The men were big gamblers at heart. When visiting Indians came from the coast or east of the mountains and camped nearby, it wouldn't be long until Chall chall or similar games were in progress. I have often watched but never joined into the games of chance. When I was a boy of 12, Chief Trujons (often called True Johns) asked Celly, my older half brother, to take him across the river in a rowboat. Celly invited me along. We landed on the north bank just above the chutes and walked down around Bradford's Landing to the small lake later known as Icehouse Lake. Here on the meadow alongside the lake were hundreds of Indians camped. This lake is at the north end of the man-made Bridge of the Gods, and before the railroad and highway came through there was a nice meadow alongside of the lake.

"The Chief joined the other chiefs there and Celly went around sticking his head in each tent or tepee until he found the one he wanted and went in and soon a young buck came running out with Celly hitting him over the head with his own shoes. Celly stayed in the tent; this left me alone with strangers but I soon made friends and played with the Indian kids. When the kids stopped to eat, I was fed with them.

"Great games of gambling were in progress so I might tell a little about one of these games. Several groups were in separate places with much noise going on. The players sit opposite each other, usually three on a side; sometimes they sit cross-legged and other times they kneel facing each other, three on a side. Each side has a number of small sticks stuck in the ground for keeping score and the players have two small polished bones like beaver teeth. When all is ready and the stakes or prizes are put up, a song is struck up with the pounding of sticks on a piece of wood, sort of keeping time; this not only makes more excitement but also adds to the confusion. One side starts passing the small bones from one fist to another with great speed, nimbly crossing and recrossing arms. The players muffle their wrists, fists and fingers with bits of fur or leather in order the better to elude and deceive their opponents. The quickness of the motions and the muffling of the fists make it almost impossible for his opponents to guess which hand holds the bones, which is the main point of the game. While the player is doing all this maneuvering, his opponent eagerly watches his motions, trying to discover which fist contains the bone. He points with lightning speed at the fist he thinks the bone is in, the player at the same time extends his arm and opens the fist;

if it is empty the player draws his arm back and continues, while the guesser must forfeit one of his ten score sticks. If the guesser hits upon the fist that contains the bone, the player must give the guesser one of his ten sticks and cease playing while the opponent trys his hand at juggling the bone from fist to fist. When one side wins all ten sticks of his opponent, the game is over.

"Before another game starts the winner collects his winnings, which could be blankets, horses, canoes, slaves, or even wives. Wealthy losers often come out without even their clothes, losing everything; the gambling fever had such a hold on them. Just before sunset, Chief Trujons asked me where Celly was and I pointed out the tent, so he walked over and called Celly and we three walked back to the boat and crossed the river home.

"The local Indians used the Chinook Jargon to communicate with the settlers. It was a universal language between all the river Indians. One tribe only a few miles from another tribe would find their native tongues so different that they would have trouble understanding each other, so Jargon was the universal language between them. The Indian's native tongue is very difficult to speak as it has guttural sounds that a white man has trouble with. I learned this native language but was never able to get the right throat action into it.

"Chinook Jargon is simple to learn and the early settlers soon learned it. Counting in Jargon as an example is: ikt = 1; mokst = 2; klone = 3; lokit = 4; kwinnim = 5; taghum = 6; sinamoxt = 7; stotekin = 8; kweest = 9; tahtlum = 10. To count above 10 was to use a combination, 11 would be ikt ikt; 12 = ikt moskt and so on. Meeting an Indian with a greeting like 'How do you do,' would be, 'Cla hyum,' here in the gorge but 'Cla howya', on the coast. If you were to greet a male friend it would be, 'Cla hyum sikhs'.

"Many jokes were told on the newcomer, like the following. 'The new pioneer on meeting the Indian woman with two fine salmon, offered to buy them by laying down 50 cents and pointing to the salmon. The Indian woman smiled and said, 'Sitkum dolla hyas close.' (One half dollar, alright, yes.) The newcomer: 'Sixteen dollars and all my clothes? No deal, but I will give you two dollars and my undershirt.'

"The Indians had their own religion. They believed in a future life and a happy hunting ground. When they died, their belongings were placed alongside of them at their burial so that they would have them over the Great Divide. A wicked Indian would not be taken to this happy hunting ground, so this kept the Indians on the correct path.

12

"When a local Indian died there was much mourning and grieving. Under no circumstances would anyone remain in the house or tent where one had died, as the evil spirit that had caused the death goes into the ground and would enter the person who foolishly remained where the death occurred. The body would be wrapped in that person's best clothes and all is rolled up in a new blanket. In a few days the wrapped body is placed on a board and placed in a canoe and several men take it out to one of the 'Memaloose Islands'. Here on a scaffold several feet above the ground would be the final resting place for the deceased, and alongside the body would be placed all the dead Indian's belongings. If a man, his canoe, bows and arrows, scalps and blankets; if a woman, her beads, blankets, pots, pans and jewelry. These were left with the deceased to go with them over the Great Divide. No Indian would ever take a thing from a burial site, but when the white man came, some of the very lowest type of relic hunters robbed many of these sacred burial sites. Tomahawks, axes, bows and arrors, beads of many sorts and other treasures, and often the Indian's bones were taken.

"There was a large memaloose island just above Hood River. If no island was near, high scaffolds were built and often dead houses were constructed so as to keep wild animals from bothering the memaloose tilukum. Sometimes new blankets were put around the corpse as the old one rotted away.

"If a mother was to die during childbirth or while the baby was only a few days old, the baby might be rolled up in the blanket with the mother so that they could go to the Great Beyond together. These people loved their children and often took orphan children to raise as their own, but a baby so small and young could not live without its mother's milk as it could not eat acorns or dried salmon or roots and would soon die without its mother. Chinook Jargon for their burial site is Memaloose Illahee, meaning dead, and earth or island. Large Memaloose Island is above Hood River opposite Lyle. Small Memaloose Island was at the head of the rapids.

"It is not known how long ago it became the custom to bury the memaloose as they did, but the old Indians said their 'papa yaka papa' and 'mama yaka mama' were buried this way. Sometimes as many as 50 canoes, filled with Indians attired in their beaded finery and plumed war bonnets, would accompany the 'hearse' or dead Indian canoe to the burial on Large Memaloose but at the Little Memaloose Island where the water was so swift at the very head of the rapids, only the best paddlers delivered the memaloose while the waiting mourners remained ashore, beating their tom-toms.

13

"At first the dead wrapped in their blankets were placed on the ground on these islands, but after the white settlers built sawmills and lumber became available, they often built platforms and placed the dead on these to keep them off the cold ground.

"Perhaps the last burial on little Memaloose Island was for Princess Virginia Miller about 1927. When she was 16 she married a white man and lived in Skamania County for 80 years. She had asked to be buried there and later her faithful friends removed her body before the back water of Bonneville Dam covered the island a few years later. Instead of being wrapped in beaded buckskin finery, she was clad in a silk dress and wrapped in a Persian shawl, a valued heirloom of her father's people. The shawl was brought from Asia in a sailing vessel by traders who exchanged it with the Indians for furs.

"The Indians used to catch mammoth sturgeon at the rapids, often 6 and 7 hundred pounds each. After they were able to secure steel hooks from white traders, a large sturgeon hook 3 inches across would be secured to a wooden thimble; this thimble was fitted on a 20 foot pole so that it would come loose with a hard pull. A rope was secured to this thimble. The Indian would lower the hook on the pole down into the water below a large rock, keeping the hook near the bottom so as to be under the fish. The fish are not disturbed with anything touching them underneath, while touching them on top will frighten them into flight. Leave the hook turned down and then coming up under the fish's stomach, one can feel the fish with the end of the pole and determine its size and length. If it is a large sturgeon and you hook it just behind the head you will have a tug of war, so to place the fish at a disadvantage and have less trouble landing him, sock the hook in near his tail. When you decide where to hook the fish, turn the hook upward and sock the hook into it, and now the ingenious device shows its merit. The thimble with the hook is jerked free of the pole which is tossed onto the bank; the fish now has a large hook socked into him with a rope secured to it. If it is just a thirty pound salmon, it is shortly hauled out on the bank, but if it is a 700 pound sturgeon you had better have help or the rope tied to a tree. I have caught many fish this way myself and have often massaged a fish's belly with the pole which they seem to enjoy until the hook is socked into them.

"Indians from east of the mountains would join the local Indians at the huckleberry fields south of Mt. Adams. Many different tribes would camp near each other at these fields. Horse races and gambling were at their best. One tribe would bring their best horse to race another tribe's best horse. The races were much like the white man's races at an early fair. One chief would enter his best horse and another chief would bring his greatest horse. Bets were wagered and at a signal, the two fast horses were off.

"There were always a few young bucks along the sidelines with their own horses, and after the champions passed, they would take off after them but were soon left far behind. Between the races the famous wild huckleberry was picked. Cedar trees were stripped of their bark for making baskets to bring the berries home in aboard the horses.

"In the early days when we went to the huckleberry fields and camped near the Indians, we always hired an Indian boy to care for our horses. He would be delighted to do this for 25 cents a day. If you staked the horses out yourself the visiting Indians from Yakima or some other place would steal them before morning, but they would not steal them from another Indian.

"While walking by an Indian tent near ours, I noticed that they were cooking venison. An old squaw was sitting in front of the tent, so I spoke to her in Chinook Jargon and she answered me. I asked her if they had any extra venison that we could buy and she only laughed. Just after dark a hand slipped under the side of our tent and left a package and when we unwrapped it, we found it to be venison. So we wrapped two loaves of bread and took them over to their tent and slipped them under the side of their tent.

"The Indians on both sides of the gorge were peaceful during my youth. The Yakimas caused the only trouble here to speak of, in Mar. of 1856. Three blockhouse forts were built at the rapids on the north bank but none on the south bank. My father, who was one of the first settlers here, never carried a gun or wore a side arm. One time I did see the Indians all stirred up. It was caused by other Indians and not the whites. This was in the 1860's at where Cascade Locks is now. The warriors were painted in their war paint and armed for battle. I joined the Indian kids my age and watched from the sidelines. Several warriors danced through the fires and one warrior cut pieces of flesh from his own breast and roasted them in the fire and ate them, showing how ready he was to meet the enemy. In a few days all was peaceful again so some settlement had been made.

"Their war garments of elk skin, dressed and worked to a thickness of $\frac{1}{2}$ inch, is arrow proof. Their implements of war at this time were guns, bows and arrows, knife and tomahawk. A Flathead Indian armed cap-a-pie is a most unsightly and hideous looking being with his war paint added.

"The Indian's bow was usually made of yew wood and finely tapered giving it great spring action. It was not a long bow like the paleface makes for himself today. It was short so that it was easily carried through the brush; bear sinew from a bear's muscle

15

was glued on the back, making it strong as steel. The arrow shafts were of arrow wood and tipped with the proper arrow head or point. Small ones for birds or squirrels and larger ones for deer, wolves or bear. These were secured to the arrow shaft so when the arrow was pulled from the game the head would remain on the shaft and be retrieved. However, for killing a man, the arrow head would not be secured to the shaft, so when the victim or his companions pulled the arrow shaft out, the poisoned arrow head remained in the victim. If possible, it was best when receiving the arrow to leave the shaft in the head and push it on through the flesh until the head was exposed and removed as soon as possible.

The arrows are neatly made with feathers secured to the tail end for guiding them straight as an arrow.

"They were excellent river men from boyhood. They made small gad-about canoes for hunting and fishing near camp and for the young to learn and practice paddling, and they gouged and burned out large war canoes from cedar logs.

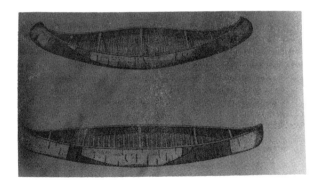

"The Cascade Indians did not have many horses like the Indians east of the mountains, but they had a few. I have often watched them break a horse to ride. They rode bareback and did not have saddles until the white man brought them. It is near impossible to

16

stick aboard a wild horse without a bridle and saddle so they over came this by blindfolding the horse until the young buck was aboard, then a couple of bucks would tie his feet together under the horse's belly and the horse was unblindfolded and turned loose. The wild horse could not throw the rider and as long as it didn't go completely over backward the young buck survived and the horse wore itself down. The young buck might be bleeding from his nose and ears but he had won the match.

"Chief Banaha of the north bank tribes was always friendly with the settlers and always liked me as a boy. He would often come over to the south bank and visit with the Indians there, and nearly always stop at our home. Mother always gave him hot bread with prune jam which he loved. Before the white man settled on the north bank of the rapids, the area was known as Wa Banaha Village.

Early Roads and Trails
As Told By J. F. McCoy

(Ref: John McCoy...Compiled by Mrs. R. W. Van Valin.)

They arrived at The Dalles of the Columbia River the first of November 1845. Here, greatly to the surprise and delight of the company, John McCoy opened a chest containing a complete kit of carpenter tools, consisting of a broad-axe, augers, saws and so forth necessary for the work, and superintended the building of a flat boat of sufficient capacity in which to bring his family and that of Dr. Maley and their effects down the Columbia to the Cascades.

This lumber from which this boat was built was whip-sawed by the emigrants from timber brought in from the foothills of the Cascade Mountains. After the boat was completed, the wheels were taken off the wagons and placed in the bottom of the boat and the running gears and beds placed on top. A steering bar on the stern and 2 oars, one at each side near the bow, were provided with which to, in some measure, control the movement of the boat. In this way they came down to the Cascades, carried most of the way by the current of the stream. It was on this voyage that the submerged forests were seen standing upright in the bottom of the river.

At the Cascades a portage of some five miles had to be made before the open river to the end of their journey could be reached. On their arrival at the upper end of the portage, the boat was unloaded and the wagons set up. The road around this obstruction being on the north side, oxen with which to draw the wagons were brought across for the purpose. After the wagons were hauled around to a point below the rapids; the animals were taken back and again crossed over to the south side and brought down with the stock. Our provisions running low, an animal was brought across and slaughtered.

The trail over which the stock was brought was cut out by Dr. Whitman and the emigration of the year previous. Up to that time a dim trail, rarely used even by the Indians, was all there was. It was afterwards called the Shell Rock Trail and most of its way lay close to the river.

The empty boats above the Cascades were turned loose and on their own accord run over the rapids. Some of them survived the trip and were caught and used again, while others were broken up on the rocks by the violence of the current and the crookedness of the channel. John McCoy's boat struck a slanting rock, the bow ran up out of the water while the after part sank below the surface, the swift current pinning it fast to the rock. For a good round price he secured the services of an Indian with a canoe, and at the risk of their lives, succeeded in reaching the rock on which it was lodged, but the current proved so strong that their united efforts could not avail, and it was necessarily abandoned. They secured the services of a Hudson Bay Co. bateaux in which Dr. Maley with the two families embarked and continued their journey while John McCoy returned to the stock and assisted in bringing them down the trail.

The boat proceeded down the Columbia River with its precious cargo, past Vancouver, to Oregon City. Here they waited the coming of the stock and men with it. After a fortnight or so had passed with no news from the stock, no little uneasiness was felt by the two families. On the 20th of November the stock reached the Wallamet at a point called Linnton, some six more miles from its mouth. Here they crossed over to the west side of the river. They then took their way up through timber past what is now Portland, out onto the Tualitan Plains near the present site of Forest Grove where they settled.

CASCADES--NORTH BANK OF RIVER

This little settlement was first established while it was still in Oregon Territory. It was the landing place in portaging around the impassible rapids. In 1851 the mail route, established in 1850 from Independence, Mo. to Salt Lake City, was extended to The Dalles.

In Mar. 1851, proposals for carrying mail from Columbia City (Vancouver) once a week from 6 a.m. Mondays, the 30 miles to Cascades and back again the following day. In the same proposal was for delivering mail with celerity, certainty and security at 6 a.m. on Tuesday from Cascades to The Dalles, 35 miles and back again the following Monday. Chenoweth's bid was accepted. The mail to be delivered by boat, probably a canoe. For over 13 years this was the only post office in Skamania County.

Cascade Post Office established Nov. 5, 1851, Francis A. Chenoweth; Sept. 6, 1852, Daniel F. Bradford. Mar. 1853, Congress created Washington Territory from Oregon Territory. The W.T. first legislature created Skamania County so Cascades became the only town in Skamania County. Sept. 3, 1853, Isaac H. Bush became postmaster; May 18, 1855, Daniel Bradford; Sept. 8, 1862, Isaac Bush; Oct. 21, 1863, Samuel Hamilton; Mar. 7, 1887, John Andrews; June 2, 1893, Mrs. Ida E. Jones; Mar. 6, 1894, Miss Minnie Jones; Dec. 4, 1895, Mrs. Minnie Stevenson (Mrs. Momen Stevenson); name to Moffett Springs, April 16, 1907.

The rapids or cascades being a natural obstruction which stopped all boats from passing, canoes and bateaux had to be unloaded and everything they contained carried around the rapids. Frances Chenoweth, after watching party after party toil, carrying their precious belongings, over two miles of slippery, muddy portage, decided there should be a better way, so he constructed two miles of the Northwest's first railway, wood rails with a small, four wheel flat car pulled with an old faithful mule in 1851.

Bradford brothers bought the portage from Chenoweth two years later, doubled the charge for handling freight over the line and added another car and another mule. Dan Bradford filed on the land grant at the upper end of the portage and remained in charge while his wife and his brother remained in Boston. The portage was a big money maker and dissatisfaction grew along the river at the exorbitant charges for the short portage. Gold mines discovered in eastern Washington and Oregon gave a vast increase in business over the portage. High prices bring competition where big money can be made.

Joseph Ruckel and the Oregon Portage

Early in the spring of 1855, Joseph Ruckel moved to Oregon, taking a homestead on the south bank of the Columbia River, east of the mouth of Eagle Creek. He built his home at the place known as the "Middle Cascades" but his land extended farther east and was partly located in Wasco County. He was not a wealthy man but he possessed some means, good business ability and an abundance of energy and perseverance.

Soon after Ruckel had secured his land, Harrison Olmstead took a claim joining him on the west side and extending one mile farther down the south bank of the Columbia River. This land included the mouth of Eagel Creek and Tooth Rock, but did not include the site of Bonneville, which was owned by John C. Tanner.

Ruckel worked quite rapidly. He and Olmstead formed a partnership. The steamer "Fashion", formerly used by Bradfords, had been sold by them to J. C. E. Williams. Col. Ruckel interested J.O. Vanbergen--her former captain--and together they purchased the "Fashion" and put her in service between Portland and the Oregon Portage in July, 1855.

Steamboat "Fashion", built in 1853, was 80 feet long; her engines were from the former little steamer the "James P. Flint". She ran until 1861.

Captain McFarland of The Dalles was also interested in a like manner and ordered the "Wasco" to be built at the Attwell boat ways and to run between the upper portage and The Dalles. Both Vanbergen and McFarland took stock in the portage. The sidewheel "Wasco" began running August 1, 1885. In the meantime, W.R. Kilborn had been busy in road making and furnishing teams, warehouses and other road equipment for moving freight between the boats.

Entry No. 2

John Chipman	*LEASE*
	Dated, August 29, 1857
to	*Filed, August 29, 1858*
	Vol. A of Deeds, pge 95
J. S. Ruckle and	*Wasco Records.*
H. Olmstead	*Vol. A of Deeds, pge 5*
	Hood River Records.

Signed: John Chipman, J.S. Ruckle, Harrison Olmstead, signatures are seaied; two witnesses.

.....grant, demise and doth lease unto....the exclusive right of way for the term of fifty years to build or construct a railroad from the landing known as the "Wasco Steamboat Landing" at the upper Cascades, from thence along the most practicable route on or near the banks of the Columbia River to the most westerly line of the land clain belonging to the party of the first part, also the said party of the first party doth agree to grant and lease unto the said party of the second part, their heirs, executors and assigns for the same period (fifty years) the further exclusive Right of Way to build or construct a Railroad or Wagon Road or Roads from the point described Wasco Landing and the most westerly line of said claim, and the party of the second part, their heirs, executors or assigns, doth covenant and agree to pay to the first party the yearly rent of fifty dollars, the same to be paid yearly in advance on or before September lst. and the party of the second part, their heirs, executors and assigns further agree to have the main line of the Railroad that is to say, from Wasco Landing to the most Westerly limits of the land claim on the Columbia completed within a period not exceeding fifteen months from the frist day of September next, and it is further agreed by the parties of the first part that the party of the second part shall not be limited as to time in constructing the railroads and wagon roads to the big eddy or other points on the Columbia River.

BUGLES IN THE VALLEY

(A story of Garnett's Fort Simcoe by H. Dean Guie.)

Capt. and Mrs. Heger...Mrs. Heger wrote to her sister, Miss Kate Whitney at Pottsville, Pa., from the Middle Cascades on Nov. 27, 1857. ..

"From Portland by little sidewheeler "Fashion", wind so violent the Captain hauled to over night and the following evening we landed at the Lower Cascades on the Oregon shore." (The "Fashion" on downward stream run, struck a reef and sank, was afterwards raised and repaired.)

They traversed the portage accompanied by a soldier...Behind a 4 mule team "with trunks and all (they) jolted over a road much worse than at home" for about a mile...rowed in a small skiff about 2 miles on a lake-like branch of the river, then walked a mile "over the most lonely road through nothing but dense woods, not a habitation in sight with such feelings," said Mrs. Heger, "as I cannot describe." Came to a house, the headquarters of Joseph S. Ruckel and Harrison Olmstead, operators of the portage route and owners of the "Fashion" and "Wasco", which ran between upper Cascades and The Dalles.

Surprisingly, this Mr. Ruckel was an old acquaintance of Mrs. Heger, whose brother had married his cousin. The last Mrs. Heger had heard of the now "very stout and healthy looking but quite as handsome as ever" co-operator of the transportation system, he was living in Cal. Mrs. Ruckel gave her "a box of yeast powder and a pound of precious butter" when they continued their trip to Ft. Simcoe

*****

Col. Ruckel had secured a contract for the transportation of government supplies for March 8th, so the Weekly Oregonian referred to him as "Agent of the Quartermasters Department at the Cascades on the Oregon side".

For a time (after the massacre) the Washington Portage was unable to do much business, so the Oregon Portage became very busy.

The Bradford Company was not long in recovering and soon substituted the "Senorita" and the "Hassaloe" for the "Belle" and "Mary", both being bigger and better boats.

The Transportation Co. met this improvement by building the "Mountain Buck", a better boat than any other on the river. They also began a railroad similar to Bradford's. In Sept. 1857, Ruckel and Olmstead entered into a lease with John Chipman for

21

the use of land from the landing place of the "Wasco" to its most western point for a term of fifty years at $50.00.

This new rail portage probably alarmed the Bradfords for in Nov. 1857 they made overtures to the Oregon Transportation Co. for a combination of their forces. A truce was called, and the "Senorita" was withdrawn below the Cascades and the "Wasco" was removed from above, and the Oregon Portage was closed.

This arrangement lasted less than a year, and the Oregon Portage was resumed in the fall of 1858. The "Wasco" and the "Mountain Buck" were connecting the Oregon Portage, while the "Senorita" connected Bradford's.

Captain Vanbergen, on August 28, 1858, contracted to clear the land within thirty days, preparatory to laying the tracks for the Oregon Portage. The plans for the portage were made by John W. Brazee, a civil engineer of Portland A mill was erected and accommodations made for the employees of the railroad and mill. Other buildings were provided for the horses and mules. There was one covered passenger car and all the cars were small with four wheels. The mules were driven tandems, as many being used as the occasion required. The railroad was constructed of wood, which was supplied by the Eagle Creek sawmill. The rails were of fir in sections six inches square and laid at a gauge of five feet and covered with scrap iron. The spaces between the rails were covered with planking. The bridges were solidly built; the Eagle Creek bridge being a frame cantilever. A large amount of bridging and trestle work was used because it was easier to furnish the lumber than to hire labor for dirt work.

Dynamite was not then in use, and Tooth Rock was a formidable obstruction which was overcome by building a trestle around it.

Late in 1856, General Wool issued an order prohibiting all whites, except Hudson Bay employees and those having ceded rights from the Indians, for settling or staying in Indian Territory. The Indian country was defined as all land east of the Cascades on the Washington side and east of the Dalles on the Oregon side.

June 29, 1857, Brigadier General Clarke (Wool's successor) defined Indian country as the land east of White Salmon River in Washington and the Deschutes River in Oregon.

In October 1858, General Harney issued an order opening up the entire eastern country to settlers. This order meant prosperity for the portage interests.

The Oregon railroad was opened late in 1858 or early 1859. The Portland Advertiser of June 14, 1859 says: "Three hundred feet of Ruckel and Olmstead railroad near the upper warehouse, and all trestles around Big Tooth Rock was swept away with a damage estimate of $10,000. This damage was probably repaired promptly for competition was keen between the rival portages, and Ladd and Tilton was furnishing money for the Transportation Company."

John C. Ainsworth, a lower steamboat man with good backing and much ambition, found these two money-making, mule-drawn portages intolerable. Ainsworth was not a man to sit idly by; he wanted his finger in the pie. He could be called a wheeler-dealer, and seeing the north bank portage the most vulnerable, he approached Ben Stark who jointly owned the portage with D.F. Bradford. The north bank portage's steamboats could not run the swift river current to their railway so it was necessary to land at the lower end of Hamilton Island and then haul the freight with ox teams and wagon through axle deep mud up to the railway. Ainsworth offered to join forces with them and offered his powerful steamer "Carrie Ladd" to replace their less powerful boats on the Portland to the north bank portage. The "Carrie Ladd" (Ladd was a Portland banker) could run the swift water and land at the Middle Cascades and eliminate the slow and costly ox team freight haul.

Entry No. &

John Chipman and Amanda M.   *WARRANTY DEED*
his wife   *Dated August 31st, 1861*
    Filed, September 9, 1861
to   *Vol. B of Deeds, pg. 305*
Harrison Olmstead   *Wasco County Records*
    Vol. A of Deeds, pg. 9
    Hood River Co. Records
    Cons. $11,000.00

Signed: John Chipman Amanda M. Dhipman; Signatures Sealed;
two signatures witnesses.

Acknowledged by same as above on August 31st, 1861, before Addison C.
Gibbs, NP, Seal, Multnomah County, Oregon.
.....bargain and sell and convey.....to-wit: The Fractional NE½ of SW¼ of
Section 12, River lots No. 3, 4, and 5 in Section 12? the NE¼ of NW¼ of
Section 13, River lots No. One in Sec. 13, and River lot No. One in Section
14, all in Township 2 North Range 7 East, being an entire donation Land
Claim at the Cascades of the Columbia River in Wasco County Oregon No.
(8035) containing 320 acres more or less, excepting a Deed to Amos
Underwood for lot 70 by 100 feet.

To have and to hold....
.....free from all uncumberances.....warrant and defend.....

Bradford and Ainsworth worked through Ben Stark. Bradford went along with the deal, hoping to curb the Ruckel portage from encroaching upon the business of the older portage.

As Ainsworth planned, it wasn't long until the Ruckel portage felt the crushing effect of the new combination of the Bradford portage. Ruckel and Olmstead agreed with Ainsworth that bitter rivalry would end in a steamboat and portage war so they agreed to joining into a 'Union Transportation Company'. Ainsworth finally managed to bring the feuding rivals together which worked fairly well for a year. Ainsworth with his constant push wanted Thompson with his big steamboat on the upper river, the "Colonel Wright" to join into the new merger. Ruckel was against it but the Oregon Steam Navigation Company was chartered in 1860, with a capital of $172,500. Ainsworth was named president, while on the board were J.S. Ruckel, D.F. Bradfrod, S.G. Reed and L.W. Coe; Thompson replaced Coe six months later.

The feuding Bradford and Ruckel sat on the O.S.N. board, yet would vote together, often seemingly blind to everything except their portages.

In the spring of 1862, the opportunity presented itself. The spring highwater halted the Bradford portage. The Idaho gold rush was on. The south bank portage was now handling all the business and collecting the big revenues. Ainsworth knew this was the time to get two fingers in the pie. He and Thompson had taken over the upper portage at Celilo and announced plans to construct a railroad there. Ainsworth wanted the O.S.N. to finance this up river portage and he needed the board's approval. Bradford was the first to bite; he supported Ainsworth in having the O.S.N. finance The Dalles portage railroad. Ainsworth acquired 20 miles of railroad iron and the little locomotive, the PONY. Some accounts credit Ruckel for bringing the PONY to Oregon, but it was Ainsworth who made the $4,000 purchase possible.

Ainsworth had purchased more iron rail than was needed at The Dalles, and Bradford was eager to have the extra rail on his portage, hoping the O.S.N. would build him the better railroad. What a blow to Bradford when he found the PONY was unloaded on Ruckel's portage May 10, 1862, the engine was fired up and soon began hauling freight and passengers over the south bank portage; Ruckel's stock was rising and Bradford had been out-smarted.

Ainsworth, the master dealer, convinced Bradford that if he sold his portage and railroad franchise to the O.S.N. that they would built a railroad on the north bank and make it a better portage. Bradford yielded and Ainsworth shifted a 200 man crew from The Dalles to the Bradford portage

Ruckel and Olmstead were furious knowing that the railroad activity on the north bank would leave the south bank portage valueless, so they sold to the O.S.N. The little PONY had played its part in bringing the two portages under one head, the O.S.N.

The north bank portage became a railroad with iron rails and steam locomotives. A small locomotive was purchased from the Vulcan Iron Works of San Francisco, who had also made the PONY. This new locomotive was half flat car so was used to haul rails and construction material in rebuilding the mule railway into a steam, iron-railed railroad. Two more modern locomotives were ordered from Danforth & Cooke of Patterson, New Jersey, and brought around Cape Horn, S.A by ship and then brought to the Lower Cascades on a barge towed by two steamboats.

Parts for the passenger and freight cars were made in San Francisco and assembled in the car or 'round house' at the lower landing. A turntable was also purchased and assembled there. Monty Attwell, an early locomotive engineer on this portage, said, "The turntable worked so smooth that when a locomotive was driven onto it, one man could turn the locomotive around to head in the opposite direction.

This was the first locomotive used on the north bank portage for the laying of iron rails. It was then taken by steamboat to the Dalles and Celilo portage.

At the Upper Landing, the track was laid in what was called a "Y" for turning the locomotive around."

Ainsworth had the steam railroad opened for traffic April 20, 1863. Six miles of iron rails with a 4-1-0 locomotive (which indicated it had only one drive wheel on each side). The rails were laid at a 5 foot gauge. In 1880 the gauge was changed to standard 4' $8\frac{1}{2}$'.

Monty Attwell told, "I had been driving the mule on the Ruckel portage since I was 16. I was 21 when Ainsworth put me on as fireman on the North Bank portage April 16, 1876. The locomotive had only one drive wheel on each side, but the drive wheels were large so while the engine wouldn't pull many cars, it was fast on the track. The tender was part of the locomotive and added more weight on the drivers.

"Captain Ainsworth was the 'big brass' on the O.S.N. which included the Cascade Railroad. He was so proud of his organization of steamboats and portages that he decided to show that he could leave Portland in daylight on a steamboat, go over the portage and get on a middle river steamer to The Dalles and return to Portland the same day. He left orders for the locomotive

to be waiting for him at the Lower Cascades. We were waiting for him when the boat arrived. The engineer had a coach behind the locomotive but Mr. Ainsworth jumped on the locie.

"The engineer pulled the throttle and we were off. Mr. Ainsworth put his arms around an iron post in the tender. We made the 6 miles in 6 minutes to the Upper Landing. Mr. Ainsworth jumped off with a wave to us, and rushed on board the "Daisy Ainsworth" which dropped its holding lines and with a whistle was on its way to The Dalles.

"That afternoon the fast steamer returned from The Dalles and Mr. Ainsworth again crawled aboard the locie. Mr. Ainsworth rode on this return trip with his arm on the engineer's shoulder telling him that a new and larger locomotive was on its way, so the engineer did not make quite the speedy return to the Lower Landing where the steamboat was waiting. Ainsworth had made the first round trip between Portland and The Dalles in one day's daylight.

*****

TAKEN FROM OLDE RECORDS:

The Bradfords sold their wooden track railroad and the survey for the steam operated iron track railroad (the Cascade Railroad Co.) to the Oregon Steam Navigation Co. for $20,000 in May, 1862

Dan Bradford soon left the Cascades. His wife in Boston had mailed her signature to the deed and he left to be with her. While at the Cascades he had taken a young Indian wife known as 'Nettie' as many white men had done. He bid her and their half-breed daughter, Mary, 'Adieu', saying, "Her people would not let her leave." When Mary became a woman she married Chief Warcomac, and raised a well known family at the Cascades.

Middle Landing Cascades

28

Picture taken about 1898, and given by courtesy of Maggie McLaughlin. Left: Mary Bradford Warcomac, Margaret (Maggie) McLaughlin (granddaughter of Bradford), Georgia Miller, Alice Warcomac Williams, George Foreman, Josie Corner, Henry Thomas, Joe Corner, Chief Warcomac (sitting), Virginia Miller, Ed. Thomas, little old lady unknown. Identified by Maggie McLaughlin.

J.C. Ainsworth always liked a challenge. He was a licensed steamboat captain who loved boats and he was a capable business manager and made money for his backers. The O.S.N. grew under his leadership and later became the Oregon Railroad and Navigation Company Besides managing the Cascade portages, he built and managed The Dalles and Celilo portage around the upper falls.

Monty Attwell said, "While firing locomotive on the north bank portage, one time a Wells Fargo agent came down the river as guard over $50,000 in gold. It was placed in the tender under the wood used for fuel. When we arrived at the lower landing, the engineer and the Wells Fargo guard got off the locomotive and walked down on the wharf. The locomotive setting with a fire under the boiler and a full head of steam, I noticed the water getting low in the waterglass, and this was before the steam injector had been invented, so to add water to the boiler against steam pressure, a pump was mounted on the axle and the locomotive needed to be run down the track to replenish the spent water. I would take the throttle and run the locomotive down the track a half mile and back again, always expecting armed robbers to come out of the bushes before I could reverse the Johnson bar and get back to the landing.

Skamania County as it was first created by the territory legislatures in 1853, extended from the present Clark County boundary into Montana, taking in Missoula.

Territorial Legislature establish powers and duties of the board of commissioners for the new county in 1853. It could be said that they were the people's only contact with the government, for the affairs of Territorial Government then were vastly farther away from the daily lives of the state's people than they are now.

A new primitive county without a court house, it appears that the Bush Hotel served that purpose for some time, making the Upper Cascades W.T the first county seat.

County officials changed office on some very short terms, and it may have been partly because of the salaries paid.

First school above the Cascades in the present Skamania County. Dr. Whitman had a school at Waiilatpu in 1843 which was in Skamania County in 1853.

Felix G. Iman and John (Nels) Nelson built this little log school house in 1863. It was located about three hundred feet west of Rock Creek on the secondary highway and on the now Skamania County Park property.

The desks and seats were roughly chopped out of logs, and the floor was dirt. School was held three months during summer and the first teachers were John Denver and John Bull, they received $15 a month.

The first pupils were Theadore and Flora Iman, Henry and Malisia Shepard, Ellen and Mary Nelson, and Monty Attwell. Monty lived at Cascades, Oregon which did not yet have a school, so he rowed across the river to school. His half-brother Celly went with him one week and then decided it wasn't exciting enough for him, but Monty continues crossing the river to this school until a school was built on the south bank of the river.

Credit must be given Felix Iman for helping build the first school near Stevenson and on his land. Felix could not read or write but still was one of the first school directors in Skamania County.

*****

Thirty two years later J.A.A. Bull was found dead in his burned home Feb. 7, 1895. Charge of First Degree murder served on Lysanias Anderson by G.W. Stapleton, Prosecuting Attorney for Skamania County. Anderson and Bull had had a disagreement about ownership of a tract of land. Anderson was acquited and left the country.

Commissioners received $12 per year for the four commissioner meeting prescribed by the first legislature W.T.

Thompson takes the Probate Judgeship after Salmer and he is followed by E.C. Hardy, an early settler who filed on a donation land claim where Mr. and Mrs. Lawrence Pierce live now.

The first county government was very primitive with no court house, and records stored in the fruit cellar or pantry of a log cabin or the bar room of the Bush Hotel

The following is a sample of the new county's bookkeeping. Question asked when E.C. Hardy took over as Probate Judge in 1856.

Question: In whose possession did you have the Probate Records and Papers at the time you became a non-resident and resigned your commission as Probate Judge?

E.C. Hardy, Probate Judge and Ex officio Clerk.

Answer: I left the records and papers of the purpose in the house of I.F. Bush.

J.W. Thompson

*****

George Griswold was shot and killed by the Indians March 26, 1856, when the Yakimas attacked Fort Rains at the Cascades.

List of property set aside to the widow of the late George Griswold, which is allowed by law.

2 yoke of oxen (2 oxen to the yoke)

1 ox wagon

All Kitchen & Cupboard ware

All wearing apparel

2 beds

Probate Judge E.C. Hardy

Received from Benson & Jenkins for 2 yoke of Oxen, the sum of two hundred and fifty dollars this first day of July A.D. 1856.

Ex officio Clerk

*****

The first commissioners were appointed by the 1st Legislature of Washington Territory were S.M. Hamilton, Joseph Robbins, Jacob Scroder. The first sheriff was E.F McNell; Treasurer was J.H. Bush; Auditor was George Johnson; Probate Judge was Cornelius Salmer; Justices of the Peace were B.B. Bishop, N.H. Gales and Lloyd Brooke.

The county road book shows that the commissioners met in the Bush Hotel at the Upper Cascades until 1867; this would be 14 years

Turner Leavens says an election was held in the Ferguson Hotel, Upper Cascades, Washington Territory, on 'Territorial Election' June 1864.

Captain J.C. Ainsworth, in a generous moment, loaned the commissioners a portage railroad box car as a courthouse.

It is not recorded how long the box car was used for the county government court house. When the Army moved out of the garrison at the Lower Cascades, the commissioners moved from the box car into the Army building. It has been told that a fire destroyed this building and some of the county records went up in smoke. Then an old building was rented for the county courthouse from Tom Moffett until 1893.

The Territorial Legislature created more counties in Washington Territory, decreasing the size of Skamania County.

An act to Create and Organize the County of Clicatat. Sec. 1.--That all that portion of Washington Territory embraced within the boundaries Commencing in the Middle Columbia River, 5 miles below mouth of Clicatat River; thence North to the summit of the mountains, the divide between the waters of the Clicatat and Yakima rivers; thence east along said divide, to a point north of the mouth of Rock Creek; thence south to the Middle of the Columbia River; thence along the channel of

river to the place of beginning, the same to be constituted into a separate County to be known and called Clicatat County.
Passed Dec 20th. 1859

The first jail in Skamania County was built at the Cascades. A wooden building about 8 feet wide and 10 feet long, one room with bunks on two walls. The wood door was of several thicknesses riveted together with iron rivets. The iron bars were set in wooden sills. This olde jail stood until after 1926.

Word did not reach Washington, D.C. for several months and when the government 1960 Census was taken, Erastus and Eleanor Joselyn of Bingen were still listed under Skamania County.

Clicatat was changed to Klickitat and the county is now known as Klickitat County.

*****

A request was made in 1853 to Major Rains for forming Wasco County with boundaries running from the Cascades (Cascade Locks) south to the California line, thence east along this line to the Rocky Mountains, thence north to the Columbia River and west to the Cascades. The major turned down the request with saying, "It is too large a territory for only 35 white people in the area."

The need for local government prompted the territorial legislature to create Wasco County, January 11, 1854, comprised all the territory east of the Cascades and south of the Columbia River in Oregon.

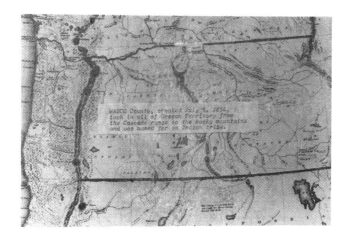

Dalles City, afterward called The Dalles, was named the county seat. About the only settlement here was a small mission established by Jason Lee but transferred to Dr. Marcus Whitman for $600. In 1848 the mission was transferred to the Methodist Missionary Society. The army established a military reservation that occupied a part of the site. The government paid the mission $24,000 for this property. Wasco County Commissioners had The Dalles surveyed and the town was incorporated in 1857.

*****

Road Book 1. The Dalles

Pg. 4

Road from Cascades to Dalles City.

Report received from viewers appointed to view a road from Cascades to Dalles City handed in a report which was laid over until next meeting of commissioners.

April 5, 1858

At a special meeting of the Board of Commissioners held at Dalles City, Wasco County on the 22nd. day of May 1858, board all present, the clerk absent, Wm. C. Laughlin was appointed Clerk pro-tem, the board proceeded to examine a report of C.W. Shang and others of road located between Dalles City and the county line at Cascade falls, the said report was considered insufficient and they then proceeded to appoint R.G. ATTWELL, JAMES ALLEN & DAVID WATTERS to view, mark and locate a county road commencing at J.S. RUCKLES house near west line of Wasco County, thence on the nearest and best route to Dalles City in said county.

22 May 1858

Report of R.G. ATTWELL, ALLEN and WATTERS of road from Cascades to Dalles City read twice and adopted and ordered to be opened & established as a public highway without survey and issue orders to open same to the supervisors.

Dec. 8, 1858.

*****

Dec. 1866.   Petition for road to Rowleys Canyon in Dog River Valley via Mosior's mill. O.K.ed May, 1867.
Complaint...Many Indian raids along canyon stage road. Stealing mules and horses.

*****

Aug. 1867.   Petition for road to Rowley's Canyon or Horn's Landing (distance 27 miles) O.K.ed Sept. 1867.

*****

It was possible to take a wagon around the rapids as early as 1844 as Parrott's story relates, a passable portage on the north bank about 4 miles long.   This appears to be the all and only road in the gorge at this period.

1851--Frances A. Chenowith built a wooden railed portage $2\frac{1}{2}$ miles long around the swift rapids on the north bank. The little rail car was pulled with a mule.

1852--Griswold and Hamilton built an ox team road from the lower end of Chenowith's portage to the lower end of Hamilton Island.   Yokes of oxen pulled freight wagons through axle deep mud from the boat landing up to the rail portage.

1855--A military road was started from Fort Vancouver to Dalles City.   The Army used pack animals so it was more of a trail than a road.

1856--After the Indian attack at the Cascades, the Army under Lt. Derby started a 4 mile road, around the rapids and had it passable in 1857.

In late 1856 a narrow hilly road was built on the south bank from Tanner Creek to the Upper Cascades, Oregon; 6 miles for portage around the rapids by Col. Ruckle.

1861--Ruckle built 4 miles of wooden railed portage on the south bank with mule power.

1862--The first steam locomotive in the northwest was placed on this wooden rail railroad...the little 6-ton PONY, now on display at the Cascade Locks Museum.

1863--Joel Palmer built and operated a toll trail and wagon road from the mouth of the Sandy River to the Upper Cascades on the south bank. Old timers used north and south bank for the reason that it was all Oregon Territory, and could not be called Washington side or Oregon side until after 1853. However, the old steamboat captains used the south or north bank expressions until as late as 1900 rather than the Oregon side or the Washington side. When the S.P. & S. Railway came through in 1908, it was called the North Bank Road by nearly everyone.

1883--Construction of the O.W.R. & N. Railroad on the south bank was completed. Joel Palmer sold his south bank wagon road to the railroad in 1879. Construction of the O.W.R. & N. destroyed much of the old crooked wagon road. It had been a possible summer wagon road but in rainy season it was almost impassable on horseback. When the Columbia River Highway was started in 1913, the old wagon road had almost disappeared with only traces of it found in places.

Building a road up the Columbia was delayed for years by the influence of the steamboat tycoons on the legislature. They contended that the steamboats furnished ample and best transportation along the river.

Several times when the river froze out all steamboat operation and Cascade Locks, Hood River and The Dalles and other towns which depended on boats were left without provisions for a month at a time. Pressure was put on legislation to repair the old road.

Again with the high river flooding in 1894 when the O.W.R. & N. was washed out in many places, the people started real pressure at the state house.

*****

One of the first important duties of the commissioners was to get wagon roads located and built between the settlements. There were no road funds and very little money available. Roads had to be built with pick and shovel where ox teams were unable to pull a plow or scraper, which were most cases. Brush and trees were removed by man power, and roadbeds roughed out before teams could work on them.

There was a provision that a man might work on the county roads in lieu of paying taxes

The commissioners were directed to divide their counties into convenient road districts and to appoint annually at their April session a supervisor of roads in each district. The super-

37

visor of roads in each district. The supervisors were to list the names of all persons liable to the performance of road work, which meant every able bodied man between 18 and 50 years of age, except ministers. Each of these persons was to perform a basic three days work each year. The supervisor received $3 per day for the time worked in his district. This was not a popular post but he must serve under penalty of fine.

Locating the best route for a wagon road from Monticello, which is north of Vancouver to the Baughman Land Claim, where the Stevenson Co-Ply is now located, was acted on with the cooperation of Clark and Skamania counties.

"Chako humamokst nesika kopa muckamuck kopa tenas polaklie."
("Come join us for supper.")
"Nesika mitlite delate muckamuck...mahsie sikhs."
("We have just eaten...thanks friend.")

ROAD BOOK FOR THE COUNTY OF SKAMANIA
January 15th 1860

We the undersigned having been appointed by the legislative
Road Commissioners to view and locate Territorial road from or
near Monticello in Cowlitz County W T by Vancouver in Clark
County to Daniel Boffman's claim in Skamania County W T Provided on the 18th day of June 1860 to view said road commencing
at Maxons Lower Mill through the Mill plain by Salmon Creek to
Lewis River--Was sworn as the law directs on the 21st of June
by H L Caples a Justice of the Peace -- Joseph Godard was
appointed, on recommendation of S Strong to fill the vacancy
caused by the resignation of S. Strong. H J G Maxon was appointed surveyor to locate the Road. We examined the Country
near the Columbia River as the trail runs to Monticello it was
inexpedient to start at Monticello on account of overflowed
land by the Columbia River--We found the nearest point at which
we could intersect the Military Road to bee bout 3 miles above
Monticello at Mr. Leonards Land Claim. Thence across the Cowlitz River as shown by the notes as per surveyor's Report. We
found a good and practical Rout from place of beginning to Wm
H Martins then for two miles there will be considerable side
cutting or grading the balance of the way to Vancouver there
is but little work except removing under brush and trimming
timber, and a few bridges to make. From Vancouver we followed
the County Road as near as practible (varying) only to mend
the road in a few places) to the Eastern boundary of Clark
County--We found a good Rout over Cape Horn Mountain avoiding
the canyon of the old trail, and we discovered a better decend
on the Eastern slope of the mountain than that of the old
trail--For a mountain Road we consider the whole rout a very
good one. The Rout is plainly marked by blazes on the trees
and loping the underbrush we recommend that when we left the
County Road only for a short distance, that the County Road
be vacated. The amount due each person for services viewing,
is as follows:

	H.J.C. Maxon	27 Days	$ 100.00
	J.E.C. Durgin	27 Days	$ 108
	J. Godard	24 Days	$ 96
	Wm H. Martin	13 Days	$ 52
	P.W. Crawford	12 Days	$ 48
	Amount		$ 304

For surveying the account is as follows:

	H.J.G. Maxon	32 Days	$ 160
	All the employed as chainmen and axmen		$ 208
	Amount		$ 368
	Total		$ 672

Of the above amount there is due to each person as follows from Cowlitz County:

J.E.C. Durgin	4 Day	$ 16
Jos Godard	4 Days	$ 16
Wm Martin	4 Days	$ 16
P.W. Crawford	4 Days	$ 16
H.J.G. Maxon	4 Days	$
	at $5 per Day	$ 20
James H. Poland	4 Days	$ 16
James S. Bennet	3 Days	$ 12
Samuel Spencer	3 Days	$ 12
James B. Croly	2 Days	$ 8
Total due from Cowlitz County		$132

*****

There is due from Clark County as follows:

J.E.C. Durgin	20 Days	$ 80
Jos Godard	19 Days	$ 76
Wm H. Martin	9 Days	$ 36
P.W. Crawford	8 Days	$ 32
H.J.G. Maxon	24 Days	
	at $5 per Day	$ 120
J.H. Poland	5 Days	$ 20
Samuel Spencer	5 Days	$ 20
James Burk	1 Day	$ 4
Vost	2 Days	$ 8
John Kinder	2 Days	$ 8
John Messenger	1 Day	$ 4
Charles Godard	1 Day	$ 4
S.D. Maxon	3 Days	$ 12
Lon Durgan	3 Days	$ 12
Allen Austin	3 Days	$ 12
Making a total due from Clark County		$ 448

*****

There is due from Skamania County as follows:

J.E.C. Durgan	3 Days	$ 12
Joe Godard	3 Days	$ 12
H.J.G. Maxon	4 Days	$ 20
Lon Durgan	2 Days	$ 8
Allen Austin	2 Days	$ 8
John Rurner	2 Days	$ 8
Arthur Kincelly	2 Days	$ 8
John Stephenson	3 Days	$ 12
E.C. Hardy	1 Day	$ 4
Making a Total for Skamania County of		$ 92

We the undersigned H.J.G. Maxon, J.E.C. Durgan, Joseph Godard, Wm H. Martin and P.W. Crawford Road Commissioneers solemnly swear that the facts set forth in the foregoing Report are True to the best of our knowledge and belief so help us God.

H.J.G. Maxon
Jos H. Godard
J.E.C. Durgan

Subscribed and Sworn to before me this the 28 Day of July A D 1860

Jno. D. Biles
J.P.

*****

Notes of a Report of the Territorial Road leading from Monticello to Daniel Boffmans Claim.

The Territorial Road viewed and located by H.J.G. Maxon, J.E.C. Durgan, J. Godard, Wm H. Martin and P.W. Crawford and surveyed by H.J.G. Maxon in June and July 1860. Intersects the Military Road leading from Steelicoom to Monticello at Mr. Leonards on the Right bank of the Cowlitz River about 2 Miles above Monticello. Commences at a Post marked T R Thence Southerly 43 miles to Vancouver Thence Easterly a little over 21 miles to the west line of Skamania County from Mile Post 21 Thence

	Chains	
N 92 E	50,000	West line Ska. Co.
	6500	B F Tanners imp'ts.
East	8000	Post Marked T.R.22 M.
East	900	
S 73 E	3400	
East	7200	
S 45 E	8000	Red fir tree 6 in Diam Marked T.R. 23 M.

*****

	Chains	
S 45 E	2500	
East	5500	
N 65 E	7700	
N 85 E	8000	Red fir tree 36 in Diam Marked T.R. 24 M.

*****

	Chains	
East	1700	
N 79 E	2600	
N 60 E	33,50	
N 33 E	40,00	
N 58 E	51,50	
N 68 E	8000	Post marked T.R. 25 M.

*****

```
             Chains
N 70 E       1000      Chases Field
S 80 E       17,50     Top of Easterly slope of Cape
                         Horn Mountain
S 20 E       5350
S 26 E       6000
S 70 E       67,00
S 30 E       8000      Alder tree 5 in Diam Marked
                         T.R. 26 M.

              *****
             Chains
S 30 E       9,00      Foot of the Mountain.
East         37,00
N 75 E       4500
N 78 E       7500
East         80,00     Maple tree 12 in Diam Marked
                         T.R. 27 M.

              *****
N 30 E       1300
N 63 E       2600
East         4000      Charles Frece's improvements.
N 60 E       80,00     Alder tree 10 inch's Diameter
                         Marked T.R. 28 N
```

*****

Then the Territorial Road intersects the County Road which was
surveyed by Lieut Derby's party. And it was deemed inexpedient
to survey the Road further as there is but one Rout for a Road,
and the distance is known to be nine miles from the last
Marked tree to the Landing at the Lower Cascades.

The Road continues above high water Mark in an Easterly
Direction about one mile when it intersects a small mountain.
Thence Southerly along the foot of the mountain about 1/4
mile.   Thence Easterly 1/4 mile along the base of the mountain.
Thence Easterly across bottom land and a small creek and across
Arthur Kincelleys claim to the foot of a small mountain 1 1/4
mile.   Thence over the mountain to avoid some bad Canyons 1/2
mile.   Thence Easterly a winding way to get by bad Rocks 1/4
of a mile to what is known as the Schroder Place.   Thence
Easterly on bottom land and Easterly along a good Ridge way
1/2 mile to Marr's Creek.   Thence along the Ridge to the north
of the town line of Town. 2, N.E. 6. E to N.E. Corner of Sec.
33.   Thence Easterly along the Ridge and on level bottom land
one mile to a small creek.

Thence Easterly North of the Duncan Lake and North of
Castle Rock and south of Widow Snooks house. And north of
E.C. Hardys Housecroping Lake creek above where the Columbia
backs the water.   Thence a straight line across the Prairie
to intersect the Military Road to the Landing at the Lower
Cascades.   Thence 4 miles.   Thence along the Military Road to

the Landing at the Upper Cascades. Thence westerly above
high water mark 1/2 mile to blue creek. Thence Easterly
above high water mark to Daniel Hoffmans Land Claim.
   Distance in Skamania County 22 Miles and 30 chains.
Distance from Vancouver to Daniel Boffmans, 44 miles. All
of which is most Respectfully Submitted to the Honorable
County Commissioners Court of Skamania County, W.T.

                         H.J.G. Maxon
                         Surveyor
       Recorded on this 17th Day of January A.D.
       1861
                         E.C. Hardy
           Clerk of the board of County Commission
                         Pro Tem

This is to certify that you E.C. Hardy are hereby
appointed Road Supervisor of the Territorial Road, through
Skamania County, given under my hand and Seal this 6th Day
of May A D 1861.
                         C.E. Mayo
                         Auditor
Regular Term Tuesday May 7th 1861
Be it ordered that the Territorial Road here Recorded be
opened according to Law.
                         Approved
       Attested   Henry Shepard
         E.C. Hardy   C.B.C.C.
           Clerk Pro Tem

                         *****
   H.J.C. Maxon, the head viewer of this road location was
not a civil engineer but an early settler near Washougal. In
1852 he built a sawmill near the mouth of the Washougal River
where LaCamas Creek enters. It burned the year it was built
but was rebuilt again and sawed lumber for many years.
   J.E.C. Durgin came west in 1854, taking up a donation land
claim 5 miles east of Washougal.

                         *****
   While the road was layed out, it never was improved much.
Twenty years later in 1860, the road was declared almost
impossible. The road was narrow, rough, crooked and often
dark for it wound among stumps and forested areas.
   People traveled by boat whenever possible from Portland to
Monticello rather than travel over the road with more bear
tracks on it than human tracks. The road from Vancouver to
the Cascades had so little work done on it that it was still
almost impassible with a horse and buggy into the 1900's.
Boat travel here was still preferred until the north bank
railroad was built in 1908.
   In 1863 the commissioners appointed viewers to locate a
wagon road between the Cascades and Rockland (Grand Dalles).

These viewers walked over the forty miles and estimated the total cost of cutting brush, grading and building bridges to not be over $3,900. However, this appears to be too much money for the commissioners to part with, so the building of the road was delayed for forty years.

*****

Credit must be given Felix Iman as a viewer because he could not read or write his own name.

To the Honorable Board of County Commissioners of Skamania County. Greeting.

We the undersigned Territorial Road Commissioners would respectfully submit the following report of view and location of a Territorial road from Cascades to Rockland Monday Feb. 15th, 1864. Henry Shepard, Felix G. Iman's and E.C. Hardy met at the house of I.H. Bush, at the Upper Cascades. Henry Shepard being unable to attend to view said road Felix G. Iman and E.C. Hardy appointed Samuel Snook in his stead. On Wednesday the 17th of February Sml Snook and E.C. Hardy proceeded to Rockland to view on the Upper end while F.G. Iman viewed on the lower end of said road.

Commencing at the town of Rockland at the Columbia River, and followed the public road back on the second bench or what is known as the Rockland flat, thence followed a waggon track down the Columbia River running to the right of Rev Mr. Ransdelle farm. Thence up Clickitat Mountain following a road used by the settlers to haul wood over. Thence along the South side of Clickitat Mountain to a narrow ridge. Thence along said ridge until we come to a right hand Indian trail leading down said hollow to Clickitat river crossing said river about 1/2 mile from its mouth. This stream can be bridged very cheap as the banks are solid rock and project over so as not to require more than forty feet of the bridge. Thence up the hill on the west side of the said river and passed by the north side of Mr. Townsends farm. Thence to Bed Creek Rock crossing it where the old Indian trail crosses it. Thence to the right up a mountain, and along on said mountain crossing down the same near E.S. Joselyn's farm,

44

(Bingen). Thence followed the Indian trail to Little White
Salmon Creek. Thence along the foot of the bluff to Collins
wood yard. Thence followed an old way on road to lake where
there had been hay mowed. Thence on nearly on a straight
line through the timber to the North side of Wind Mountain.
Thence through brush and timber, to a hollow leading to
Joseph Robins Farm. Thence along near the foot of the hill
crossing Wind River above the Murphy Farm. Thence bearing
to the right on an angle up Wind River hill and along a flat
to a hollow crossing it on an old bridge that has been used
to haul out wood across. Thence along near an upland trail
to a place known as the George Fields place. Thence up a
hill and down a hollow and along above the high water mark
to a creek. Thence on high ground to a place known as the
Ginder place. Thence to Nelsons place. Thence on westwardly direction to due north of Henry Shepards. Thence
south to near the house. Thence west to Rock Creek. Thence
westwardly through the timber and brush to the Old Saw Mill
Seat. Thence around the Columbia River bottom above the
high water mark to the Upper Cascades intersecting the Military Road at the Saw Mill Stable.

We do hereby report that portion of the rout lying
between the Upper Cascades and a point of rocks above
Collins Wood Yard as being practicable to make a good wagon
road, and make the following estimate of cost of building
the same coin rates.

FOR CUTTING AND CLEARING BRUSH, TIMBER AND LOGS

Grading		$ 300.00
Bridging	Rock Creek	1000.00
"	Wind River	800.00
"	Galentine Creek	1000.00
		800.00

These streams are fordable over nine tenths of the year,
except Wind River which is fordable over 4/5ths of the year.
There can be a good trail made above the Collins wood yard to
Rockland for a very small expense the county being generally
prairie.

Expense of locating			
F.G. Iman	6 Days	18.00
Samuel Snook	9 Days	27.00
E.C. Hardy	10 "	30.00
Henry Shepard	4 "	12.00
Joseph Robins	1 "	3.00

Of the above expense there is due Samuel Snook and E.C.
Hardy each 2 days from Clickitat County the remainder to be
paid by Skamania County.

                          Signed (F.G. Iman
March 12th 1864   (E.C. Hardy
                               (Saml H. Snook
              Territorial Road Commissioners.

March 12, 1864
     At a meeting of the Board of County Commissioners held at
Upper Cascades Skamania County W.T. It was ordered that that
portion of the road described in the above report as lying
between Collins wood yard and Upper Cascades be declared a
public Highway.

                     Attest   T.E. Andrews
                               Auditor

     At a meeting of the Board of County Commissioners of
Skamania County W.T. held at Upper Cascades W.T. on the 12th
of March A D 1864 it was ordered by the Board that Road
District No1 extend from the west line of Skamania Co to
Castle Rock thence north as far as inhabited.
     Ordered that Road District No 2, shall embrace the boun-
daries lying between the eastern boundry of No 1, and a point
of rocks immediately above Collins Road Yard.
     An act Declaring the Road now running from John W.
Stevensons Farm, on Cape Horn Mountain, to the Columbia River,
a Territorial Road.

Section 1
     Be it enacted by the Legislative Assembly of the Territory
of Washington, That the Road now running from John W. Stevensons Farm on Cape Horn Mountain, in Skamania County, to John
W. Stevenson on the bank of the Columbia River in said County
be, and the same is hereby declared a Territorial Road.

Section 2
     Be it further enacted that it shall be the duty of the
clerk of the Board of County Commissioners of Skamania County,
upon receiving a copy of this act, to record the same in the
road book of Skamania County.

Section 3rd
     This act to take effect, and be in force from and after
its passage. Passed Jan. 24th 1864.

                         C. Crosby,
                  Speaker of House of Representatives
                         O.B. McFadden,
                  President of the Council.

     At an election held at the home I.H. Bush of Upper Cas-
cades Skamania County W.T. for Road Superviser for Road
District No 2 A.H. Simmons was duly elected and has this 26th

                           46

day of April A.D. 1864 taken the necessary oath and entered
upon the discharge of his duties.

John E. Andrews
Auditor

Cascades W T June 18th 1865

At an election held on Monday the 5th day of June A.D.
1865 John Johnson was elected to the office of County Road
Superintendent, and had duly qualified by taking the oath of
office and giving bonds for the faithful performance of the
duties of his office.

John E. Andrews
Auditor

Cascades W T June 28th 1865

At a meeting of the Honorable Board of Co. Commissioners,
of Skamania County W.T. held at Upper Cascades, on Monday the
6th day of May A.D. 1867, a petition was received from the
inhabitants of Road District No 1 for a change of District
Lines, which petition was granted and it was ordered that
Road District No 1 shall commence at the Clark County line,
and extend to Woodwards Creek. John W. Stephenson was
elected Supervisor of No 1.

Road District No 2 shall commence at the Eastern boundary
of No 1 and extend to a point opposite Memoluse Island at
Upper Cascades. Philip Snook was appointed supervisor of Road
District No 2.

Road District No 3 shall commence at a point opposite
Memoluse Island, Upper Cascades and extend to Klickitat County
Line. Henry Shepard was elected Road Supervisor for Road Dis-
trict No 3.

In witness whereof I have hereunto set my hand and caused
the Seal of the County to be affixed.

John E. Andrews
Auditor

An election held at Upper Cascades W.T. for Road Supervisor in April A D 1867 Henry Shepard was elected Road Supervisor for Road District No 3. Road District No 1 elected
John W. Stephenson as the Supervisor for said district.

Philip Snook was appointed Supervisor for Road District
No 2.

Attest   J.E. Andrews
Auditor

At an Election held at the Home of Moses Boleman for the
purpose of electing a Road Supervisor April 16 1868 Henry
Shepard was elected Supervisor for District No 3 for the year
1868.

John W. Stephenson was appointed by the Board of County
Commissioners, Supervisor for Road District No 1 for the year
1868 and James H. Stevens Supervisor for Road District No 2.

47

Thomas Monoghan was appointed Road Supervisor for Road
District No 3, Henry Shepard being disqualified from holding
said office.

Attest   J.E. Andrews
Auditor

At a meeting of the inhabitants of Road District No 1
held at the Home of Charles Freeze on the 5th day of April
A D 1869, for the purpose of electing a Road Supervisor for
District No 1, George J. Stephenson was elected Supervisor
and duly qualified for said office according to law.

Attest   J.E. Andrews
Auditor

At a meeting of the inhabitants of Road District No 3
held at the Home of Neil Anderson on the 5th day of April
1869 for the purpose of electing a Road Supervisor for Road
District No 3. Thomas Monoghan was duly elected Supervisor
as by law required, Jason Hamilton was on May 3rd 1869, by
the County Commissioners appointed to fill the Office of Road
Supervisor for said District No 2.

Attest   J.E. Andrews
Auditor

Cascades May 3 1869

DEED FROM E.C. HARDY TO SKAMANIA COUNTY W.T.
    Know all men by these presents that I, E.C. Hardy of the
County of Skamania and Territority of Washington, for and in
consideration of the sum of Fifteen Hundred Dollars to me
paid by the said County of Skamania, have this day and by these
presents, do hereby bargain, sell, and convey unto the said
County of Skamania, all my right title, and interest in, and
to the Toll Road now owned by me, lying and being in said County of Skamania, Commencing at the West boundry line of said
Skamania County and intersecting the U.S. Military Road at
the Cascade Portage. Together with the Charted granted by the
Legislature of said Territory Jan. 26th 1863, under which said
Toll Road was built, with all the amendments to said Charter
granted by the said Legislature.
    To have and to hold the same unto the County of Skamania
forever. In testimony whereof I have hereto set my hand and
private Seal, at Cascades Skamania County, Washington Territory this 25th day of Feb. A D 1867.

Signed in presence of   (
    J.W. Brazee   (E.C. Hardy
    Saml B. Jones   ((Seal)

#2 U.S. Internal Revenue Stamp

Territory of Washington   (
County of Skamania   (S S

Personally appeared before me the Undersigned, on this 25th day of Feby 1867 E.C. Hardy to me personally known to be the person whose signature is attached to the within foregoing instrument, and who acknowledged to me that he executed the within instrument or conveyance freely and for the purpose therein stated.

In testimony whereof I have hereunto set my hand and caused the County Seal to be affixed this Feby 25 1867.

John E. Andrews, Auditor, in and for Skamania
County, Territory of Washington

(County Seal)

KANAKA CREEK
(Courtesy Mrs. Bud Ramsay)

This small creek just east of Stevenson has always been a curiosity for its naming. In the 1870's a few Kanakas took Indian wives and settled along this creek.

Romantic stories have been told of these first Kanakas being shipwrecked with Spanish sailing ships along the Pacific Coast and the Spaniards being killed and the Kanakas being taken in by the Coast Indians, later taking Indian wives and setting up their own settlements. This story is not correct.

The Hawaiians aboard the "Tonquin" were killed along with the white men by the Indians on Vancouver Island. Several working with the fur traders were killed, and a Kanaka was killed during the Whitman Massacre, which shows the Indians had not accepted them with open arms as the romantic story told.

The English were the first to take the Hawaiian or Sandwich Islanders aboard their ships as employees. In May, 1787, the British ship "Imperial Eagle" took aboard a Hawaiian woman as a servant to the Captain's wife. Her name was Winee, and she was the first recorded Hawaiian to leave the Island. When the Captain's wife decided to return to England, Winee was returned to the Islands.

In 1788, William Douglass sailed the "Iphigenia" into an Island harbor and thereafter the Islands became regular stopping points for all ships crossing the Pacific. Ships needed fresh water and food as well as replacement of crew members. Kanakas, Owyhees or Blue Men, as these Hawaiians were called, were often hired aboard these ships. They were natural seamen and quickly learned 'the ropes' of these early sailing ships.

When Captain Robert Gray discovered the Columbia River, a Hawaiian was a member of his crew. When Astor's men voyaged on the "Tonquin" to the Columbia River to build Astoria, some Kanakas had signed on for a three year stay with Astor's men while the ship was in Honolulu Harbor. Their wages were room and board, clothing and $100.

When Astor's Pacific Fur Company sold to the Northwest Fur Trading Company, these Kanakas worked with this company collecting furs. They were at home in a canoe or bateau, and also valued ashore at other work. When the Northwest Company and the Hudson Bay Company merged in 1821 under the name Hudson Bay Company, there were 35 Kanakas at Fort Vancouver, 32 at Walla Walla, and others at several stations. 1828 the Hudson Bay Company employed 28 Kanakas in their sawmill a few miles upriver from Vancouver.

As more white settlers came into the Northwest, anger fell upon the Kanakas for taking jobs away from the new pioneers at far less pay. In Dec. 1845, the Provisional Government's legislative body considered an act providing, "That all persons who shall hereafter introduce into Oregon Territory any Sandwich Islanders, for a term of Service shall pay a tax of five dollars for each person so introduced. An additional section of the bill called for an annual $3.00 tax on persons already employing Kanakas and not returning them to the Islands."

These Kanakas who settled on Kanaka Creek found work on the sailing wood scows that hauled cord wood from Shepards Point (Stevenson) to The Dalles. They were excellent boat men so handled these clumsy scows with ease. They could be heard singing while sailing up or down the river, their voices carried the songs ashore.

Barges which carried firewood to The Dalles

WYETH, HOOD RIVER COUNTY

Wyeth, a small railroad station, received its name for one of the notable early pioneers.

Nathaniel J. Wyeth, trader and patriot, who had a definite plan to counteract the British fur-trading monopoly in the Columbia River regions. Wyeth crossed the plains from Boston in 1832, the first American after the Astor overlanders to make the crossing. On a second expedition in 1834, he convoyed the missionaries Jason and Daniel Lee, built Fort Hall near Pocatello, and named it for one of his financial backers. On Sauvie Island he established a trading post known as Fort Williams.

Wyeth worked out plans for a combination fur trade and salmon and lumber exporting business. Hudson Bay Company did not want Wyeth cutting in on their monopoly so they offered his men better offers in pay. Wyeth soon found himself so shorthanded that he was forced to return to St. Louis and hire more men which he contracted for at $250 per year to return with him. They arrived at Fort Walla Walla in September 1834. They came on down the Columbia to Fort Williams where he met his ship the "May Dacre" which brought him 20 Kanakas.

Wyeth and his new employees started back up the Columbia River in Oct. He made a foreman out of Joe Thing and gave him 8 whites and 13 Kanakas and sent him on to Fort Hall. Wyeth soon learned that the Kanakas had stolen 12 horses and $3,000 in supplies and deserted Thing, which left him stranded until Wyeth gave him 4 more Kanakas and another 10 whites.

Wyeth started a search for the deserters and in February he received a report that they had taken a trail over the Blue Mountains, one had frozen to death, one had drowned, another had died, and the rest had gone down the Columbia to Vancouver. When Wyeth reached the fort, he found the Kanakas there completely sick of their escapade, so he decided not to punish them severely.

This was not the only problem that faced Wyeth, and as he was running out of finances he offered to sell to the Hudson Bay Company, his Columbia River property, including Fort Hall. The Hudson Bay Company agreed to buy Wyeth out and he accepted the offer if the company would agree to return the Kanakas back to the Hawaiian Islands. Some of the Kanakas did not wish to return so were allowed to remain here.

*****

History has not always classified the Indians fairly. They were not all villains. Many chiefs spoke with great wisdom and showed great leadership in war and in peace.

Chief Sealth (Seattle was the name given him by the early settlers) may best be remembered for his oratorical masterpiece spoken in the Duwamish tongue in 1854, when Governor Isaac Stevens came to Seattle to present a treaty to the Indians.

Chief Sealth arose, solemnly and, placing one hand on the Governor's head and pointing heavenward with the index finger of the other, made his famous speech. (It was interpreted to the governor and recorded by a newspaper reporter).

"Yonder sky that has wept tears of compassion upon my perople for centuries untold, and which to us appears changeless and eternal, may change. Today is fair. Tomorrow it may be overcast with clouds. My words are like the stars that never change.

What ever Sealth says, the great Chief at Washington can rely upon. The White Chief says that the Big Chief at Washington sends us greetings of friendship and goodwill. This is kind of him for we know he has little need of our friendship in return. His people are many. They are like the grass that cover the prairies. My people are few, they resemble the scattering trees of a storm swept plain. The great, and I presume, good White Chief sends us word that he wishes to buy our lands, but is willing to allow us enough on which to live comfortably. This indeed appears just, even generous, for the Red Man no longer has rights that he need respect, and the offer may be a wise one to accept as we no longer have need of an extensive country.

"There was a time when our people covered the lands as the waves of a wind-ruffled sea covers it's shell-paved floor, but that time long since passed away with the greatness of tribes that now are but a mournful memory. I will not dwell on or mourn over our untimely decay, nor reproach my paleface brothers with the charge of hastening it, as we to may have been somewhat to blame.

"Youth is impulsive. When our young men grow angry at some real or imaginary wrong and disfigure their faces with black paint, it denotes that their hearts are black and that they often are cruel and relentant, and our old men and women are unable to restrain them. Thus it has been. Thus it was when the white man first began to push our forefathers further westward. But let us hope that the hostilities between us may never return. We have everything to lose and nothing to gain. Revenge by young men is considered gain, even at the cost of their lives, but old men stay at home in times of war, and mothers who have sons to lose, know better.

"Our good father at Washington, for I presume he is our father as well as yours, since King George has moved his borders further north, our great and good father, I say, sends us word that if we do as he desires, he will protect us. His brave warriors will be to us a bristling wall of strength, and his mighty ships of war will fill our harbors so that our ancient enemies far to the Northland, will cease to frighten our women, children and old men. Then in realty, he will too be our father and we his children. But can that ever be? Your God is not our God! You God loves your people and hates mine. He folds his strong protecting arms lovingly around your people and leads them by the hand as a father leads his small son, but, he has forsaken his red children, if they are really His. Our God seems to have forsaken us, while your God make his people wax strong every day. Soon they will fill all the land. Our people are ebbing away like a rapidly receding tide that never will return. The white man's God cannot love our people or He would protect them. They seem to be orphans who can look nowhere for help. How then can we be brothers? How can your God be our God? If we have a common Heavenly father, he must be partial.

"To us the ashes of our ancestors are sacred and their resting place is a hallowed ground. You wander far from the graves of your ancestors and seemingly without regret.

"Your dead cease to love you and the land of their nativity as soon as they pass the portals of the tomb and wander beyond the stars. They are soon forgotten and never return. Our dead never forget the beautiful world that gave them being. They will love it's verdant valleys, it's murmuring rivers, it's magnificent mountains, sequestered vales and verdant lakes and bays and ever yearn in tender fond affection over the lonely hearted living, and often return from the Happy Hunting Grounds to visit, guide, console and comfort them.

"Day and night cannot dwell together. The red man has ever fled the approach of the white man, as morning mist flees before the morning sun.

"It matters little where we pass the last remnant of our days. They will not be many. Grim fate seems to be the red man's trail and whereever he goes, he will

hear the approaching footsteps of his destroyer and prepare stolidty to meet his doom as does the wounded doe that hears the approaching footsteps of the hunter.

"A few more moons. A few more winters, and not one of the decendants of the mightly hosts that once moved over this broad land and lived in happy homes, protected by the Great Spirit, will remain to mourn over the graves of a people once more powerful than yours. But why should I mourn at the untimely fate of my people? Tribes follow tribes and nations follow nations, like the waves of the sea. It is the order of nature and regret is useless. Your time of decay may be distant, but it will surely come, for even the White Man whose God has walked and talked with him as friend, cannot be exempt from destiny. We may be brothers after all. We will see."

JOHN M. MARDEN AND FAMILY

John M. Marden was born in Georgetown, D.C., November 30, 1828. His parents were Nathaniel M. and Mary (Lutz) Marden. He attended the public schools of Washington, D.C., and later entered college. When his school days were over he learned the carpenter's trade.

In 1849 he joined a party of men going west; they were known as "Washington City and California Mining Association", and numbered sixty-four men in their company. They crossed the plains with mule teams, arriving at Lassen ranch in California on Oct. 13th, 1849. He mined at Bidwell's Bar untill January 1, 1850, when he went to Sacramento in hopes of getting letters from home.

In February he went to Marysville and helped to build the first frame building erected in that town. Later he went to Shasta with pack train, then to Scotts Bar, Weaverville and again to Marysville.

In 1856 he sold his mules and returned to Shasta, filing on a placer claim on Whiskey Creek where he washed out considerable gold in nuggets, one nugget being worth $800. That fall he went again to Marysville and up the Yuba River to Trask Bar, working there successfully for six months. In July 1858 he went to Fraser River with three men, traveling from Victoria, B.C. in an Indian log canoe as far north as Fort Langley, B C. He then returned to Olympia, going across country to Monticello at the mouth of the Cowlitz River and then to Portland and up the Columbia River to the Cascades on the south bank of the Columbia River. This land was formerly occupied by a warlike tribe of Indians under Chief Walluchian, the place being called Polally-Illahee, which in English means sand land. In later years it was given the name of Ruthton by a lumbering company that operated a planer on the place. For ten years Mr. Marden lived alone on his farm, then on February 13, 1869 at The Dalles, he was married to Miss Harriet Reed of Troutdale, Oregon.

Their farm was isolated from Hood River Valley, and if they wished to ship their produce on the steamboats, they had to take it in a small boat to the steamer landing two miles east of their place.

They had no road in those days, only an Indian trail, following the river, came through the farm and wound its way up a precipitous bluff to the valley nearly four hundred feet above. Theodore Perham made his home with the Marden family for a time, and twice each school day he dared its perils, attending the Hood River school which was located on the southwest corner of Wm. Jenkins' claim.

Mrs. Armstrong of New York was the teacher and left an impress for good on the characters of her pupils.

Their nearest neighbors were Amos and Ed Underwood, who with their wives, lived on the north bank, nearly two miles distant. Amos Underwood had filed on Polally-Illahee before Mr. Marden came, but preferring the north bank had moved across the river where he made his home. The wife of Amos Underwood was a Cascade Indian woman, baptized by the missionaries as Ellen, daughter of Chief Chenowuth. Col. Lear, of the U.S. Army, had married her according to Indian rites, but when the army was ordered away, Ellen and her daughter were left behind. Amos Underwood befriended her and later married her with the Indian ceremony, saying that later he would have the ceremony repeated by a minister when one could be found. Ed Underwood, while on a visit to his brother at White Salmon, met and loved Isabel Lear; an Indian marriage ceremony followed, and a new home was founded near the home of Amos Underwood.

At the close of a cold, disagreeable day, two forlorn travelers stopped at the Marden home and begged for shelter. For three weeks they had been traveling over rough Indian trail along the bank of the Columbia River. The man was about thirty years old, the girl sixteen; her home had been at Hillsboro in Oregon and she had run away with her lover when her parents had refused their consent to her marriage. They had found no one to perform the marraige ceremony and the girl was exhausted. Mrs. Marden listened to their story, then made them welcome to her home. Rev. Thomas Condon, Congregational minister of The Dalles was sent for and a message was also sent to Amos and Ed Underwood. Mrs. Marden made three wedding cakes and when the minister arrived a wedding was solemnized at the Marden home, and soon after two more at the homes of the Underwood brothers.

In 1872 the Marden farm was sold to Haynes and Sanders. Later Mr. Marden purchased a tract of land east of Mosier which he soon developed into one of the most valuable ranches on the Mid-Columbia River. In 1883 this farm was sold and the family moved to The Dalles.

UNDERWOOD

Amos Underwood was born in Cincinnati, Ohio, Dec. 10, 1834. The Coe Diary says that Mr. Underwood gave his arrival to 'Dog River' as Sept. 9, 1852, at 18 years of age. In 1855 he was a Corporal in Co. B of the Oregon Volunteers. In March 1856 he received his discharge from service and then came on down the river on his horse, seeing the Joslyn home at Bingen in flames and knew it was the work of Indians. He traveled on down the south bank trail, arriving at the Cascades, Oregon, and was staying with the Attwells when the Indians on Mar 26, attacked Bradfords

On Aug. 5, 1859, he filed on a claim at Polalla Illahee, now Ruthton. He soon afterwards sold this claim.

Oct. 15, 1860, he purchased property from John Chipman at Portageville (now Cascade Locks). This may be when he courted Ellen Lear, the daughter of the late Chief Chen o wuth. Capt. Lear had taken Ellen as wife while stationed here with Phil Sheridan's soldiers. Lear, like many other officers, left his Indian wife when he was transferred. He also left her with a small daughter, Isabel Lear. Amos liked the grass widow so took her as wife by Indian rites.

*****

ENTRY NO. 8

John Chipman	DEED.
	Dated, October 15, 1860
to	Filed, October 18, 1860
	Vol. B of Deeds, page 203,
Amos Underwood	Wasco County Records
	Vol. A of Deeds, page 8,
	Hood River County Records
	Cons. $150.00

Signed: John Chipman, Amanda M. Chipman, Signatures sealed; Two witnesses.

Acknowledged by John Chipman and Amanda Chipman on October 15th, 1860, before John Chipman, JP, Wasco County, Oregon.

...bargain, sell and quit-claim unto the said Amos Underwood...all and singular my right, title, interest, estate, claim and demand both in law and in equity and as well in possession as in expectancy of and in and to all that certain lot or piece of land situated and being in Wasco County, Oregon, and known as Lot number one in the town of Portageville being on Front Street in said town and being a corner lot and bounded as follows: One hundred and forty feet on first street, by seventy feet on Front Street with all and singular the houses, buildings and improvements thereon situated and thereunto belonging or in anywise appertaining to him the said Amos Underwood and to his heirs and assigns forever. No 4425, pg. 10.

*****

In the summer of 1861, Amos Underwood moved up river to the mouth of the White Salmon River, taking up a homestead there. They built a log house and cooked their meals over a fireplace.

His brother, Ed Underwood, came out from Iowa and took a homestead also, and seeing Isabel developing into young womanhood, took her as his wife. Both Underwoods then built frame houses. Later both families were married by a minister.

Amos and Ellen had three children; Jefferson Underwood, born Jan. 28, 1862; Mary Underwood, born April 17, 1864, and John Underwood, born Oct. 23, 1868. Ed and Isabel raised a family of eight children.

Harry Olson married one of the Underwood daughters, sold his homestead and moved down on the river. He ran the ferry for many years.

The first post office was established at the little town of UNDERWOOD, May 25, 1900. Mrs. Grace Dark was a daughter; Dec. 13, 1904, Charles Robards; June 13, 1905, Myron Smith; April 22, 1911, Herbert Adams; May 16, 1923, Charles Brannon; Nov. 9, 1923, Omar Claypool; Mar. 19, 1924, Ken. Schweitzer; Aug. 11, 1926, Omar Claypool; Dec. 31, 1926, Miss Julia Kapp; May 19, 1927, Clifford Cordier; May 26, 1943, Mrs. Elmer Sooter.

One night in May 1946 the whole village was mostly destroyed by fire.

The "Daisy Ainsworth" was the first large, beautiful steamboat on the Middle Columbia (Cascades to The Dalles) She was built in 1873 at The Dalles, her engines and hull built for speed, her elegant cabins covered with Brussels carpets, giant chandeliers glowed in her cabin and dining room. For three years this fine steamer ran daily between The Dalles and the Cascades.

One cold wintery day in November 1876, a herd of 200 head of beef cattle was driven into The Dalles for shipment to Portland. The "Idaho", another steamer at The Dalles was too small for such a shipment, so it was decided the larger "Daisy Ainsworth" would transport the cattle and the smaller "Idaho" would take the passenger and mail run the next morning. Captain John McNulty, the regular captain on the "Daisy", would then step over to the "Idaho" and allow his first officer and pilot, Martin Spelling, a fine young river man, capable and efficient, to take command of the "Daisy Ainsworth" for this night trip with the load of cattle.

The night was dark and stormy, but the cattle must be delivered to the portage railroad at the Cascades that night. At midnight the cattle were aboard and young Spelling took his place in the pilot house and bells sounded in the engine room and the steamer was soon on its way down the river.

In November the river water is very low at this time, before the Bonneville Dam raised the water level in this section of the river. A pilot must know where he is at all times, for every few miles was some obstacle directly in his path which could destroy his boat; rock islands in the center of the channel, rock points along the shores, and sand and gravel bars on both sides of the river. It would be necessary to change sides of the river often in the forty mile run. The skipper would be alone in the darkened pilot house, his eyes trained to pick out each bend in the river; he must know within a very short distance as to where he is at all times.

This night not a star shown and the air was full of snow, a tail wind and current increased the speed of the fast boat. Not a single light showed on either bank.

Forty miles down river he neared the Cascades; he could hear the roar of the rapids as it cascaded over and around the large rocks in its fall of 33 feet in one-half mile. Also at this point, a very large sand bar took up one-third of the river on the south bank and this caused the channel to narrow, with two rock islands which he must pass between; he had to know exactly where he was at this time.

The story told later, that he mistook a light in a wood scow's cabin on the south bank (Oregon) of the river for Bradford's Landing, is very false. Captain Spelling knew just where he was at this time when he passed the two rock islands in the north quarter of the river. He knew from the roar of the rapids that in minutes he had to be near the north bank to head into the

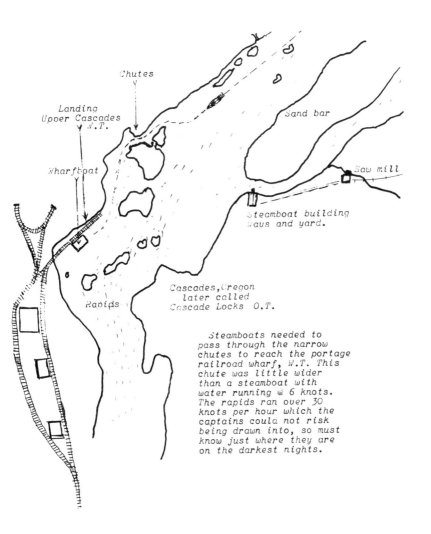

Chutes

Landing
Upper Cascades
W.T.

Wharfboat

Sand bar

Saw mill

Steamboat building
ways and yard.

Cascades, Oregon
later called
Cascade Locks O.T.

Rapids

Steamboats needed to
pass through the narrow
chutes to reach the portage
railroad wharf, W.T. This
chute was little wider
than a steamboat with
water running @ 6 knots.
The rapids ran over 30
knots per hour which the
captains could not risk
being drawn into, so must
know just where they are
on the darkest nights.

narrow rock chutes. These chutes at this time were little wider than a large steamboat, and about one quarter mile long through rock islands to the railroad incline and wharfboat. Here the water widened with room for a steamboat to turn around and tie up to the wharfboat. This was at the head of the rapids and the water ran quite swift, picking up speed as it raced on over the falls.

Monty Attwell was fireman on the portage locomotive and was a witness to the accident of the "Daisy Ainsworth" wrecking at 3 o'clock in the morning on the rocks at the head of the chutes, and this is his account: "We were waiting for the "Daisy Ainsworth" to come into the landing. A cold east wind was blowing down river and the air was full of snow. After a long wait down near the wharfboat, the old engineer backed the locomotive up the incline. The headlight, which was a 'presto light' and not much brighter than a lantern, was burning. The watchman on the wharfboat had hung a lighted lantern out on the east end of the wharfboat to direct the "Daisy's" captain to the landing and then went inside the wharfboat where he had a wood stove fire going and laid down and had gone to sleep.

"We could not see the lantern from the locomotive so did not know that the strong east wind had blown the lantern out. Captain Spelling, on nearing the Chutes, mistook the locomotive's dim light for the lantern on the wharfboat and innocently headed into the Chutes a few seconds late. This one quarter mile difference in the position of the light caused him to misjudge the entrance, by less than one hundred yards and pile the steamer upon the rocks at the entry of the narrow Chutes.

"As she broke up on the rocks, the wild cattle broke out of their pens and stampeded overboard; some drowned; some came out on the north bank, but seven head went completely over the falls and came out on the Oregon side of the river below the falls. Deer hounds were used to run them out of the mountains so that they could be corralled again."

Captain Spelling was an excellent riverman and pilot, but after this fateful night, his spirit and health went into rapid decline and the youthful captain died of a broken heart within a few months. The accident was not the young captain's fault, and had the wharfboat's lantern remained burning he would have avoided the rocks, but a tricky gust of wind had snuffed out the lantern's small flame, unknown to the watchman or the train crew.

*****

Ross, in 1811, set down on paper: "We stayed over night at the 'Washougally Camp'." The French-Canadian fur traders a few years later named it 'La Prairie du' for its wild mint that grew there, and which was found as a good substitute for tea by the early fur traders.

Michael T. Simmons built a crude cabin here in 1845 where the first white child was born in Washington, and christened Christopher Columbus Simmons. Joseph Parrott and his wife Nancy, the Kindred family, and the Simmons had arrived in Oregon City 23 Dec., 1844. With them was a free Negro named Bush. The new Oregon laws would not allow a Negro to own land so the hot headed Kindred and Simmons moved into Washington Territory. The Simmons stopped at Washougal while Christopher came into the new world. While the families remained at Washougal, Simmons led the party of men to Tumwater. (Complete story in Volume One.)

In 1845 David C. Parker either took over the Simmons cabin or erected another log cabin; with his wife and four children, they became the first white family to set its roots down here. They cleared a garden spot and planted potatoes purchased from the Hudson Bay Company store in Vancouver. The first steamboat landing was known as Parker's Landing. A boat launch ramp, boat anchorage, and a fine restaurant are located at this place today, 120 years later.

Next white people to settle here were named Doan and White who built a log cabin and then left for other places. Then in 1847, Joseph Gibbons settled on the banks of the Columbia River, near where Gibbons Creek enters the river, now Port Property. He purchased the White property and hired a man named Charles Carter to help him build a log cabin 18 x 20 feet and costing $15. His family were soon established in the home. Gibbons soon brought in cattle and started raising them on the bottom land.

In 1849, Richard Howe, a sailor from His Majesty's Navy, settled in the area. Howe, who was born in England, soon fell in love with the beautiful 'White Wing', daughter of Indian Chief Schlyhouse. It was said that she was a granddaughter of Soto. Howe, with his blarney brogue, dropped the "H", so was known by everyone as 'Ough', and this name came down in records.

A July 22, 1911 article in the Journal gave this interview with White Wing; she was then 103 years old. "When I was about 12 years of age, my mother told me to go down to the river and pick berries. I no want to go, but mamma she say, 'You go down river, you see new country, new people, new things.' I go down river, and I never go back to Cascades; I never go back."

She stayed at the home of the McDonalds, connected with Hudson's Bay Co...they persuaded her to stay and work for them.

Richard Ough worked for the fur company and met White Wing who had changed her name to Betsy. Ough was engaged to sail along the coast of Oregon to pick up furs. Whenever he returned, Ough gave her his earnings to keep. Betsy: "They all laugh and say, 'Ough he no marry Indian girl.' Then I say, 'Then why he always bring his money to me to keep?' and I shut my ears and don't listen." A few years later they were married.

Mrs. Latourell, next to oldest child. Grace was wife of Joseph Latourell.

*****

Camas' history began when Jacobo Hansaker settled where Camas now sets, in 1846. He hired Parker and Ryan to help him build a sawmill.

The first post office was established at Parker's Landing, Aug. 6, 1852 with Joseph Watkins as postmaster, next was Hamilton Maxon, Oct. 11, 1853; William Kelly, Mar. 16, 1861; Joe Gibbons, Aug. 22, 1865; Discontinued Sept. 10, 1868, and re-established, Aug. 17, 1874 with George Hart, postmaster. Benjamin Hancock, Aug. 7, 1877; Henry Carpenter, Sept. 9, 1878; E.C. Durgin, April 5, 1880, with the post office moved to the town of Washougal. David Gary, Dec. 21, 1889; Tom Sampson, Nov. 11, 1893; John Herzig, Nov. 15, 1897; Charles Cottrell, Feb. 7, 1901; David Wright, June 15, 1903; David Hutchinson, April 17, 1907; Charles McClure, June 27, 1914; Elmer Armstrong, Feb. 6, 1923; Bill Ruettgers, May 13, 1935; Reginal Jones, July 1, 1939; LeRoy McClain, Mar. 17, 1940; Richard Ross, Aug. 1, 1942; LeRoy McClain, Nov. 24, 1945.

Joseph E C. Durgin platted the town of Washougal on April 2, 1880. The first house was built by A.H. Kersey. Durgin built a store at the new town site, with a post office in the building. The store was at the S.W. corner of 2nd. and Main St. Durgin was appointed postmaster and met the steamboat and carried the mail to the post office. The new location was nearer and more convenient for a large number of settlers.

*****

In 1886 a contract was let to carry the mail to Fern Prairie to D.K Webster for $96 a year. Durgin sold his store to Mr. Gary and Tom Sampson became postmaster and moved the office to 211 Main Street in 1889.

In 1898, mail was brought from Vancouver by horse and buggy

62

rather than steamboat.   F.H. Smith was the mail carrier and brought the mail daily for $530 per year.

CAPE HORN
This little village was located in one of the most beautiful spots along the Columbia, at the base of a massive rock bluff. From the rocky mass standing in the river and reaching skyward, it reminded the first boatmen of the tip of South America.
The post office was established June 4, 1883, with Loren Wright's home the office.   John Stevenson went to Bridal Veil with his sail boat twice a week and walked to the depot for the mail sack.   Dec. 11, 1892, James Haffey had the office in his home near the dock; Nov. 8, 1897, Grant Hadley took the office to the little store he had at his home. John Stevenson sailed his boat to a new location for the mail, as the mail came via horse and buggy to Mt. Pleasant.   Stevenson cut a trail up to the road far up the mountain and carried the mail sacks both way to his boat.   Dec. 29, 1900, Iongeld McPherson was postmaster; April 15, 1912, George Breslin with the mail being dropped off the S.P. & S. Railway.   Feb. 26, 1915, Mrs. George Breslin, with the post office discontinued July 31, 1942, mail to Washougal.

*****

Dr. Candiani was reputedly of noble Italian birth. He doctored the early settlers, and started a manufacturing plant to use the produce grown by the settlers. His colony of Italian people were the ancestors of many still found in the community.
John W. Stevenson, Cape Horn, at the age of 16 crossed the plains with his parents in 1853.   He first lived on Clackamas River.   At age 28, worked on first railroad, Oregon Steam Navigation Co. between Eagle Creek and Cascade Locks. He became head sawyer in Eagle Creek sawmill.   The trestles, and even the rails were made of wood. The Headquarters Building of the railroad and sawmill was a large boarding house near the mill, accommodating 13 employees.
Homesteaders took land back on the hills and spread the community out.   In 1844, James Walker crossed the continent by ox team from Pennsylvania to Vancouver.   Then in 1846 he and his family moved to Cape Horn, thus becoming the first settlers.   They were later followed by the Stevensons in 1855, the Fosters, the Smiths, the Nevins, the Hanlons, Haffeys, Buslachs, Gunthers, McCues in 1875, the Breslins, Daughtertys, McCartys, Mascons, Baraccos in 1882, Mackeys in 1885, Del Grossos, Martells, Tavellis, Wantlands, Andersons, Loomis',

Seated--Mr. & Mrs. Jim Walker
Standing--Elmer, Austin, Clarence, Mrs. Clarence, Orvis &
Albro (Lila Taylor)

Peter Klinicks, Rupkies, Hutchinsons, Wrights and Dr. Candianni, who came about 1880, hoping to establish an Italian colony. He first settled on what later became known as Froeschle place. Later he built a factory at Mud Flat on the bank of the river between Cape Horn and Prindle. This factory was to make starch and syrup from potatoes grown by the settlers. It is said that hidden under a bushel basket was a still to manufacture spirits to brighten the times for the local blades. He later operated, on the island opposite Cape Horn, the first seine fishing. Amanuel Baracco recalls that his father worked on the seine with his team of oxen.

The first school in the community was a log cabin beside Canyon Creek near the Sam Angelo farm. Later a building was built on a knoll near the Elliott home, later known as the Walter Dugan place. This building served the community until 1911 when the present school house was built. (A new school is under construction.) Some of the early day teachers were Nellie Wright, Mary McGreel, Katherine Daugherty Breslin, Mr. Waterman in 1881. In late times, Mrs. Mason, Ed Hollis, Lena Strong, Lillie Miller, Mr. Hinkle, Miss Blackwood, Anna Monaghan, Alice Hawkins and Buslach Trimble.

The settlers raised practically all their food, buying only such staple items that they could not raise.

64

Elmer Walker recalled that his brother Clarence built a box boat and he and his father loaded it with wheat and corn to take to Vancouver to be ground into flour and meal. On the way down the Columbia the boat swamped, but they managed to land it on the island. It took them several days to dry the grain before resuming their journey. In the meantime the said grain was all they had to eat.

Most of the farm work was done by the sweat of the brow and help from a team of oxen or horses. In those days, lack of machinery little daunted the hardy homesteader. It is told that Mr. McCue cut his hay with a scythe, raked it by hand and then carried it to his barn, shock by shock, on a rope slung over his back.

In the early days, Protestant Church services were held in the school house and every Monday a priest from Vancouver held Catholic mass in the Nevins' home. Mr. Nevins was a man with some education and took the papers. He read these papers to some of the other settlers who were eager for news but could not read. Some of these early pioneers were from foreign lands of good, intelligent stock but had not had the opportunity for schooling.

The first store at Cape Horn was operated by Ordway Logging Company. When they left, Jim Haffey, father of Irene Hoffman, took over. Mr. Haffey sold to Grant Hadley. Next, McPhersons had the store and took George Breslin as a partner in 1905. In 1907 Mr. Breslin bought out McPherson and Mrs. Breslin took charge of the post office. Mr. McPherson built a store up on the hill.

In 1957 the Stevenson farm had been lived on by the same family for 100 years.

L. Wright owned what was known as the Barret place because his daughter married a Barret, but later it became the Elliot place.

STORIES THAT I HAVE HEARD MY FATHER
TELL IN MY CHILDHOOD
by
Mrs. Minnie M. Levens
June 17, 1922

My father used to tell stories about the pioneer experiences in early days, some of which were quite comical, but to them at that time were very perplexing.

One I remember that always seemed very funny to me, happened while his people, in company with others, were on their trip down the Columbia River from The Dalles, which they had made as far as the Cascades by some kind of a boat, that is, all except the oxen which had been driven down the south bank and ferried across the river to the north bank where they had their wagons and equipment landed. They then drove around the Cascade Falls where they again were obliged to embark by some kind of craft, as they were going still farther down the river. When making such trips, the women and children and equipment and part of the men would go by boat, but a part of the men would have to go by land to drive the oxen, as at that time there were no boats large enough to carry the whole outfit. The men that went by land would usually tie their blankets and what provisions they had on some gentle oxen's horns during the day to make it easier on themselves.

It happened that my grandfather was one of the party that was with the oxen. He had made his bundle ready and tied it on his favorite ox. This was early in the morning and no boat was available yet, and while the party was getting ready for their final departure, the old ox wandered away out of sight in search of food. When the party was ready to go, my grandfather's ox was not to be found, and a search which was fruitless, lasted all day. All the other oxen were in sight, and when night came, there was a big row in my grandfather's family as bedding was very scarce anyway, and the ox had quite a portion of it with him. Poor grandpa was feeling very blue. But then as now, what could not be cured, had to be endured. When morning came, the ox was in camp and the journey was commenced which, however, was not a very long one as my grandfather found a location that suited him near what was later known as Parker's Landing, and near the present town of Washougal, where he stopped and waited for his family to arrive, which they did after some delay and worry.

Some time that fall he took us a Donation Land Claim, I think on what was later known as Lower Cape Horn Mountain, about six miles east of Washougal. Then alone in December or January, my father was sent to Portland to buy supplies for the winter as there was no place nearer than Vancouver to get them. At that time my father was a mere boy. He went with another man in a small boat. After they got their supplies loaded in their boat, one item of which was a barrel of molasses, they found their boat was loaded to its full capacity. The weather was very cold and a strong wind blowing; a winter storm was in full bloom. My father and his partner started on their return trip in spite of the storm, knowing that it was very necessary that they should get their provisions home as soon as possible.

The wind was in their favor until they reached the mouth of the Willamette River, then they found that they had to face it, and they soon found that it was too strong for them. They managed to cross the river to where there was a house on the bank and carried their provisions to the house, all except the molasses, which they were obliged to leave on the river bank with the boat.

After staying all night, they started up the river bank on foot. By this time the snow was about two feet deep and the weather bitter cold, but my father and his partner, Tam O'Shanter decided to go. They finally reached home without any fatal disaster but I do not remember how long they were making the journey. I do remember hearing my father say many times how badly disappointed he and many others were in Oregon weather for they had been told that there was no cold weather in Oregon.

This cold storm wrecked the confidence of a great many emigrants in regard to Oregon climate for the time being, but it came back like the cat, for it was of short duration as are the majority of Oregon cold spells and a Chinook wind soon came and melted the snow and ice.

My father and his partner lit out for their boat and provisions, but none too soon for the river had raised like it always does when a thaw comes and their barrel of molasses was in the river. They had a hard time getting it into their boat but finally succeeded and made their way home without any serious accident that I remember now.

There was a man, I think his name was Brown, who I think crossed the plains in the same train with my father. He was a bad man to swear; a husky old fellow of forty or fifty years of age. During this same storm, he was sleeping out of doors as he had done all the way across the plains. He wore a heavy pair of buckskin pants which kept the cold out very well. One night during the storm, he froze fast to the ground. When he did not come in as early as common, some of the family with whom he was boarding went out to see what was the reason. They soon discovered it and they could hear him cursing and swearing, so they listened to what he was saying and it sounded like this: "Here I have followed them d----d oxen all the way across the plains to this perpetual summered Oregon, and here I am froze down to the ground and can't get up."

My father remained with his father on his claim until 1855 or 1856 when the Eastern Oregon Indians went on the warpath against the whites. He then volunteered with the other Indian War veterans to settle with the Indians. He furnished his own

67

horse and gun and went east of the mountains with the others. But that country was not like it is today; it was wild and woolly then. My father was taken sick before the expedition was finished and was sent back to civilization. He left his gun and horse to others that had lost theirs and he did not get any pay for them until 1918.

I think he was tardy about asking for his pension and lost his discharge, so when he did apply for it, all the officers of the company were dead and the records were defective. His discharge was lost and to this day, he has not received it and he is now eighty-six years old and helpless as he has been for years. He is at the Soldiers Home in Orting, Washington. His name is Hogn M. Turner. There are perhaps many other incidents of his life that might be of interest if I could remember them.

Minnie Turner Levens

FISHER'S LANDING ESTABLISHED

Solomon Fisher took a donation land claim in 1851 on the north bank of the Columbia River about 12 miles up river from Vancouver.

Prune trees were planted and this area became a prune center years later. One year 50,000 sacks of potatoes were shipped from here.

One of the oldest land marks here was the old 'Love Flour Mill' built around 1860. Roger G. Attwell built the mill for the owner. It was powered by a large, overshot water-wheel which turned two large stone grinding wheels. The water wheel remained standing as late as 1920 and the

Grand-daughter of the master carpenter who built the mill. Adele Attwell and her husband, Joe.

68

grinding stones were a historic novelty placed alongside the old highway, and enjoyed by thousands of tourists who often stopped to examine and photograph the historic grinding wheels of the very early flour mill.

MT. PLEASANT

It was first called "Staggerweed Mountain" by pioneers who did not know the reason that livestock grazing there soon staggered; later they learned that it was the wild larkspur that was eaten that made the livestock stagger.

The first settler, John Tompkins, raised and sold $1,500 worth of potatoes the first year, 1878. He is the one who named it Mt. Pleasant. Cottrell built a small sawmill using water from a small stream as power.

Mail came over a trail by horseback from Washougal. Augustus Kruckman carried it for many years. Mrs. Tessie Smead filled in as carrier later.

Post office was established May 17, 1890, Charles Cottrell, in his home; Aug. 1, 1892, William Gillett, a relative; Aug. 24, 1893, Mrs. Julia Moore with the office in her home; Aug. 6, 1900, Robert Turk; discontinued June 15, 1904 with mail to Washougal. After the S.P. & S. became operating, a post office was set up just over the Clark County line at what was known as lower Mt. Pleasant where mail was dropped off the trains. Oct. 26, 1912, Alf Leroy Emmons; Mar. 20, 1918, Harry Brooks; May 20, 1921, Charles Berthea; discontinued Sept. 30, 1926 with mail to Washougal.

*****

Caleb John Moore was born March 11, 1849, in Iowa, and was educated at Waverly High School and Academy. On October 19, 1875, he started west for Oregon Territory. He looked over different places in the northwest until he came to the wilderness of Mt. Pleasant; there were no roads, only wild animal trails.

After climbing the mountain, he came upon the Tompkins log cabin. The Tompkins let him know that they did not want bachelors for neighbors, but he assured them that he had a girl picked out in Iowa. They then encouraged him to stay. He then selected a homestead site, a place with lots of water, good soil and some timber. April 8, 1879 his rude log cabin was completed and he learned his girl friend would not come so far west. He began to clear land with an axe and grub hoe, and put in his first crop. He then left to find work for a few months, and on his return he found a good crop of carrots, potatoes, squash and pumpkins.

His cabin was rather loosely built as the climate had been so mild. He was surprised to awaken one morning to find several inches of snow all over his bed and cabin; the strong east wind had blown it through the cracks between the logs.

He batched for five years and was elected County Commissioner on the Republican ticket. One day as he was inspecting a road in Cape Horn Valley, he stopped at a cabin to ask for a drink of water, and there met a girl who, a year later, became his bride. She was Julia Foster, a real pioneer daughter of a Civil War veteran, Fenner Foster.

Mr. Moore had a notation in one of his diaries telling of the easy going life in the early days. Captain Love, of the old stern wheel steamboat "Calliope", was making a trip down river. He came in to Parker's Landing, and there was met by a woman whose eggs he regularly picked up for a Portland man. This day the woman met the Captain, exclaiming, "I lack one egg of having a dozen, Captain, but if you'll wait awhile I'm sure another hen will lay one." So Captain Love allowed the boat to wait for the hen to lay that egg.

Caleb Moore was elected to the Legislature four times. He and Julia raised three daughters; Mollie, Zetta and Josie. Mr. Moore belonged to the Grange in Iowa in 1873. When he came to Washington Territory, he brought the Grange spirit with him and he helped organize the Washougal Grange in 1883. He and Mollie organized the Mt. Pleasant Grange, and he helped organize the State Grange at LaCamas. His grand-daughter, Della Miller, has carried on the good work and is Master of the Mt. Pleasant Grange at this time.

*****

In the next few years came the Turks, Marbles, Powells, Chandlers, Kruckmans, Alldridges, Pettersons, Grouts, Sampsons, Baileys, Ledstrones, and Rathbornes. Descendants of most of these families still live in the county or in nearby Clark County. Sampsons operate a large acreage in both beef and dairy cattle.

The pioneers built a little church in 1886, and the first school was held in the church with Mrs. J.O. Wing as the teacher. The term was three months a year, and salary $15 per month.

Travel was by boat and horseback and buggy where possible. Many farmers worked out their poll tax by working on the roads. C.J. Moore spent 8 years in the legislature working for better roads.

Portland was the closest market for these farmers. Butter was the major product shipped via boat across to the Oregon side of the river, thence by rail. Whenever the river froze over, as it did in those days, the produce would be sledded across to the railway.

PRINDLE

Ernest H. Prindle, a native of Vermont, had a fish market at 3rd. and Washington, Portland. He also did some commercial fishing. In 1884 he made a trip on the steamboat "Calliope" and landed at Fresedale. He liked the place so well he purchased 280 acres of the Charles Frese' D.L. Claim. Prindle and his wife worked at the Bridal Lumber Co. across the river until 1892. Lewis & Clark called this place Cruzatt in 1805; Frese called it Fresedale, and now Mr. Prindle named it Prindle.

Mr. Prindle donated land to the S.P. & S. for right-of-way through his property and built a store. A post office was established in his store Aug. 26, 1909; his son was postmaster Jan. 3, 1930, with the post office discontinued Dec. 31, 1938 to Washougal. Ernest Prindle died Jan. 1, 1930, and his son Robert took over the store, operating it for 36 years. He was Skamania County's first horticultural agent and was very active in getting orchards started in Underwood.

A number of Polish families moved into this area. They settled in Prindle and worked across the river at the Bridal Veil Mill, crossing in small boats in all kinds of weather. Later some of them turned to fishing. They were Frank Knopski's, Julius Gory, Soboski, Ketchmarks and Zawistowski.

Before the area was named Prindle, in 1880, J.J. Mackey, then 7 years old, came to the area with his parents. The elder Mackey worked for loggers, Ordway and Britchford. The logs were hauled with oxen over a skid road and then floated down the Washougal River to Camas. The Mackeys homesteaded what is now known as the St. Cloud Ranch, later owned by Vials.

*****

The little town of Skamania has changed names many times: Fresedale, Marrs Landing, Mendota, Butler or Butler's Landing, Edgewater and Skamania.

Fresedale: Mrs. Charles C. Frese established a post office April 27, 1882, which was discontinued April 30, 1883. Charlie Frese, a German, settled here and purchased 65 acres alongside the Columbia River and built a cabin and planted fruit trees. He visioned raising fruit for the early settlers and also the river travelers. As the orchard matured, he built a two story house alongside the cabin. Charlie's wife, Louise, was a medical doctor but enjoyed family life more than following the profession. They raised two sons, Carl, a pilot on Puget Sound, and Herman, a river pilot on the lower Columbia.

The Frese home and property was purchased in 1905 by William F. Sams and a family was raised there. In 1930, Elmer and Grace Walker purchased the Frese place from Mr. Sams.

There appears to be a lapse of about nine years before mail again was distributed here. Marrs Landing, which received its name from the Marrs brothers, became the post office station for the area. Mrs. John Clark became the postmaster Oct. 18, 1892. It was one of the most primitive offices ever; it is said that she sorted the mail into a three foot square box in her bedroom. While it was a steamboat landing, boats seldom stopped because the place was so scarcely populated. The mail came by a primitive but secure method. Mary Stooquin, an Indian woman, carried the mail on horse back in all kinds of weather from the Cascades. The mail came from Portland to Warrendale, Oregon, and was picked up by a row boat at the fish cannery dock and taken across the river to the Lower Cascades. The boat carriers were Johny Baughman, Fred Wise, Carl Lindstrom and William Davi.

Nov. 16, 1898, Edward Hughey took over the post office and renamed it Mendota; May 16, 1899, Mrs. Hattie Yettick became the postmaster and the office was set up in her name (which is still standing behind the Grange Hall at Skamania).

Dec. 18, 1901, Billy Butler moved the post office to his store which was located at Butler's Landing on the river (now Skamania Landing). He called the office Butler. The steamboats picked up and delivered the mail here. William Fredrick Sams took the post office Feb. 24, 1911 to the Thomas Reath store (Skamania General Store), and it is said that Tom Reath named it Edgewater, honoring his home town in Michigan. Mar. 2, 1915, Alen W. Andrews with the post office name Skamania; Mar. 26, 1915, Thomas Reath; Sept. 23, 1927, Arch Sams who placed the office in his service station just west of Duncan Creek alongside of the Evergreen Highway; Feb. 18, 1943, Mrs. Stella Hazard, postmaster, with her Aunt Eleanor McDonald finishing with the office closing in 1974 and the rural route established from Stevenson.

Logging and fishing were the main industries in this area. The Barr Logging Company with 6 steam donkey engines was the big operator. Sweeny and Kupler logged here with teams as did several other small companies.

Several fishwheels operated along here as they did on both sides of the river, catching hundreds of tons of salmon, as Hi Reed tells later.

One story that shows the abundance of salmon in the river. An old timer tells, "Many stationary wheels were in use when two brothers built a floating scow wheel which could be easily moved and also remain at the right level when the river raised or lowered. Shortly after building the wheel it was tried out and proved to be a great fish catcher, in fact, too good.

As soon as the wheel was lowered into the water, fish were dipped aboard with every turn of the wheel. When the scow became loaded to the gunwale, they decided to raise the wheel but found the scow so loaded that hoisting the wheel added weight which the loaded scow could not carry. It was necessary to leave the wheel in the water which kept revolving and dipping salmon until the fish load sank the scow and wheel." The scow above is not the same scow wheel.

About 1915, a carnival stopped at the one store in Skamania to water the animals   An ape decided that he was getting tired of carnival life in a cage, and when the cage door was opened, he knocked the attendant aside and took off for open spaces. No coaxing with choice food could entice him back to his prison. An oil truck driver was bitten and mauled when he tried to lasso the new Skamanian.

A local mother out walking with two of her small children, met the sasquaquach in the road going to her home. She turned and fled back to town with her children, screaming, "My God! A gorilla is coming down the road!"

All efforts to catch the ape failed as he roamed through the forests. Traps with his choice tidbits were set about, but he disliked the carnival and wanted no part of it. A reward of $100 was offered for his capture.

Sometime later, a Cape Horn resident watched the ape go into their root cellar so he closed the door on him and called the carnival people, who came out and recaptured the ape and left without paying the reward. The root cellar owner called the sheriff who soon overtook the owners and made them return and pay the reward.   But. .while the ape was locked in the root cellar, he enjoyed himself and busted 400 jars of canned fruit which the $100 reward would not replace.

Che che optin was the Indian's name for this second largest monolith in the world, next to Gibraltar. Lewis called it Beacon Rock when they sighted it in 1805. The Astor fur traders called it 'Inshoach Castle' in 1811. The early pioneers called it Castle Rock and it was known by that name until the 1930s when the name was changed to Beacon Rock.

An old Indian story of the wind's wail on the rock:

"Wehatpolitan was the beautiful daughter of the principal Indian chief in the area. As she matured into young womanhood, she fell in love with a young chief of a neighboring tribe who also loved her. The young chief sent a messenger seeking the girl in marriage but the stern father would not consent to the request. This great love did not end here and the two lovers met clandestinely and were secretly married. The father was unaware that this had happened, so he gave Wehatpolitan to a chief whom he favored. The latter kept silent and constant watch of the girl and one night he saw her stealing away and he followed her and watched her meeting Penpen and fall into his arms. He returned telling the father what he had seen.

"The big chief then sent word to Penpen and the girl that all was forgiven and if they would return to her people, all would be forgiven and that he, Penpen, and Wehatpolitan would be rightfully wed. Rejoicing at the good news and happy that Wehatpolitan could see her people, Penpen hastened to see the father, but no sooner than he arrived, he was seized and executed.

"Not long after this, the heart broken girl gave birth to a child. The father decreed that the child must share its father's fate. On learning this, Wehatpolitan took her baby in her arms and disappeared. The stern chief had his executioners search in vain for the child which they could not find. In a few days the Indians heard wailings from the top of Che che optin (Beacon Rock), and they soon discovered that the poor girl with her child had climbed to the inaccessible top of this monolith. The old chief, repenting of his harsh actions, called aloud to his daughter to come down and he would forgive her. But fearing treachery, she paid no heed, and the wailing continued. Overcome with grief, the remorseful chief offered all kinds of rewards to anyone who would climb the rock and save his daughter's life, and that of the child. Many tried but none could succeed. After a few days, the half crazed father decided to climb the rock. He was seen near the top as he disappeared over the summit. He was never seen again; the Indians thought that on reaching the lifeless bodies of his daughter and grandson that he just had lain down beside them and died. Even yet the heart-breaking wailings can be heard coming off the rock when the wind blows, the wailing voice of the unhappy Wehatpolitan spirit."

FIRST WHITE PEOPLE TO CLIMB THE ROCK
It has been told that in 1901 the rivalry between the two steamboat lines was at its height, Frank Smith, with two helpers of the Regulator Line, managed to climb the rock with ropes and rock hooks and placed the Regulator Line's flag on top where it could be seen from passing steamboat passengers. George Maxwell later placed the O.R. & N. flag alongside the first flag. Afterwards, Mr. Whitney of the McGowan Salmon Cannery placed the Stars and Stripes on the very top.

Turner Leavens' goats were seen on top of the rock before anyone else other than Wehatpolitan had scaled the rock. Turner was unable to go after the goats at milking time, but when they decided to come home, they came down where a man dare not take the risk.

Beacon Rock is located on the North Bank Highway, 5 miles west of the Bridge of the Gods. This monolith is second in size to Gibraltar, stands 850 feet high, and its base covers 18 acres.

Rock was needed for constructing jetties in northwest ocean harbors. Henry J. Biddle, philanthropist, nature lover and a wealthy business man with a large stone quarry at Fishers, to stop competition from others who had plans to buy and blast down Castle Rock as it was called at that time, purchased the monolith and had a winding trail built to the top. He then gave the property to Washington State Parks.

Charlie Johnson, known as 'Tin Can Johnson' to his friends, was the construction foreman on the trail. He had two burros that he used to carry tools, cement and sand and gravel up the trail during construction. They would be loaded in the morning and started up the trail at their slow pace. The workmen would go on ahead and the burros proceeded on their own. If they became tired, they would lay down and rest, then proceed on to where the material was needed and be unloaded and fed. Many places concrete bridges and steps were built.

It was a generous gift of Mr. Biddle; the rock was saved and thousands of hikers walk up the trail to the great view and the thrill of reaching the top.

Come see it when you can, and try the climb.

Hamilton Creek Logging Co. built an incline railroad from the river just above Castle Rock (now Beacon Rock) to the top of Hamilton Mountain. This incline was so steep, 65%, that a logger with his cork-shoes (spiked shoes) could stand on the end of a log, aboard a log loaded car coming down the incline.

A large steam donkey with steamboat boilers furnishing steam for it, the 2-inch steel cable from the donkey drum was chokered around the logs rather than the car, otherwise they would slide off the car while letting the load down the incline. After the car was unloaded, with the logs dumped into the river, the big donkey would pull the empty cars back to the top of the mountain for another load.

Thousands of carloads of logs came down this mountainside until the mountains were logged off in the early 1900's.

The abandoned rails were taken up during World War II. Two logging locomotives on top of the mountain were cut up and hauled out for the iron.

James P. Grenia, born 1859, was married to Ella Johns, born 1862, and was the daughter of the Methodist minister that St. Johns, Oregon was named for.

They settled near Hamilton Creek about 1880. The nearest town was at Garrison Eddy, or Lower Cascades, and about 150 people lived here and at the Middle Cascades.

Mr. & Mrs. James P. Grenia and 3 of their 8 children. L. to R. Ella, George, Claude, Jim and Mary.

George Grenia, a son born here, told this to Marie Knight for History of Skamania County.

"Steamers have been known to come up Hamilton Creek in high water and go through Greenleaf Slough and back into the river above. Some books refer to this as a dangerous portage the boats had to make below the Cascades in high water.

"In the early days there weren't any banks so the settlers each had their own means of hiding their money," Mr. Grenia recalled an incident about Louis Marr. "Mr. Marr had built on the stairway a little box under one of the steps. The way he had built it was not noticeable. It was rumored around that Mr. Marr had a lot of money in his house. This news reached the ears of two robbers. They lined up and both fired when Mr. Marr came out of his house, killing him instantly; they searched the house but did not find the money. Later the money was found in

78

its hiding place and amounted to $1,700. The Marr family had one of the first orchards in the area, a huge barn, a prune drier, and a fine home.

"One of the first mills here where North Bonneville now stands was built by the Kemp brothers. Orey Kemp was a silent partner. They later had a mill north of Carpenter's Slough, some distance east of the house and flumed lumber down to the planer mill just east of what is now the Moffett Springs road. This mill was built about 1905 and had a contract to cut ties for the new railway. The planing mill belonged to Table Rock Lumber Co.

"Porter Bros. had a forty mile contract on the railroad and borrowed fill dirt from the Hamilton Donation Land Claim.

"The cemetery near North Bonneville is the oldest in Skamania County. There is one grave marked 1854. The cemetery was larger before the railroad came through; they moved some of the graves out of the right-of-way. There was a military barracks on the Hamilton place, thus soldiers were buried here. Also when the Bridge of the Gods was raised, three graves by the bridge approach were moved. There was a grave near the bridge that had a tombstone that said, 'He went over the rapids and was scared to death.' The story behind this is that a man went over the rapids in a canoe, as sometimes daring men did. Later this man's canoe was found downriver with him quite dead, apparently from a heart attack. Thus the epitaph on his tombstone.

"The cemetery was part of the old Bishop claim. Some of the old families have kin in the cemetery; Leavens, Hamilton, Reed, Grenia, Walker and others.

George Grenia married Lura Wantland who was for many years County School Superintendent. Joe was married to Carrie Williams, a pioneer girl of Skamania.

*****

Dr. Hiram Leavens, the first doctor on the middle Columbia, came west in 1851, leaving his wife, Pluma, and two children, Turner and Emma, with his mother in Illinois. He first took out a donation land claim near Dodson and under St. Peter's Dome (mountain). Several years later he moved to the north bank across the river and took up a homestead just east of Beacon Rock. In 1858 he returned to Illinois for his family and remained there a little over a year. Anna was born to them Feb. 9, 1859. In May they joined a wagon train west, arriving at Cascades in late August and settled on his homestead.

Anna spent her childhood here just below the Cascades. In her teens she had a fall down the stairway of their home which injured her spine. When she reached 17, she fell in love with and married Monty Attwell, April 18, 1876, who was firing locomotive on the Cascade Portage Railroad.

A son, Rutherford, was born to them Mar. 5, 1877, and the little fellow died April 10, 1877, only 35 days later.

"Mercy" enters the picture, as told by Myrtle Hamilton many years later.

"Doc Leavens had attended the childbirth of a baby girl to a young woman in July. The woman's husband had drowned a few months before and the young widow was living in a cabin near the Hamiltons. Mrs. Mary Hamilton often looked in on the young mother as she wasn't well. This morning when Doc Leavens came by, Mrs. Hamilton accompanied him to the woman's home. They knocked on the

door as usual, and this time they did not hear the "Come in" so Doc opened the door and walked in, followed by Mrs. Hamilton.

What they saw was almost too much for Mary, but Doc had already handed her the little baby that was all bundled up by the mother before she died. Two house cats that had been in the house with all the windows and doors closed, had eaten part of the woman's cheek and nose. Doc pulled a blanket over the woman's head and relieved Mary of the half dead baby, taking it over to his daughter Anna. When Anna took the little baby from Doc, she said, "Mercy, mercy, mercy." This is the name the little baby girl was known by from then on. Her real name was never recorded. Even with the loving care, Mercy died in October."

Maude, a girl, was born to the unlucky couple Mar. 21, 1878, and poor Anna died Dec. 7, 1878 of 'spinal meningitis' which had developed from her fall several years before. Monty was so broken up with such tragic happenings, that Pluma, the grandmother, took Maude who was then only nine months old, into the Doc Leavens' home. A little over a year later, Maude died. It appeared that all the children had contracted the meningitis from the young mother. The graves are all in the Pioneer Cemetery at North Bonneville, and on Mercy's stone is the epitaph, "She climbed the golden stairs."

Seven years later, Monty married Bertha Blackwood, whose older sister was teaching school at the Cascades. Bertha, with her loving and unjealous nature, always left Monty's first wife Anna's picture hanging in their front room. The picture is now in the Cascade Locks Museum in its original mounting.

LEWIS MARR WAS MURDERED
(Portland Oregonian Paper)

Lewis, sometimes spelled Louis by early settlers, lived near where Skamania is now. The 1860 census showed him as being a farmer from Missouri and a newspaper article on his death claimed him to be an old Hudson's Bay Frenchman.

Lewis lived alone and it seemed well known that he always kept considerable money stashed away in his cabin. He was around 70 years old when he let Ed Gallagher move in with him. This was around 1892 and Ed was working at Dodson across the river helping build Cape Cod dories for Eph Winans. Gallagher was a morose sort of fellow and did not talk much, yet he was a satisfactory worker; weighing only 90 pounds, he could do heavy work. Ed would row across the river to Dodson and put in his days work and return at night to Marr's cabin. Ed often bought the groceries at Dodson and took them in his boat to Marr's place.

After a time had passed and Ed was not seen around, nor was Lewis, a neighbor paid a visit to Marr's place and found old Lewis with his head blown off from a shotgun blast.

Sheriff Clarence Walker of Skamania County, when Lower Cascades was still the county seat, investigated the murder. Since Gallagher had been living with Lewis, he was considered a likely suspect. Sheriff Walker found that Marr's own shotgun had been used for the crime; it was an old-fashioned muzzle loader. This old gun, designed before cartridges were invented, was found in the room where Lewis was murdered A 'wad" was used in this old type of gun to tamp the powder down and then the bullet placed in on top of the powder. Sheriff Walker found this 'wad' in the far corner of the room. A small piece of paper had been used for the 'wad'. On inspecting the piece of paper, Sheriff Walker noted that it had been torn from a Milwaukee, Wisconsin newspaper.

Sheriff Walker set about to locate Gallagher and his description was telegraphed around to different counties. Gallagher was found and arrested in Tacoma and returned to Vancouver for trial. The Milwaukee newspaper was found among Gallagher's possessions. It had a notice of the death of his mother in that city. During the trial Sheriff Walker brought forth the wad of paper which had been used to tamp down the powder. He spread it out over the paper Gallagher had carried and the torn piece fitted in perfectly. When they had him dead to rights, Gallagher confessed, and he was duly sentenced to be hanged.

In his confession, he told why he had killed Lewis Marr. He wanted to get money to buy a saloon.

When the day of execution came at Vancouver, a general invitation was made for anyone to attend. The 14th Infantry was stationed at this time in Vancouver and, with the soldiers watching, there were about 500 people present for the hanging.

Without any show of emotion, Gallagher moved quietly up the 13 steps between the sheriff and his deputy. On the west side were about 200 soldiers and at the front were the citizens.

All of a sudden, Gallagher broke loose, knocking down the two men guarding him. He made a break for freedom but chose the wrong direction. The soldiers, not wanting to be deprived of a show, caught him and returned him to the platform. His feet were tied together. The noose went around his neck and the sheriff kicked the trap--but the excitement wasn't over yet. Gallagher only weighed 90 pounds; he was muscular and had a strong neck. The fall did not break his neck as it was supposed to do. The sheriff and the deputy, being kindly men and not wanting to see the cold blooded killer suffer, they grabbed him around the shoulders and added their weight which soon sent the murderer into different hunting grounds. However, it is many minutes before the doctor pronounced Gallagher dead.

Kinsey Marr was an heir, and came from Missouri and was awarded the estate in Mr. 1885. Value of estate estimated $3,400, 380 acres in Sec. 4 through 3, Town   N, Range

WILLIAM HIRAM REED REMEMBERS
EARLY DAYS IN THE COLUMBIA RIVER GORGE

"Hi" Reed as he was known to a host of friends he had made during his colorful lifetime. In 1952 he was given the honor of being the oldest marine engineer at the gathering of the Veteran Steamboat Men at Champoeg. He was 86 years old when he gave the following remembrances. He, along with his old friend Henry Latourelle at Latourelle Falls who was past ninety

years of age, were two of the oldest pioneers remaining in the gorge. His parents lived at the Lower Cascades, and later settled on a farm in the shadow of St. Peter's Dome on the Oregon side of the Columbia River. He engaged in Commercial fishing and, at one time, owned Wahkeena Falls. His interesting story of the early days in the Gorge follows:

"Yes, I believe I should be classed as a pioneer, being born in the year 1868 on the 4th day of March in one of the buildings of the Garrison at the Lower Cascades on the Columbia River. The Garrison was built by the government to house soldiers for a time after the Indian Massacre of 1856. After being abandoned by the army, emigrants would occupy the buildings, some which were made of lumber, but most of the buildings were built of hewed logs. There were holes on all sides of these buildings to shoot through if needed. The post office was called 'Lower Cascades' and was the place from which the pioneer settlers rafted down the river after making the portage around the Cascades from the Upper Cascades. These rapids were situated just below Cascade Locks and are now covered by water from the lake formed when the river was damned by Bonneville Dam.

"Bradford Island, now the site of Bonneville Dam's powerhouse, was used by the Indians as a burying ground. One time my grandfather, Dr. H.A. Leavens, was on board a steamboat that attempted to make a landing on Bradford Island but was greeted with such a volley of bullets that they gave it up.

"Granddad and his partner, Tommy Pierce, were active during the Indian trouble. Tommy Pierce was shot and wounded, but not badly, when he was helping to move women and children out of reach of the Indians. He was using a rowboat. The bullet went through a leather knapsack at his side which saved his life. After he was shot, the people in the boat went into panic. Some of them insisted that they push off while a woman with a little child in her arms was running toward the boat. An Indian was trying to catch her. Some of the people cried, 'Push off', but Mr. Hamilton who owned the farm, drew his gun and declared that he would shoot the first man who tried to push the boat off before the woman and child got aboard. The Indian did not have a gun so did not come closer. The boat was rowed down river to Vancouver, which was the nearest place of safety and where medical aid could be had for Tommy, who recovered quickly.

"When I was 2 years old, my parents moved onto a farm 5 miles below the Cascades on the Oregon side of the river. We still had to cross the river and go up to the Cascades for our mail. When I was 9 years old, my folks moved back to the Lower Cascades so that we children could go to school.

"During the first year there was another Indian outbreak in Eastern Washington, and while the Cascade Indians were friendly, there was some anxiety about other Indians attacking us at the Cascades. I remember being shown the holes in the walls of the log buildings.

"Salmon were so plentiful in the Columbia in those days that they could be dipped out of the river with a dip net. I became quite interested in the manner in which the Indians caught salmon. The Indian would stand on a large rock or a dip-net stand which was made by the Indians out of small trees. Usually four trees would do the trick. Two poles would be tied together at the top by twisting small vine maple which were used as rope. They were placed in a V-shape out in the river and held in place by two poles, one on each side of the V, and about 5 feet from the top and extending 3 feet outside the V poles and covered with boards making a place to stand on.

"The nets were shaped something like a sack but with a taper and were fastened onto a sort of a bow made of wood and shaped like a balloon, the small end fastened to a small pole which served as a handle. The binding was made from the spinal column from a sturgeon, which when removed and dried made a very strong, waterproof binding.

"In the year 1875 or 1876, the first salmon cannery to be built in this area was built about 3 miles below Bonneville by a Mr. Warren; ever since the place has been known as Warrendale.

The price he paid for salmon weighing 25 pounds was 25 cents. Salmon weighing under 25 pounds brought 12 $\frac{1}{2}$ cents each. Bluebacks sold for 3 cents each. Business was not so good for Mr. Warren for the first several years.

"When my folks moved back onto our farm on the Oregon side from the Cascades in 1879, our former renter, a Mr. Sam Wilson, built the first fish wheel. It was a weakly constructed thing and it washed away during the spring freshet, but it caught fish while it lasted.

"The next year the Williams Brothers built a wheel that stood the test and caught an enormous amount of fish. From then on there were a number of fishwheels on the river. Some were built stationary, others were built on scows. There were 3 dippers in each wheel. At one time I counted nine blueback salmon in one dip.

"The fish wheels could only be operated in swift water. There arose the problem of getting the fish to the cannery. I never knew whose idea it was, but someone conceived the idea of floating the fish to the cannery. The fish were strung on cords which were passed through the heads of the fish. The string of fish was then attached to an empty barrel about half the size of standard barrels. They were then dumped into the river and picked up by a steam launch and towed to the cannery. As I remember the average weight of fish attached to each barrel was about 1,000 pounds.

"In the years 1896 and 1897, I worked as fireman on the steam launch "Nerka" (in Japanese meaning Blueback). Part of my duties were to loosen the ropes on the side of the barrel and pull the fish into a boat, a string at a time, which had to be done fast.

"The banner year for salmon was 1896 when we picked up 81 barrels in one day. The cannery was packed to capacity. The Chinese laborers worked day and night. Some worked until they dropped in their tracks rather than have the contractors lose money. For several days a large steamboat was loaded with fish and taken to Cathlamet for Warren's other cannery there, but many tons of salmon spoiled and were dumped into the river.

"From then on Mr. F.M. Warren became rich but he did not live long to enjoy his riches. He went down on the maiden voyage of the steamship "Titanic".

"Now something about sturgeon. In the pioneer days they were so plentiful that some people were ashamed to be seen carrying a piece of sturgeon home. An old pioneer said that he and his brother would buy a piece of sturgeon from the Indians and take to the woods when passing a neighbor's house so that they would not be seen taking a sturgeon home for fear that they would be considered poverty stricken.

"In early days sturgeon grew to be of enormous length and I recall seeing the carcasses of two sturgeon that had been killed by blasting of rocks by the Government on the upper Columbia. They had drifted ashore on our beach and were as long as father's rowboat which was 16 feet long. They must have weighed 1,000 pounds each.

"It is a shame how they got exterminated. Fishwheels were the cause of a lot of waste. A big sturgeon would stop the wheel which was quite a loss when it stopped. It was dangerous to try and get the sturgeon out of the wheel alive, so it would have to be killed and then thrown back into the river, being valueless. But in the year 1896 a Mr. Prescott came out from New York and began to buy sturgeon and ship them back east. He paid 75 cents a piece for sturgeon over 4 feet long.

"I remember catching a sturgeon weighing over 500 pounds which I was glad to sell for 75 cents as it enabled me to get it out of my boat. The fish when opened had 90 pounds of prime roe in it. When it had been sieved and salted, it brought the buyers (not me) 25 cents a pound.

"Now about trout. All this I remember is in the Columbia Gorge. There was an abundance of trout in the creeks in the vicinity of Castle Rock, now known as Beacon Rock, three miles above and three miles below. An uncle of mine caught 300 trout in one day in Duncan Creek There was never any great amount of trout in the creeks on the Oregon side of the Columbia River. Herman Creek was the exception. The falls in the creeks on the Oregon side may be the reason that there were few trout in these creeks."

*****

William Hamilton, son of Sam Hamilton, tells the story--a little more complete than Hi's story--of the woman with the child racing for the boat with the Indian after her.

"When word was received that the Indians had attacked the Cascades, Father (Sam Hamilton) unyoked the oxen, came to the house and told Mother to get the children ready to board the boat. Several neighbors came running to the house. Father took his rifle and everyone went with him to the boat which was a large rowboat about the size of a lifeboat and would carry 20 people. Tom Pierce and Doc. Leavens also arrived as the people were climbing into the boat. Father had not yet climbed into the boat when a woman with a small child came running

86

across the field and a dozen Indians following her, yelling their war whoops. One warrior was ahead of the rest and almost catching her. This panicked the people in the boat and one man called, 'Shove off,' but Father answered, 'I will kill the one who shoves the boat off before this woman gets here.' The woman set the child over the rail fence and went over herself just as the leading warrior reached the rail fence. As he attempted to climb the fence, Father shot him and this stopped all of them, but one shot Tom Pierce before the boat got away."

*****

The olde Cascades post office was changed to Wacomac, then to Moffetts and then to North Bonneville. Wacomac misspelled for the Indian Chief Warcomac. The name had been sent in as Wacomac so the postal department let it remain. The post office was established July 18, 1917, and Henry Hostetler was the first postmaster. Hostetler was a partner with McGregor and McClaren in Western Pacific Logging Co.

May 29, 1918, Ernest Nelson; Nov. 10, 1918, Henry Sprague, who moved the office to North Bonneville to the office of the Sprague Lumber Co. Roy Winston, Nov. 6, 1919; Ray Matlock, July 19, 1920; Miss Marie Schick, Mar. 4, 1922, changed the name to Moffetts, Mar. 29, 1922, and set the office up at Moffetts Hot Spring, where she was a nurse. She picked the mail up at Cascades depot in her car.

Moffetts Hot Springs Hotel

May 1, 1934, name to North Bonneville; Aug. 25, 1934, Roy Emerson; Dec. 1, 1951, Norman (Wid) Senter. When death took Wid, his wife Gil, was appointed postmaster. Trains brought the mail until Oct. 31, 1959, and from then on the mail was brought by truck.

Cascades, a small town with many Indian houses, was renamed North Bonneville with the construction of Bonneville Dam in the early 1930's. The S.P. & S. Railroad maintained a depot here called the Cascades until 1932 when it was changed to North Bonneville. Don Brown owned part of the first town and refused to have the name changed, so retained the pioneer name Cascades which is still listed as a voting precinct.

Potter Lumber Co. was out near Moffetts Hot Springs. The railroad had a large water tank here for filling the tenders; after filling, the engineers had difficulty getting the trains started because of a curve and incline; sometimes it was necessary to back the train and try again, so the water tank was moved to Skamania at Duncan Creek on a more straight track.

For years, starting about 1909, Porter Bros. Table Rock Bottling Works had a bottling works at Moffetts. Carbonated soda water, and later all kinds of flavored drinks were bottled, then hauled to the Cascades flag stop depot with horse and wagon and shipped around the country.

*****

NOTES ON STEVENSON
by Mrs. Henry Harding
(This was written when Mrs. Harding was very old.)

1911--Railroad had been built 4 years--trestles--to Lyle. Two trains east and two west.

No parsonage. One little 4-room house--just the walls--4 partitions inside and a little pantry--no closets. No furniture. Ladies Aid just formed--gave a little furniture--not too good. Was in the house seven years. Bought some furniture and organ for Harry.

After about one or two years, started the Carson Church. Had services Sunday afternoons. Both of us went on Tuesday until we left Stevenson. We visited around all day--walked there and back. Harry went with his father on Sundays.

In those days the Cascade Locks were in use, being the only way the boats could go up and down. From Stevenson to Cascade Locks there was a small ferry boat run with a motor. Dad was going across to officiate at a funeral and half way across the motor gave out. The captain tried everything he knew but it seemed useless. All the time the boat was drifting nearer the rapids. It was dangerous. They were nearly in the current when the motor sputtered. I do not know how many were on board. Dad said how he gave thanks to our heavenly Father for His care. That was the nearest he had been to death during the years.

Men's meetings started once a week--were very successful.

First sane Fourth of July: Over the railroad tracks, barber shop, four saloons, two hotels, cafe. All burned except one saloon. All of our family sat on the bank across the tracks nearly all night as we watched the places go one by one. Along that road was the only way out of Stevenson. Could go as far as home Valley--no farther east--poor road--no road west farther than Cascades. Many trails.

Funeral up on the mountain; the first one. It was about 2 miles back of Stevenson. It was a Mr. Skaar, I believe. Our two boys and I had only been out here about three weeks then. The service was held in the home and many Norwegians were there. They made the coffin as there was no one to do such things nearer than Vancouver. The burial took place in a corner of one of their fields. There were several graves already there. There was a fence around it making it a small cemetery.

Dad also had one or more funerals at the Indian Reservation at Cascades. The Indians there also wanted him to come down. They were moving the body of a young girl to another spot. They had beautiful new blankets. They opened the grave, took the body out and put it, soiled blanket and all, into the new ones, tying it around. Then they all walked to the new grave. Dad walked in front as at any funeral. He read the committal that was what they wanted; a Christian burial. In the grave they put the pots and pans and china that was in the other grave.

During the first World War, we had an Indian wedding. Of course it was a legal marriage. They had gone to the Court house for the certificates. It was Saturday about noon. I looked out of the window and there were about thirty Indians coming. Among them was a man in uniform--also a young woman--My, was she dressed. Also with them was old Chief Wacomic and an old squaw; that was what she really looked like. We knew both. It was in the days when the minister asked all the questions. Dad asked the young man first (and in his uniform he looked very smart--he was 29), then he turned to the young woman. She said, "It is not me, it is her," pointing to the old squaw. She could not speak English so had the young woman come to interpret. I will never forget Dad's face, he was so embarrassed. After it was over, Dad asked the young man the reason. He answered that they had been married for years according to Indian law but he wanted to insure for the ten thousand dollars for her so they had to be married according to U.S.A. laws. (Note: The couple that was spoken of here were John Clark and Molly (Mary) Sam.)

The Reservation was moved to the Yakima Reservation after we moved from Stevenson. We moved to Skamokawa and were there three years. The church and parsonage was on the island then.

Birds-eye View STEVENSON, Washington.

POST OFFICE...NELSON TO STEVENSON

One mile east of Stevenson is a small creek called Nelson Creek An early settler, Nels Nelson, took a land claim here and built a log cabin for his wife and two small daughters. This was 40 some years before Stevenson was known by anything other than Shepard's Point.

A post office was established here at Nelson with the first postmaster, Nels Nelson, Aug. 21, 1890; Samuel Hayes, Feb. 9, 1891; Ernest Edwards, Oct 18, 1892. April 5, 1894 the office was moved to Stevenson. Mail was brought from Cascade Locks by row boat.

Stevenson Post Office, April 5, 1894, John Stevenson; Feb. 14, 1895, J.P. Gillette; Henry Johnson with his father in his sail boat carried the mail from Cascade Locks in all sorts of weather. This crossing was just above the Rapids and with a strong, icy, downstream wind in winter time, which required tacking against the wind and much know-how to keep from going over the Rapids.

John Attwell told of crossing the river here with a row boat in winter. "It was snowing, with visibility limited to 100 yards. I left the Locks, rowing upstream a mile before starting across the river. On reaching the center of the river, I ran into slush ice floating down the channel. I attempted to row through this ice which was O.K. until I reached the center of the river; here I found myself surrounded with ice that I could not row in, or row out of. It was carrying me toward the Rapids and I knew that in a few minutes I would be going over the falls. I couldn't see shore but I called or yelled for help, with no answer coming back. As I drifted into the swifter water at the head of the falls, the swirling water separated the ice and I was able to pull ashore at the head of the rapids."

Other Postmasters:

James Walker, April 1, 1898; Phillip Mitchell, May 31, 1899; J.P. Gillette, Dec. 31, 1902; Mrs. Mae O Gray, Mar. 19, 1914. Al and Charlie Salsettes carried the mail from the Locks until the S.P. & S. came into operation in 1908. Albert Sly, Dec. 15, 1918.

The office moved from Whisky Flat to Main St. and when the railroad came through, the office was moved to near where the Eagles Hall is across from Knapp's old bakery. Later it was moved above the Ash and Attwell store. The next move was into the Avary Building. Herbert Miller, Dec. 1, 1924; George Chesser, May 16, 1933; Will Lamm, Aug. 1, 1935; Richard Morley, May 1, 1947; Mrs. Alice Berg, April 17, 1951; April 9, 1954, Bert Miller with the office going into its new building in 1961.

When the Nelsons left for other parts, Mr. and Mrs. Francis M. Vanderpool settled on the land claim where the Stevenson cemetery is now, later the Bevans family took over the claim.

*****

The site of the city of Stevenson is the old Shepard D.L.C. For forty years the site had been known as Shepard's Point by all rivermen. A scow landing was operated here with thousands of cords of wood being loaded, often two scows at a time.

George Stevenson, a fisherman on the river, purchased part of the Shepard land claim in 1893 and laid out the start of the town, selling lots to the new pioneers.

Stories the Tombstones do not tell by Daphne Ramsay

Benjamin Frazer packed up his fiddle and a few possibles and headed west. He was a soldier in the Union Army; but he was young and impatient and he did not wait to be mustered out.

Benjamin loved to play his fiddle at dances and play-parties, and one night he met Mary, a girl who loved to dance.

Their romance was suddenly so intense that they planned to run away together. Mary had a husband and several small children. One can only speculate about Mary's reasons, but the story goes that Mary's husband had raised some hogs and planned to take them to market on a certain morning very early.

Mary told Benjamin she would leave a lamp burning in the window on the night she knew her husband would leave. The husband went his unsuspecting way, and Mary kissed each sleeping child   and went to join Benjamin, who waited with two riding horses not far away.

They left, never to return; Mary never saw her children again.

If is unfortunate that my story has so few details of their long trip to our community, but I am recalling bits and pieces told me by people who knew them after they came to live in Skamania County.

They owned property now comprising the Interlaken and Bowles Lakes. Their home stood for many years in the vicinity of Ash's Lake.

I have been told that they changed their names to Bently and Mary Geer, and that with Elmer Ash, they operated a store in the settlement there that was called "Bagdad," in the vicinity of the present-day Co-Ply mill.

Bent Geer was a drinker and at times he would confide the secrets of his past.

He would cry and lament that he could never go home again; he was a deserter from the army and had stolen another man's wife.

He always wore a gun because he feared he would be tracked down. Stevenson's main street below the railroad tracks was well supplied with saloons in those days and it was a common occurence for Bent Geer's team and wagon to stand in front of one or another of them.

The barkeeper would assist Bent out of the saloon, load him in his wagon and untie the horses. The patient team knew the way home and always delivered him safely to Mary.

Her neighbors knew her as Molly. Agatha Garwood told me that she remembered seeing Molly sitting on her little porch smoking her pipe.

Bent & Molly would often stop at the Attwell farm on their way to Stevenson. This is the only known picture taken of them and their team about 1908.

It seemed that Molly was deeply fond of Bent. Ethel Patterson recalls that Lizzie Fields, a neighbor of Molly in those long gone days, told her that they would pick blackberries to sell across the river at Cascade Locks. He would take them in his rowboat, and Molly would stand on the bank and call out to him, "Good-bye, Hon!" as he rowed away.

Hard times befell the Geers in their old age. They sold their property below Stevenson and went to live on the old John Anderson homestead (we know it as the Dodge place) on the loop road.

At the last they were county charges and Clarence Walker looked after them as they became feeble.

Do you think it was all worth it to Mary? Was her life with Bent Geer what she really wanted? I cannot help thinking that she may have shed many bitter tears.

Several years after their death, in the 1920's, a man came to Stevenson in search of his mother. I do not know how he had traced her here, except that he said he had inquired at Fort Hall.

An Indian there remembered the man and woman who had passed without stopping-unusual enough to remember at this remote and lonely outpost! It was a long way to another stopping place.

It is also possible that Mary wrote to someone back home, but I do not know how her son traced her here to Stevenson.

Unfortunately, the people he spoke to did not know the story I have just told and he went away without knowing his mother was here.

It might have been a comfort to know that his mother was at rest in a peaceful, small cemetery with a respectable marker:

MARY FRAZER
Born 1838
Died October 19, 1913

Benjamin Frazer
Born 1842
Died January 1, 1914

Before the far northwest had courthouses, city halls or even statehood, early records were often stored in primitive but handy places, which might be a meeting place in an old log fort or even a log home. One story of a much later date, tells of the early courthouse which lacked chairs, so the visiting taxpayers sat on boxes of records stacked around the commissioner's room Many of these old records were lost, chewed up by mice or even burned, but often an exciting old record is uncovered.

We think of Clark County being the first county with other counties cut from it. Mrs. Lottie Gurley with her persistence quality searching has uncovered information on a prior land claim.

PROVISIONAL LAND CLAIMS, BOOK THREE OREGON TERRITORY

SMITH, Seth, Vancouver County, 640 acres. At the Cascade Falls on the Columbia River . . . . commences at large rock at the main raft landing above the Cascades. Intends holding without occupancy, 31 August 1846, (Claim ½ mile wide and two miles long). Book 3 page 63

93

Land claims at this time could be 640 acres and occupancy was not necessary. The large rock at the main raft landing can still be seen just above the Stevenson Co-Ply mill where the Lizzie Fields home used to be.

We do not know what happened that Smith did not remain on the claim, was he killed, died or just went on to greener pastures. At this period he had his choice of almost anywhere.

This is the first evidence of where the main raft landing was. This large rock is at the very head of the chutes where the water picks up swiftness in 100 feet. One often wonders how these clumsy log rafts loaded with pioneer families and their precious belongings could land so near the head of the chutes without going over the rapids. After crossing the plains and fording many creeks and rivers where there were no bridges, the people on these rafts may have become fair swift water sailors and on reaching this spot, someone jumped into the water and held the awkward raft beached until it was secured.

This was the upper end of the portage around the cascades and this early, 1846 there was nothing but a trail over the portage.

Bill (Mort) Nickelson who came to Stevenson in 1896 says, "When I came to Stevenson, there were 28 people there. There was the Richard family--about 6--Sam and wife Jessie, Dan and George, Jeff and Frank who were born after they left town and went out to the ranch. The Taylor family--with 3 sons and 3 daughters. Jeff and Nora Nix; they were expecting. Theodore Iman and wife Ada, and son Jerry. They were the only Imans who lived in the town site. Old man King was the first to be buried in the Odd Fellows Cemetery. My step-father owned the cemetery at the time. He bought it from Bevans. Charlie Green was my step-father. Billy Kirkman was a bachelor. Monroe Vallet, Dod Chamberlain, Jim Harris, and John Ginder who was the editor of the Pioneer at the time. He had not yet moved his family up from Camas, but was living in the hotel. He was the one who wrote up the story of "Ground Hog's Day". It was a cloudless, sunshiny day, that is how I remember the day we arrived in Stevenson.

"My step-dad, Charlie Green, was the first to have a saloon in Stevenson. He was elected sheriff. He served two terms as clerk and auditor, and then became sheriff. He liked his 'nips' (chuckle), so he had his bottle, and he took it, set it on the table in the jury room while in session--so he was told to resign from sheriff's duties. He left town for awhile, and went to Viento, Oregon. After a short time he came back to Stevenson and opened up a saloom. He was his own best customer.

"In 1896 Frank Kale put in a store, so people didn't have to row across the river to the Cascade Locks for groceries. Mr. Jo Peters at The Dalles, was the 'King-Pin' as far as merchants were rated. All the cord-wood haulers were on his books, some perennial. Price Teal would load thousands of cords of wood at Shepard's Point.

First Grocery Store

In the autumn of 1896 the 8-foot space between the old Pioneer Print Shop and the old Court House became Stevenson's first grocery store, but not without some dickering with old Sowbelly Joe of The Dalles, Oregon.

"The 1894 flood on the Columbia River was the highest water that was known or remembered. At the Cascade Locks it took away the Terminus and railroad. The water was up to the height of railroad tracks everywhere. We were flooded out of our house. I remember, we woke up in the morning with a foot of water in our bedroom. My sister and I had to step out of bed and wade out of the place. It stayed up high for three days. It really wrecked things up at Hood River and at The Dalles."

*****

Many stories have been told of moving the county seat from the Cascades to Stevenson and many of them different. One of them was that the records were loaded into a wheelbarrow one night and wheeled to Stevenson. Another that a team and wagon picked up the records in the dark of the night and they were taken to the portage railroad and loaded onto a handcar and then transported to the Upper Landing where they were put on board a fishing boat and sailed up to Stevenson.

However it was moved, regardless of how in 1893, and the quarrel over 'the stealing of the County Seat' was quieted down with the 1894 high water on the Columbia which washed out much of the portage road and did much other damage. Frank Estabrook, a well known and well liked Indian who was 19 years old at the time, told this to the writer, "I was walking up from the lower Cascades with John W. Attwell; we were on the portage road when just ahead of us the high water took a half mile of the railroad out so we turned back. When we got to the lower landing, the water was taking out cottonwood trees that were 4 and 5 feet in diameter and breaking them up like you would matches in your hand. There was a large meadow in what is now Hamilton Island slough, and Mr. Hamilton had just cut the hay in this meadow, leaving his mowing machine and hayrake in the meadow. The river raised so fast that he was unable to recover this machinery so it was lost as the meadow was swept away.

The old army garrison was also swept away and 4 feet of earth where the garrison stood was also washed away."

Two of the commissioners were happy to see Stevenson become the new county seat as it was more centrally located.

A.C. SLY TOLD THE FOLLOWING:

"When I came to this county in 1898, there were no good houses here at all, nothing you could call modern--just shacks. Even the courthouse was just an unpainted shack. Most of the furniture I saw was home made. Some of the well-to-do families had furniture from around Cape Horn, but only a few.

"We traveled then only by steamboat. There were no roads at all, not even between here and Carson, a little town a few miles east of here. You could scarcely get around by horseback. But we had five or six steamboats a day coming in here, even as late as 1908. By boat, it took 3 days to transact business in Portland, one day down, one day for business in Portland, one day back home. No nervous breakdowns in those days because you had to be leisurely whether you wanted to or not. Boats had a lot of trouble at the Cascades. Took more fuel there than all the rest of the trip. They all burned cordwood.

"You've heard the story of how the courthouse was moved to Stevenson? The court house used to be at the Lower Cascades. The county rented a building, just a shack, from Tom Moffat. He raised the rent $5 per month and one of the commissioners objected. George Stevenson had lived at Lower Cascades, he was now a member of the State Legislature. He bought land here and laid out the townsite of Stevenson. When the rent was raised in the Cascades, Stevenson offered them ground near his building for a court house. He then loaned them his building.

"Well, the Board of Commissioners and the Sheriff and one or two others wanted the county books audited; they came to see me. You see then they had no state auditor as they do now. I found the county had $5,000 bonded indebtedness. They also had a sinking fund of $10,000 and with some other funds, they had $225,000 surplus. Well, they would not build on the lot they owned by the post office and wouldn't buy a lot as long as they owned this one. Peter Olson, who owned the land they wanted, asked $300 for it, but he was persuaded to exchange this lot for their lot by the P.O. and $100 extra, so a few good townsmen raised the $100 by popular subscription. The commissioners at first wouldn't put any more than $2,000 into the building, but after looking at court houses in 7 or 8 counties,

hey set the limit at $5,000. A Hood River carpenter, not a
contractor, looked over the plans which a Portland architect
made for us and said he could build the building for the $5,000.
Well, he went broke doing it. He was out $2,500 when he got
hrough. They wouldn't even spend the few extra dollars to
have the building wired for electric lights so the wires which
were added later are now all exposed. It would have only cost
hem $110 more to have had it wired when it was built.

"There was lots of logging here in 1900. Kelly Lumber Co.
built a mill here that year.

"I guess more overalls than anything else were worn.

"We had just plain food. No fresh vegetables except in summer
when everybody raised their own. Lots of game and fish, espcially
salmon which one could buy from the Indians. It was salted down
or winter use.

"Beacon Rock used to be called Castle Rock. Major Biddle
changed its name. When the S.P & S. Railway was coming
hrough, some Portland men bought the rock and claimed that
hey were going to blast it down for building rock. They wanted
120,000 from the R.R. for right-of-way. Turner Leavens had
here what he claimed was a paint mine of red rock. He wanted
40,000 for his right-of-way. This made people mad because
he S.P. & S. had been generous all along and besides we were
ll anxious to have the railroad built. They had to finally condemn
he right-of-way."

Courthouse in 1894, building on right was the Skamania County Pioneer print shop.

Left to right: Walter Taylor, nephew of Dempsey Taylor; Charlie Green, county clerk; Fred Denser, county judge; J.P. Gillette, postmaster; Nora Bevans Nix, lady printer and office girl of the Pioneer; Bob Carr, county auditor; Henry Johnston; Jeff Nix, third sheriff of Skamania County and an unidentified camera man

P.S.C. WILLS

He was a mystery man who came to Skamania County in 1903. Everyone considered him to be a well-educated and neatly dressed on his arrival, but as years passed his dress became more casual.

He did the first surveying around the county. With a Mrs. Winslow's patent Soothing Syrup bottle nearly filled with water, tied to a board for a level, he surveyed the first roads.

He put in the first public water works in Stevenson for ten customers. As the little town grew, more customers wanted running water so the water works grew. He then organized the first telephone system in the county. Bill (Mort) Nickolson, while a boy, worked for P.S.C. and helped him string the one wire from Stevenson to Washougal. Bill told of the time they had getting the wire over Cape Horn Mountain in winter time. The wire was strung from tree to tree and a small piece of old bicycle tire was used as insulators. The phones worked with all customers on the one line, however the system was

mproved later with only fifteen to a line   The first telephone
ffice was in Mrs. Dick Nickolson's entryway to her living room
of her home.

As the time went on, his survey instruments became more
sufficeicated.   Two vine maple sticks were hinged to a wooden
carpenter's level, a compass secured to one end and front and
rear sights secured on top of the level.

His dress now became more casual.   Old patched pants,
held up with a rope belt.   Gunny grain sacks wrapped around
his feet for shoes.   He was nearly always carrying an axe and
a lantern and a sack of tools on his back.   Sometimes he would
use a superduper pack-sack   He would take an old pair of
overalls, tie the waist shut and fill the seat of the overalls with
pipe fittings and put a leg over each shoulder, then stuff one
leg full of tools and put his lunch and can of cold coffee in the
other leg and tie the legs shut.   This then freed his hands to
carry the axe, shovel and lantern.

P.S C. surveyed many pieces of property for the settlers.
He was as strong as a horse and would come crashing through
the brush carrying his tools.   He was his own chainman, axe
man and mathematician.   His surveys were found to be quite
accurate by the later surveyors.

In 1915 he was interviewed by John Ginder, the publisher
of the local paper.   Mr. Wills said, "On account of my poor
eyes it was found to be a waste of time to send me to school.

As a man grown, I could see just enough to grub stumps, herd cows, dig roads and mind my own business."

This is one thing that always amazed all who knew him. He wore glasses with very thick lenses that were always dirty; one wonders how he could see at all.

Frank Richards tells of those early days when P.S.C. used to come by the logging camp for breakfast. When the waitress brought in hot cakes, bacon and eggs, he would take a stack of a dozen hot cakes, put butter on them, then syrup, and then pour half a bottle of catsup on top of that, and start eating them. He would repeat this process two or three times each breakfast.

He located a hot spring several miles up Rock Creek. He purchased several miles of iron pipe and carried it on his back to lay the line from Stevenson to the hot spring. Sam Samson built a hospital where the county jail now stands and Wills piped this water to the hospital. Later the hospital was converted to a hotel and called the Hot Springs Hotel. The water was thought to have a medicinal value so many people came to bathe at the hotel. For some distance the pipe had been laid along the bed of Rock Creek and in later years the raging winter floods tore out some of the line. However, Rock Creek water filled the line so it was not known for years that the spring water was not

coming to the hotel. The name of the hotel was changed from the Hot Springs Hotel to The Samson Hotel.

P.S.C. Wills always used this name as his signature so it was a long time before his full name became known. Peter Solomon Corwine Wills, however he was always spoken of as P.S.C. Wills and was well known by everyone.

P.S.C. would get on a steamboat with a gunny-sack over his shoulder and go to Portland to do some shopping. When the gunny-sack was loaded with pipe fittings or what was needed, he would often be seen walking into one of the finest restaurants to eat among the high-bloods regardless of his dress.

He was always boosting the economy of the county. He might take several boxes of polished apples to Spokane or some other city and pass them out one at a time to bankers, ranchmen, storekeepers or anyone who walked by and tell them of the beautiful Columbia River Gorge He said, "My principal enjoyment has been working for better roads and more efficient schools."

Albert Attwell, while going to high school, delivered the Oregonian newspaper around Stevenson. He said, "P.S.C. Wills was one of my best customers; he often bought 8 or 10 papers. I asked him why he took so many and he replied that he cut articles from the papers and sent them to people he knew as far away as England. After cutting the clipping from the papers, he never destroyed the papers but stacked them against the walls of his home. He had the best insulated house against the cold of anyone. Newspapers were stacked to the ceiling against the walls. You could hardly walk between the papers while walking down the hallway."

Jan. 9th, 1937, he burned to death in his home. It was said that he had 50 years of daily Oregonians stacked in his home when it burned. At the time of his death, it was learned that he and his wife separated when their son was four years old. She was remarried somewhere back east, giving the son the new name. P.S.C. tried for fifty years to locate the son but not knowing his new name was unable to locate him.

*****

CLIFTON HUGHES

"Father's name: James A. Hughes, born October 1855 in State of Pennsylvania.

"Mother's maiden name, Mary Miller, born August 1869 in State of Indiana. Moved to Kansas with her folks while a young girl. They were married in Missouri, an elopement. They did things like that in those days. They lived near Topeka, Kansas for a number of years then moved to Dodge City, Kansas where my oldest sister was born. She lives in Stevenson at present time.   My folks then made the rush to Cherokee Strip down in the Indian Territory, which is the State of Oklahoma at present.

"My folks' grandparents on my mother's side took homesteads there where they lived until 1900 when they moved to Hood River, Oregon.   Two years later or 1902 they moved to the Little White Salmon Valley in Skamania County, Washington, and brought all of us eight kids with them.

"The Oregon Lumber Company had two large sawmills. Mill A on the west side of the Little White Salmon, and Mill B on the east side.   Mill B burned and was rebuilt.   There were lumber flumes on each side of the stream to carry the lumber to the river where it was rafted and towed across the Columbia by tug boats to the Oregon side where there was a railroad for shipping to the east.   There was no railroad on the Washington side at that time.

"My uncle owned a homestead in the Little White Salmon Valley where we lived in an old house constructed with fir pole framing and shake siding and roof.   There was no store or schools there at that time.   The streams were full of trout and game birds aplenty   As a boy I had great fun hunting with a little single shot .22 rifle and an old .12 gauge, double barrelled shotgun which kicked me down every time I shot it for I was only 11 years old and not very heavy.   The timber was so heavy that we could walk on an old dirt road which wound around among the timber to the Willard place, and never get out of the shade.

"We moved to Stevenson the year 1905 so we kids could go to school.   I did not know what grade I was in so I told the teacher I was in the fifth grade and I got away with it for none of the kids were too overloaded with school knowledge, so competition wasn't too strong.

"My parents bought 7 acres just across the road north of where the Stevenson High School is located now.   Charles Zeigler lives there now.   The only building on the place was an old hay barn in which we lived until we had a house built.   The place was covered with big trees and brush.

"The town of Stevenson was located at that time south of the railroad, but there was no railroad there then.   Ash and Attwell were in partners in a general store.   Mr. Gillett had a little drug store and post office and a small variety store owned by Mr. and Mrs. Evens.   There were 3 saloons and the Valley Hotel on the south side of the street, and this was all there was of the town.

"We hauled all our belongings in a wagon, driving the cows and hogs to the landing at Cooks where they were loaded on a river steamboat and landed at the wharf at the main street of Stevenson which was a dirt road running north past the court-house. At the north end of the street was the school house, a small two-story building composed of just two rooms. There might have been thirty pupils in all. Some were eighteen and still in the eighth grade, which was the highest you could go then. Later two more rooms were added to this school. The first high school was built in 1910. The first graduation class was a single boy, Walter Attwell, in 1911. We kids walked down an old trail through the brush to school.

"We did not go to Portland by wagon for there were no roads to Portland on either side of the river. We ordered many things from Jones' Cash Store, or Rice and Phelen's catalogue in Portland and it was shipped up on river steamboats. All farmers along the river got their supplies the same way.

"Most people then made a living by working in logging woods or sawmills or cutting wood and hauling it to the river where it was stacked along the shore and sold to steamboats, for they were fueled by wood burners; or the wood was shipped to The Dalles on sailing scows. Some had a few milk cows from which they sold cream or made and sold butter. They had to ship the cream to Vancouver or Portland. They would set their cream cans on the beach of the river and the steamboats would pick it up and drop off an empty can.

"I graduated from Stevenson High School in 1913 and entered Oregon State College that September.

"Mrs. Attwell was a great one to work with the young people and taught music to those who were interested. The Attwells had a dairy farm just across Rock Creek west of Stevenson and he was a captain of boats on the river "

Timber was the main industry. The first settlers cut the fine fir trees into cord wood and hauled it to the wood scow landings. Furnishing the timber and cutting or having it cut into cord wood and then hauling it to the scow landing for $1.50 per cord. A large straight grained tree then was valued at about $2. The same tree today would sell for $500.

Wood was used to heat the homes and fuel the wood burning stoves for cooking the meals. All wood was delivered to your door in 4 foot lengths, and needed to be buzz sawed to 16 inch lengths to fit the ranges fire boxes.

Many logging camps operated around Stevenson. The first camps brought in logs with oxen as Foster did, then the Sweeneys and others used horse teams. Then big operators came with

MUSICAL RECITAL

BY THE

Pupils of Mrs. Bertha Attwell's Class at the I. O. O. F.
Hall, Cascade Locks, Or., Oct. 17,
1903, 8 P. M.

PROGRAM:

1.	Little Trooper March	Johnson
	Mrs. Bertha Attwell	
2.	Humming Bird Waltz (duet)	Schroder
	Bessie and Bertha Hendrick	
3.	Primrose Dance Polka	Krogmann
	Ella Woodward	
4.	Three Friends Sleigh Ride (trio)	Root
	Edna Washburn, Silvio Traverso, Walter Attwell	
5.	Santa Claus Guard March	Krogmann
	Winnie Woodward.	
6.	Follete Polka (duet)	Behr
	Eveline Corlett and teacher	
7.	Bailey-Gatzer March.	
	Georgia McKinnon.	
8.	A Mine of Gold (vocal)	R. Lilly
	Kindness of Prof. Isenberg.	
9.	Piff Paff Polka (duet)	Engelmann
	Sevilla nad Ervin Brolliar.	
10.	Prayer — Passion Waltz.	
	Edna Washburn.	
11.	Festival March (trio)	Behr
	Mr. Isenberg, Miss Cramer, Sevilla Broliar	
12.	Will My Soul Pass Through Old Ireland?	
	(vocal) Kindness Mrs. Traverso	
13.	Heather Bells Polka (Duet)	Kunkel
	Mrs. Isenberg, Miss Cramer	

large STEAM DONKEY engines and railroads built into the forests. We then had donkey skinners and donkey punchers, whistle punks, hook-tenders, hookers, chasers, choker setters, high-climbers, the swing and yarders, roaders, bull-blocks, cawk-shoes and tin pants, gandy-dancers and hog-heads and an important person the bull-cook, who carried in the split wood to the cook shack, carried the drinking water and swept out the bunk house and many other chores, and told far fetched tales.

All these men were strong, hard working and good fellows to be around. Ermine Cook was an excellent boss in the woods and had a little Indian blood in his veins which we liked.

*****

Skamania County Pioneer was organized by a stock company in May 1893 and the paper was published at Cascade City. The first editor was S.H. Bell.

A steam buzz saw was pulled to your wood pile with a large team and for .50 cents a cord it was cut into the short lengths. However it might burn a rick or two of the wood for steam. This picture was taken in front of John Pugh's house near his blacksmith shop where the Eagle's Cafe is now.

When the county government was moved from Cascade City to the new town of Stevenson the little paper moved also. Successive editors were: A. Monteith, Robert Carr, S.D. Dennis. The little paper with so few customers went into temporary oblivion in 1895 and was purchased by John Ginder at sheriff's sale for $6.75.

Ad. SUBSCRIBE For the Pioneer. One dollar a year.

John Ginder and his family ran the paper for many years. He kept the paper clean, and with no one-sided politics. News was often like the following.

*****
"Mt. Pleasant Squibs"
News here is as scarce as hen's teeth, and we haven't any proof that they have any. Farmers are all busy with their spring work, and if they know anything, they keep it to themselves.
*****

Morarity printer's helper in doorway, John Ginder, editor; son Gene, sitting first unknown, son Ralph, son Brick and Mort Nickelson.

Items taken from the Skamania County Pioneer

1902. "At a 1902 county commissioners' meeting, Bill Hamilton asked that the bridge across Hamilton Creek that had washed out six years before, be replaced. It was necessary to ford the creek and in winter time the water was often too high. Messrs. Graaf, Butler, Stanley and Aldrich endorsed the request. The commissioners agreed to have it rebuilt."

*****

"A bridge at Wind River was just completed by Messrs. Murray and Johnson, who built the bridge at their own expense."

*****

"The WATER WITCH sank at Sprague Landing."

*****

"Twenty men and three teams began work on the road from Stevenson to Carson."

*****

June 19, 1902. "C. Sholin will construct a barber shop between the old laundry and the Stevenson Saloon."

*****

July 24, 1902. "Carson has three stores, three hotels, two saloons and a blacksmith shop."

*****

Oct. 9, 1902. "Andrew Zurcher to build butcher shop at Carson."

*****

Dec. 4, 1902. "John Iman has meat market in Stevenson."

*****

Jan. 11, 1903. "'Hotel Cecil' new hotel in Carson."

*****

Jan. 29, 1903. "20 surveyors bound up the river--railroad a hope."

*****

Feb. 12, 1903. "Dr. Thos. Carr Avary, late of Atlanta, Ga., arrived in the city today, accompanied by Mrs. Avary, and has located in the Frank Kale house. Dr. Avary proposes to practice the profession of medicine and to become permanently identified with Stevenson and Skamania County. Calling at the Pioneer office, the editor found the doctor to be a very agreeable gentleman of about 45 years of age, of substantial build and well informed on current topics. Dr. Avary comes to our community well recommended, having letters from the Governor of Georgia and the Mayor of Atlanta, where he practiced for a period of 15 years. These letters commended him for efficiency in his calling, and for his traits as a gentleman. He is directly introduced to Stevenson by a letter from our esteemed former citizen, A.C. Sly, who recommends him highly."

*****

"J.S. Graaff asked people to consider building a new courthouse."

*****

"Robert Carr writes: 'I doubt very much if there is another such a dilapidated court house in the U.S. The old saloon that was used for a court house at the Cascades was a duplicate of the present one. The furniture at the close of 1892 consisted of a few dilapidated chairs that formerly belonged to the old saloon. There were two round tables, blanket covered, used by the patrons of the saloon as card tables. Around one of

107

these tables every three months were seated the Honorable Board of County Commissioners. One small drop leaf desk, three wooden benches completed the list of furniture at that time. These benches and the floor were used to hold the records At the sessions of the court, the attendants either stood up or sat on the records. What improvements have been made? The same chairs, table and benches are doing service. One room 16 x 30 feet served the purpose of auditor, clerk, treasurer, sheriff, commissioners' meetings and sessions of Superior Court. The same conditions that existed ten years Ago."

*****

Feb. 19, 1903. "Prof. A.C. Sly is back in town."

"Petition for new court house. Mr. Olson offers site, a square block atop 'Capitol Hill'."

"Carson House--New, complete, clean beds 25 cents, hot meals all hours 25 cents. H.H. Olmstead.--Adv.

"P.S.C. Wills sounds out the populace on a phone company."

*****

Feb. 26, 1903. "Cooperative phone company meets much favor."

*****

March 5, 1903. "Belcher strikes hot water. Will build hotel at Collins."

"Subscriptions pouring in for phone company. Meetings held over whole county."

*****

March 19, 1903. "The Skamania County Cooperative Telephone Association is now an accomplished fact Frank Marble, chairman; A.C. Sly, Sec."

*****

March 26, 1903. R.R. survey completed to Camas. Tunnel at Cape Horn is contemplated."

*****

108

On March 24, 1901,a mannamed James G. Green, employed at one of the mills east of Stevenson, decided to go to a dance.

Arriving at the hall, he looked through a window and saw his sweetheart, Nellie Underwood a breed, at supper with a married man, E.V. Benjamin. Green waited for no explanations. He shot through the window, killing Benjamin.

Sheriff John Totton, aided by others present, gave chase and captured Green, who was hiding in brush nearby.

Green was brought to Stevenson and lodged in the jail house.

The trail was set for April 11, lasted two days. The jury found Green guilty of murder. Cost of the trail to the state was $128. Witnesses for the prosecution were paid $2 per day and 10 cents per mile.

Green's attorneys, McCredie and Rand, requested a retrial on the grounds that Green did not have sufficient time to prepare a defense, that the jury had not assembled according to law and that the presence of the widow of the murdered man in court, weeping and dressed in mourning, had been prejudicial to his case. The motion was denied October 1, and Green was sentenced to be hanged December 6.

It is said that Totton, feeling that Benjamin needed killing, repeatedly left the door of the jail unlocked and gave Green every chance to escape. Green however failed to avail himself of the opportunity and finally was hanged on schedule. Totton refused to tie the knot and the job was done by Bert Beavans.

Benjamin's wife appeared at the last minute and wanted to see the hanging, but permission was refused.

The county commissioners, at their meeting on January 6, 1902, allowed the following bills in connection with the case:

Chicago Clothing Co., suit for Green, $12.50; Totton's Store, underware, $3; IOOF cemetery grave, $5; L.B. Bevans, lumber and digging grave, $4; W.L. Gray, scaffold, $10.50; L.B. Beavans, enclosure, $2; Holman Undertaking, casket, $18.50; E.W. Hall, deputy sheriff, $1.50; Monroe Vallett, same $1; James Totton, deputy sheriff 62 days $124; Mrs. Thomas, boarding Green and deputy, $69.

April 2, 1903. "Strawberries a possibility for Wind River."

"Stevenson Meat Market--W.A. Hickey, Adv."

"New court house turned down."

"R.R. surveyors at upper Cascades."

"Cemetery bids let for clearing the I.O.O.F. Cemetery in Stevenson."

*****

July 9, 1903. "Bath house built at Collins. Belcher's bath house 87 x 33 feet, 16 porcelain tubs, reading room. Two stories."

"William Drano (French Billie) died at the home of J.M. Coulter at Cook's Landing. William Drano born Apr. 6, 1834 in France, came to The Dalles in 1864, then to Collins where he worked in the wood yard. In 1868 he homesteaded. He was a contemporary with Capt. Amos Underwood, Edward Underwood, Capt. G.W. Thompson, V.C. Trivet, Hon. E.L. Smith, Felix Iman, and many other old timers. His place is left to Mr. Coulter who was to care for him until his death. He died July 6, 1903.

*****

July 30, 1903. "E.P. Ash of Cascade Locks, sells his business."

*****

Aug. 6, 1903. "Phones a reality."

*****

Dec. 10, 1903. "Belcher starts hotel, 3 stories, 75 x 100, 96 rooms. Store 45 x 60 finished and the barn near completion."

*****

Jan. 7, 1904. "$6,000 frame court house, say commissioners."

"Robt. Carr--Assayer, Collins, Wash."

*****

March 17, 1904. "Cape Horn. The Far West Logging Co. will resume operations."

*****

March 24, 1904. "Aalvik Bros. install a planer in their mill at Stevenson."

*****

April 14, 1904. "F.F. Foster has a contract with the Portland H T.Z. Co. for 600 cords of cottonwood for excelsior purposes and an additional 200,000 feet of logs for other purposes. He will run same over the Rapids at high water.

"F.F. (Ike) Foster uses ox teams to haul his logs into the river."

*****

June 9, 1904. "Alex McKeighan and Miss Bertha Williams of The Dalles were married June 1."

*****

June 16, 1904. "R.M. Wright opens an office as attorney." (He practiced law in Skamania County for 60 years; was prosecuting attorney and judge.)

*****

June 30, 1904. "Stevenson needs a new school."

*****

July 7, 1904. "Amos Underwood lays off a townsite. Brisk demand for property."

Milton Harlan, editor, gives farewell, moves to Heppner, Oregon."

*****

July 14, 1904. "School District No. 3 has 87 pupils."

"Courthouse is progressing."

"R.M. Wright clearing land for home."

"Avary buys lot from Olson beside court house."

*****

Feb. 28, 1907. "Potatoes shipped by Marble and Smead at Mt. Pleasant."

"Miss Nelda Miller is teaching her first term at Thomas school near Prindle."

*****

111

March 7, 1907. "John Baughman of Cascades married Edith Andrews."

*****

March 14, 1907. "Doumitt will pay 70 cents per pound for butter "

*****

March 28, 1907. "Carson--The Grand Central Hotel owned by Haffey and Wigal has been leased by H. Gray."

Carson--L.T. Smith, merchant and postmaster of Carson, was married March 21."

*****

April 4, 1907. "Stevenson is out of butter and eggs."

*****

April 11, 1907. "A.L. Douglass buys the dray business from C.F. Slater, adds several horses."

*****

April 18, 1907. "Tom Moffett appointed postmaster at Cascades. Minnie Stevenson resigns."

"Butler--Miss Emma Kock has returned from Warrendale and will stay with her mother."

*****

June 13, 1907. "Whylie Quinick Tomult (Mrs. Virginia Miller), daughter of Chief Ta-honah Tomult, has returned after visiting Ska-mon-i-ack which she says gives our county its name. She was a guest of Mr. and Mrs. Waukomach (Warcomac is correct spelling)."

*****

June 27, 1907. "The Maiden and King mill, two miles northwest of Stevenson, will install new machinery. The mill will have a capacity of between 25,000 and 30,000 feet per day with a 60 horse power boiler and 50 horse power engine."

*****

Jan. 7, 1909 "J.H. Ginder takes over the Pioneer again."

*****

112

August 1908...Stevenson has been lit before with 7 saloons and coal-oil (kerosene) lamps, but now you can throw a switch and have light.

Samson and Orsen build an electric light plant below the first falls on Rock Creek.

Samson and Swanson were full brothers, when they came to this country, they went to work for a farmer who called one Sam and the other Swan. Not yet being used to this country, they just added to their new names the 'son' as was done in their home country. One became Sam Samson and the other brother Swan Swanson. Swan operated the light plant for Sam for many years.

*****

Mar 4, 1915. "Sam Samson, to-whom-we-may-kick-about-the-light-bill-what's-the-use, neglected to get his weekly new corn cob pipe. If a chain is as strong as its weakest link, and Sam is as strong as his pipe's strongest stink, he would have his burly forefather faded to a whisper." All in fun.

*****

Mar. 25, 1915. "The exact amount of taxable property in Skamania County is $4,345,036."

*****

Dec. 30, 1915. "Saloons to quit. Tomorrow is the last day for the licensed saloon in Stevenson. Lou Iman will open a soft drink emporium and pool hall in his building. Pete Peterson will lease the Stubling building. L. Ottestad has the big Stevenson Hotel."

*****

June 1919. "The North Bank Highway is now open through to Underwood. Eastern and Western Skamania are now united. Sam Samson drove his Oldsmobile over the new road as the first car."

*****

Nov. 18, 1915. John A. Griffin told Mr. Ginder: "The first of September 1885, I landed at Waitsburg from Yreka, Cal. The railroad from Portland to San Francisco was not finished and I came up the Sacramento River with a freight wagon. Deer were plentiful then in Northern Cal. and I met two four-horse teams loaded with deer hides The next morning after landing in Waitsburg, I borrowed a horse from the local minister and rode out to Dayton where I got a job teaching Spokane was about as big as Stevenson is today. (1915) There was only one wooden school house, 60 pupils and 3 teachers.

"Chickens were $2 a dozen. The best flour was 50 cents a 50 lb. sack. Milk was delivered for 3 cents a quart and a good steer was worth $10." (Mr. Griffin was living in Stevenson at this time.)

*****

The first automobile to drive up the North Bank road from Portland was in June 1908. E.L. Youman, always known as Ned and called Ned by everyone, was the son of a wealthy man in the east, who to keep the young Ned occupied, purchased the Skamania Lumber Co , giving Ned one half interest The mill was between Stevenson and Carson and called the Youman & Simpson Mill.

Ned ordered a new Hupmobile sport roadster and when it came in to Portland, he invited Ray Sly to go with him to Portland and drive the car back to Stevenson. The North Bank road then was little more than a trail. Not much trouble was incurred until they reached Cape Horn in the dark, but the stars were shining.

Ned, the wealthy playboy, would come to Stevenson from the mill over the cow trail and when ready to go home would often wait until the 8:10 passenger train came through and then follow it up the railroad tracks back to the mill.

Wood cutters had cut wood here and they could not tell which was the road up the Columbia from all the wood roads in many directions. Ned wanted to go back to Washougal and drive up the railroad tracks but Ray wouldn't agree to that. Ray said, "Look, Ned, there is the North Star, so this would be east; let us try this one." Ned consented and when they arrived at Butler

114

(now Skamania) they stopped at Billy Butler's store where two large dogs raised a fuss and Billy came out in his night shirt with a shotgun in his hands When they called to Billy, he called off the dogs. It was now so late at night and not knowing where the road was, they waited until daylight before going on to Stevenson.

*****

J.R. Bowles, the millionaire ship builder who had purchased Bent Geers Lakes, and they became known as Bowles Lakes, would bring his Pierce-Arrow on a steamboat to Stevenson from Portland. He would drive down the old wagon road from Stevenson to the lakes. Tom Graves, a boy who was raised in a log cabin with a dirt floor just across the county road from Mrs. Briggs' home, would hear the car coming and meet it, and Mr. Bowles would pick the bare footed, ten-year-old Tom up and take him the 3 miles to the lakes and Tom would walk home.

Bowles would spend a few days at the lakes and then retrace the trip back to Portland aboard a steamboat.

E.P. Ash had one of the first cars in Skamania County. It was a 1910 Buick, about two cylinders. Barefoot kids could outrun the car and hang on behind.

1912 Michigan...Monty & Bertha Attwell. Jim on floor and Albert on his mother's lap.

In 1914 the Monty Attwells drove to Washougal in their 1912 Michigan. The trip took the daylight hours each way; when a team of snorting horses were met, the car would need to stop or back up to a wide enough spot and shut off the motor while the team was coaxed with a whip, often, to pass the iron devil, then the car cranked again which often took a lot of cranking. It was necessary to change tires several times on the 60 mile round trip as the sharp rocks would cut the high pressure tires which cost $60 each

*****

CARSON

Sprague, also known as Sprague Landing, was the forerunner of the present Carson.

Post office records show that the first postmaster in Sprague was John H. Stone from Jan. 1879 to Oct. 1879. Thomas Monaghan from Dec. 29, 1879 to June 1, 1880.

Sept. 26, 1894, Sprague Landing, a 5-acre tract was platted here on part of the homestead of J.J.H. Mesplie.

Thomas Monaghan homesteaded land adjacent to that settled by Mr. Mesplie. Tom erected a log house in which he conducted a mercantile business. Tom, born in Ireland, came to the Cascades in 1859 and after a few years moved to Sprague Landing.

Carson Post Office was established June 5, 1894 with Albert G. Tucker as postmaster. It is said that Tucker's handwriting was somehow interpreted as Carson Creek instead of Casner Creek. The name stuck and has remained Carson.

Mail came to Cascade Locks on the O.R.N. Railway and was taken from there to Carson Landing, formerly Sprague Landing, by canoe and then carried from there to Carson Post Office one mile from the landing.

The first postal inspector said after seeing Tucker's store and bachelor quarters, "A little too primitive." Tucker soon provided satisfactory surroundings. Tucker was postmaster for almost 6 years.

Postmasters since have been, Lindley T. Smith, May 6, 1900 to June 28, 1909 when Jim M. Boyd became postmaster until Carl Smith became postmaster Dec. 13, 1913. Bill Thurston, Aug. 20, 1920; Quincy Wade, Dec. 21, 1920; Bill Meneice, July 27, 1922; Mrs. Fay Meneice (Mrs. William Meneice) Nov. 11, 1947; Lester J Ott, Jan. 1, 1948.

*****

Henry Metzger, who came to Skamania County in 1887, tells of heavy snows and hazards in mail and travel:

Coming to Skamania County fifty years ago and settling in the lumbering region about Carson, Henry Metzger, well known resident, told The Pioneer an interesting tale of the hardships encountered by the residents of that early day. "It required a full day to go to Cascade Locks for the mail," his letter says, "and the trip was not devoid of dangers, especially in seasons of the year when snow and ice mingled with the river current to make boating hazardous.

"I came to Wind River Valley on Dec. 6th, 1883, coming down from The Dalles on a sail boat. At that time there was a sawmill in operation where the town of Carson is now. They paid the mill hands and woodsmen an average wage of about $2.00 for a ten-hour day work. If a worker spent all he earned in the store and saloon that they were running in connection with the mill, then he was sure of a job, but if he wanted to be paid in cash, well, then, his job lasted until they could get someone else to take his place. Not being satisfied with those conditions myself and another young man moved into a cabin one mile west of Carson and engaged in cordwood cutting at $1.00 a cord.

"In December, 1884, we were caught unprepared in the worst blizzard that has visited the Pacific Northwest in general and the Columbia Gorge in particular, in the last 50 years. Just the week before Christmas. As we had but little provisions on hand and none to be had in the neighborhood we had to get out or face starvation, and so on Christmas morning, 1884, we started out, walked across the Columbia River on the snow-covered ice to Cascade Locks. There we found food conditions rather bad. On account of work on the Canal being in progress at that time there were many people living there. The railroad had been blocked by snow for five days already, and there was no telling when it would be opened, so it was up to us young fellows to move on.

"The next morning we started out for Hood River, walking up the Columbia River on the ice. At Shellrock, which is opposite Wind Mountain, we saw one snow drift on the railroad track where the snow was piled up, away above the telegraph wires and on the upper side the track was blown bare of snow. A few miles below Hood River we met a road clearing crew. Here they had two wood-burning locomotives with an old-fashioned snowplow in front. We saw them running into a snow drift with all the force they could get up, but they got stuck and had to be shoveled out before they could back out again. Road clearing in this way was slow work and for three weeks no train run clear through between The Dalles and Portland. That night we got into The Dalles on a work train where food conditions were not bad.

"In 1887 I came back to Wind River Valley and took up the homestead on which I am still living."

*****

Joe Gregorius, former commissioner, says,

"In 1905 and '06 Carson could boast of nine saloons and dance halls with all the girls and trimmings, much like the old Wild West on T.V., except there were no gun-slinging or killings, but plenty of fish fights.

"The Wind River Lumber Company brought timber in from the Wind River Valley and dumped the logs below a dam that they had built across Wind River, and at various intervals the dam was opened and the logs were flooded down Wind River to the Columbia and there they were boomed by O'Malley who jumped from log to log but couldn't swim a stroke. From here they were towed to the Cascade Locks mill.

Pete Stack who ran a butchershop in Stevenson was drowned while fishing Wind River when the dam was opened and the great wall of water and logs flooded down the deep channel, and he was unable to climb out of its roaring path.

In 1909 the Government Soda Springs were developed with a large hotel and became quite famous. The hotel burned down in 1937 and never was rebuilt.

*****

WIND RIVER, 1891
Remembered and written by Walter R. Horton
"While this story is about Wind River, the story starts in Bridal Veil, Oregon.

"My brother and I, two small boys, rode from Vancouver to Cape Horn landing on the steamboat. Mr. Wright lived at the Cape Horn Landing and had charge of things there. He was to set us across the river, if the east wind was not blowing. The wind was blowing but he took us across to the sand bar. It was much wider than now. We walked across to the slough and a boat came out from the Oregon shore and took us across to the main land.

"The Prindle family lived at Bridal Veil then. Mr. Prindle ran the store for the lumber company. Bob was a boy then, a little older than Alva and I. Later the Prindles moved to their place in Skamania County. Many people used to go in boats to the Prindle place to get fruit.

"The Scott family lived in Bridal Veil but moved to the Wind River district and settled on Panther Creek. We heard that Gray Scott went out hunting and was lost in a heavy snow storm and died in the storm. In the mountain valleys and hills there was much public land that was open for homesteading. A group of mill-workers developed a plan to go into the upper Wind River Valley and stake out claims. I do not know which man was the leader in the developing plan.

"I will mention my father's name first because I know him best. Henry C. Horton was a widower with two small boys.
    Sam Horton, father's brother, was a single man.
    Elgin Sleeper, a widower, with one small boy.
    George Warren, a family man, had one grown son. His name was Charlie Warren.

Frank Howard, a family man, was in the group.

Horace H Phillips, was father-in-law to both Geo. Warren & Howard.

John Hollis lived up the hill, north of Cape Horn landing but he worked at Bridal Veil. John was one of the group.

One or two of the Gilliam boys were in the group.

A man who lived on the Oregon shore of the Columbia in the vicinity of Bonneville, was also in the group but I don't remember his name.

"When the road work was finished and most of the houses built, a man by the name of Breen joined the group.

"Going back to the start of the story at Bridal Veil, we ferried across the Columbia River to Cape Horn Landing and went up the river by steamer to the Lower Cascades and landed at the lower end of the portage railroad on the Washington shore. It was about where Bonneville Dam is now. When all the luggage and equipment was transferred from the steamer to the box car, and the passengers in the passenger car, we proceeded to the upper end of the portage road and loaded onto another steamer. We left the steamboat at Sprague Landing. A man with a team of horses and a wagon picked up all the freight and started to the mountain. We all followed. We passed close to where Carson is now, and then north and northwest for several miles across a fairly level country and then down a long, rough hill to the bridge across Wind River.

"In contrast to the suspension bridge that was built later at a place downstream, the bridge we crossed on was made out of logs and poles. We went up the hill on the north side of the river. We passed several places where settlers had built their houses. The road turned to the west and we stopped at the Wetherell's place and visited there a little while and then went on to what was known at that time as the Brolier place. The Brolier house was vacant and that was to be our first camping place.

"My Uncle Sam Horton · had been injured in a paper mill accident and could not do heavy work with the heavy tools but he was a good cook and that was his part of the project. Each man made his own bed by spreading his blankets on the floor in the front part of the house.

"After breakfast the working crew would take their tools and walk along the road that was already there and when they came to the proper place they turned left and began making the new road. One man called the 'viewer', would go ahead with his ax and pick out the easiest way to open up the new road, just so we would go in the proper direction. The rest of the crew would come along clearing the brush and trees out of the road. If they

120

came to a big log that was sound and laying across where the road was to be, they would bore a hole into the log, in a horizontal direction, till they reached the center of the log, then they got on top of the log and bored a hole down to connect with the first hole. Then they would take hardwood coals out of the fire and drop them down into the vertical hole and then blow air into the horizontal hole with the hand bellows. This process would start a fire to burn in the center of the log. They would repeat this process at another place on the log, far enough from the first place so that the road could be built there. In two or three days the log would be burned through in the two places and the men would roll the piece of the log out of the way.

"The crew would walk to and from work each day and when this distance got to be too much, they built a log house by the road and a man with a team and wagon moved the luggage from the Broilier house to the new cabin. The road work continued. They soon came to a gully or a small canyon and it seemed that the best way to cross it would be by building a bridge. Small timber was cut and hewed to fit, and as the timbers were put in place they were 'pinned' together by boring big holes and using hard-wood pins. They soon came to a steep sidehill that extended from high up the mountain clear down to the river. There was not much timber in the way here but all the work had to be done with pick, shovel and grubbing hoe. Here they built another log house and moved the camp into it. Here is where Mr. Breen joined the crew. More road had to be built to the place where George Warren staked a claim.

"The next big problem was to build a bridge across the Wind River. They tried to fall trees across for stringers but the logs would break when they hit the rocks on the other side. Finally they got one log across, and with the use of a large rope they got others across and put 'punchion' on and some guard logs and the bridge was finished. The road continued across in a southerly direction until it came to Rock Creek. There was timber here and H.C. Horton and Sam Horton staked out their claims.

"A log house was built on my father's claim No house was built on Uncle Sam's claim. Other houses were built but I am unable to locate them. Some claims were located on the south side of Rock Creek. I think that very few of the claims were 'proved' up on.

"The crew 'dissolved' and became individuals again. Our Uncle Sam and my brother and I lived in our house till the snow came, then we had to walk all the way from this place to Sprague's Landing in the snow. Father left as soon as the main work was

121

done and went back to work at the Bridal Veil mill. I am writing this from memory, and it is a long time from 1891 to 1962.

"About 1897 there was a young lady by the name of Grace Gray who went from Stevenson down to Bridal Veil to work for some of the families there. Her sister, Zenobia, also worked at Bridal Veil.

"There was a family by the name of Stone that moved from Bridal Veil to a place just north of Stevenson. We were well acquainted with them. They had two boys about my age, Ernest and Vernon, and we went to visit them. Together we went down to Rock Creek, and there was a place there where the 'mineral water' was bubbling up through the creek water. I also went down to Moffett Hot Springs and stayed there a few days. This was in the 1890's.

"My Uncle Sam Horton owned a piece of land along the bank of the Columbia River a little way down stream from the Prindle place. Sam was clearing land with a horse and a stump windlass. The horse was hitched to the end of a beam and was driven around in a circle. As the horse goes around the cable tightens up and pulls the stump out. Uncle Sam was directly behind the beam when the hitch suddenly let loose and the beam struck Sam and killed him instantly.

"In speaking of Skamania County, Sturgeon City should be mentioned. It was a fisherman's camp just at the west end of Cape Horn bluff. There were quite a few fishermen living there. They fished for sturgeon in the winter and salmon in the spring and summer."

*****

HISTORY
WIND RIVER VALLEY
The Wind River Valley area seems to have had two distinct groups of settlers. Those who came to the area from about 1890 to 1900 and who took up timber claims and then the later homesteaders.

Some of these first families were G.A. Warren (Warren Creek and Warren Gap area), his brother-in-law, Frank Howard, then the Hollis family, Ed, John, Will and their mother, Mrs. Hollis. Each had timber claims in the Hollis Creek area. Celo "Cap" Anderson settled in Trout Creek-Martha Creek area in 1892, also, L.T. Smith and E.J. Weigel.

These early settlers worked with those who were about halfway out of Carson--the Wetherells, Scotts, Reynolds and Broliers, and Quincy and Xenophon Wade. They built a wagon road and a bridge across Wind River in the canyon somewhere

122

near the present logging bridge. Road building at that time was very difficult.

The timber lands were sold for very little. Most of the claims of 180 acres went for a little over a thousand dollars, and this was for the very best timber tracts.

About 1902-1916 the new group of homesteaders and settlers came. Among these Mr. Button, A.P. Gordon, Jim Hutchings, Art Davison, Annie Cummings, Warren Hollenberry, Tom and Sam Lung, A.G. Gray and F.T. Blaisdell and the last piece of land to be homesteaded was the Joe Szydlo place.

There were at least three schools out in the valley.

*****

In 1897 President Cleveland set aside an area designated as Mount Ranier Forest Reserve, and in March 1907 this area was divided into the Ranier and Columbia National Forest Reserves.

On June 15, 1949, President Truman changed the name of the Columbia National Forest to Gifford Pinchot National Forest, honoring Mr. Pinchot, who had been the first Chief of the Forest Service.

The first ranger was Horace Wetherell, who was appointed June 1, 1902, and assigned to the Wind River district and surrounding area at a salary of $60.00 per month and he was to furnish his own horse, saddle and any other equipment necessary to carry out his duties.

Other rangers, packers and Forest Guards were, George Williams, Axel Erickson, Eilert Skaar, Dan Lewis, Fred and Herbert Sether, Christ Skaar, Claude Wetherell. At first there was just the office building and one house for the Ranger, and the Ranger was the only one who worked the entire year; the rest were on a part-time basis, depending on the weather.

In 1909, E.J. Weigel, a Forest Guard was notified to hire a number of men, not to exceed three, to begin clearing land for Wind River Nursery. The first nurseryman was a Mr. Minor, next came Roland Cline, then William F. Will, and the present one, Forrest Deffenbacher.

At about this same time the Wind River Experiment Station was started with Dr. Julius V. Hofmann, as director, Vivian Brown, assistant. About 1923, A. Gael Simson, Radio operator and technician came and this was the beginning of the weather station, radio and humidity research in relation to logging and forest fires. There were changes here in about 1940 when the station became known as Pacific Northwest Forest and Range Experiment Station with main offices in Portland and Olympia.

Apparently, a man by the name of D.B. Schiller was the first supervisor, with offices in Tacoma or Olympia. He received his appointment June 2, 1902. Others were Mr. Stabler, Brundage, Wright and many others.

Evelyn O. Hutchings

This log carrier was used in the Wind River Valley. It's high wheels would allow it to run over logs and stumps with a log hung underneath, and pulled with several teams of horses.

Picture courtesy of Jake Aalvik. On top: Pete, Roy & Harold Aalvik, Johny Kannikkeberg, Anna Weinberg, 2 unknown. Lower: E.C. Hobe, Mrs. Christ Aalvik, Mrs. Kannikkeberg and Lena Aalvik.

*****

HOME VALLEY WAS FIRST KNOWN AS FAIRBANKS

The Lumber Co. had a large sawmill at Cascade Locks and held great timber interests along Wind River. About 1882 some one gave the two owners two sows and a boar pig. This would have been a very nice present to any of the local pioneers who had a few acres of land, but to two wealthy city slickers who had never even been close to a hog, it was something else, but being gentlemen and gracious receivers they accepted the three hogs. They could not take the hogs to their hotel.

They had logging operations going on at Fairbanks so they had the log booming foreman, O'Malley, take the three hogs onto the tow boat and turn them loose at Fairbanks. These hogs were allowed to run wild, living on berries, ferns, rattlesnakes and spawning salmon along Wind River. Hogs are one animal that will kill rattlesnakes and eat them without harm to themselves. It is said that the layer of fat on a hog protects them from the poison of a rattlesnake's bi .

A few years later, Monty Attwell estimated that there were two hundred hogs at Fairbanks so he called on one owner and asked him if he would like to sell the hogs. He replied, "We almost forgot about those pigs, however, we have no use for them. You see what my partner will take for his half and I will sell for the same amount." So Monty found the partner and told him what the first partner had said. After a moment, the partner said, "I will take $10 for my half." Monty paid him $10 and then went back to the mill office and gave the other partner $10 for his half. Nothing was said of how many pigs were in the deal so the mill owners may have thought that was a good offer for three pigs.

Monty contacted a Chinaman in Portland who was a meat buyer and he agreed to take the hogs for six cents a pound, delivered to the Locks.

Monty got two men from the Cascade Locks to help round up the pigs. They took a sail boat with lumber for crates and a few sacks of dry corn and wheat and headed for Fairbanks. The Wind River Lumber Co. had a large old barn that was used several years prior for their logging teams. They repaired the door and a few weak places on the barn and then strung grain in trails into the barn and then left quite a little grain in the barn. Then they tied a long rope to the barn door and kept out of sight. Soon hogs came from several directions picking up grain along the trails. They fed on the rare dessert and all crowded into the barn and the door was pulled closed behind them.

After looking the catch over--301 hogs--they found that the old grandfather had 4-inch tusks and whenever the old boy came in reach of the younger boars, he would rip them with his tusks. It was decided to de-tusk him the first thing. Monty was the smallest of the three men, so he took a three pound hammer and the other two men lowered him down head first with a rope around his feet, over the big boar. When Monty came in hammer's reach of the animal's head, he struck and knocked off a tusk, and before the boar could back against the crowd of hogs, Monty swung again and knocked the other tusk off. Monty said afterwards, "I put my life into Tom's and Kurt's hands; had they lost the ropes and dropped me with both feet tied together, those wild pigs would have eaten me in minutes."

They made crates and crated the 301 hogs and then had to return to the Locks for a team of horses and another sail flat boat large enough to haul a team and several crates of hogs.

When the China hog buyer saw the hogs, he threw up both hands, "No wantee," but when he was told that the two old sows and the old boar were gifts, he then agreed to the deal. One small hog escaped so he took the 300 hogs and Monty sold the little hog to his brother John for $2. He caught it and it grew into a fine hog.

*****

The name Fairbanks was changed to Homevalley. A post office was established there in 1892. John Kannikberg was postmaster April 20, 1892; Frank Davids, June 5, 1900; Joseph F. Monaghan, Aug. 9, 1900; David Mann, Sept. 24, 1901; Bill Hosford, Feb. 20, 1904; Bill Yoacham, Dec. 11, 1907; Mrs. M.D. Leavenworth, Feb. 4, 1918; Mrs. Grace Lavender, July 27, 1918; mail to Carson after June 31, 1919. Home Valley was reestablished as a post office, Mrs. Sarah Jorgensen, Jan. 30, 1922; Mrs. Alnida Norlin, Nov. 2, 1923. Discontinued Aug. 15, 1924 with mail to Carson. Re-established Mrs. James Peterson, Feb. 17, 1931; Virgil Geertz, Feb. 14, 1933, and discontinued Aug. 31, 1959 with mail to Stevenson.

The first post office was in John Kannikeberg's home; he had become a U.S. citizen a few days before and he was proud of his two important accomplishments. His brother Charles Kannikeberg, was the first mail carrier to and from Nelson, 5 miles west. There were no roads at this time, only a foot trail, which he walked over twice a week. After the Nelson Post Office went to Stevenson, the mail was carried from there.

Around 1902 Halvor Berge carried the mail with the help of his sons, Michael and Hans. The trail had been improved so horses were used. In 1908 when the S.P & S. came into operation, the east bound train picked up and dropped off mail.

*****

A FAMILY'S HISTORY

Martha and Halvor Berge left Norway when they were in their twentys and came to Minnesota. In 1883 they were joined by two of Martha's sisters, Agata and Ingaborg Kannikkeberg. While there Agata fell in love and married Mr. Skaalheim; in 1885 they moved to South Dakota, in the Black Hills. There Ingaborg married a Mr. Frost. While the girls were living in

126

South Dakota, their parents and three more sisters came from Norway. These later married and became Mrs. Thompson, Mrs. Wineberg and Mrs. Candiani.

Crops being poor, the men came west in search of employment. Mr. Berge being the only one to bring his family at this time. In 1888 all the sisters came west and settled at Cascade Locks. In February 1890, the husbands of Ingaborg and Agata were killed in the collapse of a railroad bridge on which they were working. Both of the women had four children each.

In May 1890, the Berges moved to Home Valley, which was then called Fair Banks; they were followed in 1891 by the widows of Skaalheim and Frost, who bought the old McKeighan homestead and shared a three-room cabin together. Ole Kannikkeberg and the Thompsons also moved to Home Valley. In 1892 Mrs. Skaalheim married a Mr. Erickson and Mrs. Frost married Tom Meneice. They divided the land and property and the Meneices built another house while Ericksons lived on in the old house and enlarged it to suit their needs.

During the great forest fire of 1902 the Thompsons were burned out and they moved to Canada where most of their descendants now live. These sisters had two brothers, one of whom homesteaded at Stevenson. One sister, Anna Soldahl, drowned at Cascade Locks.

Both Agata and Ingaborg had three children during their second marriage. They were both hard working pioneer women, with a lot of courage and a deep religious faith. Agata Erickson lived to be 94 years old, and Ingaborg Meneice lived to be 92.

Ingaborg Frost's daughter married a Hutcheson and had four children besides two stepsons. From these children came two Hutcheson families, a Beadle family and Johnson families as well as a Grenia family.

From her three Meneice children have come three Meneice families, two Jorgenson families, a Bennett, Smith, Sanzo, Falter and Degestet families.

Agata Skaalheim became Mrs. Erickson and from these two marriages have come three Skaar families, several Skaalheim families, two Murray families, two Neece families, a Bowden and Seymour family, a Richards and Wolf family, an Okeson and a Cluster family, also Sargantm Wright, Miller, Pettit and Bailey family, Tichenor, Nelson Callahan and Wilson families, Johnson, Cheney, Donner and Erickson families. There are several Berge descendants and the local residents of the Kannikkeberg family are Mrs. Agatha Garwood and her family.

Much credit should be given these early settlers for the first religious services in the area.

On the first of February 1880 a meeting was held at Fairbanks (Home Valley) for organizing a church which would be called the "Scandinavian Lutheran Liberty Congregation."

President--Nels G. Skaar

Secretary--E.A. Aalvik

Trustees--Thor Skaalheim, John Johnson, Nels O. Herreid.

Members of the congregation: Nels G. Skaar, Thor Skaalheim, Halvor Berge, Germund Skaar, John Soldahl, Ole Soldahl, Hokan Fersson, P. Pearson, Ole Thompson, Nels O. Fexon, Benj. Hilson, E. Aalvik, John B. Johnson, Sjur H. Kannikkeberg, J. Kannikkeberg, Andrew Frostad, Arne Selleset, F. Ramshe and Liver Halset.

Meeting was held in July, 1885, in the school house in Sec. 12 in the town of Fairbanks (Home Valley) under President J. Kannikkeberg, leader. Sunday School Pastor Thalberg presided.

Ladies Aid met with Pastor Thalberg. The ladies could hold their meetings in different homes.

Twenty years later the pastor's salary was raised to $100 per year.

*****

COLLINS LANDING was named for William Collins who bought the James M. Findley Donation Land Claim on May 2, 1862. A post office was established here April 2, 1875 in Mr. Collins' home. Five years later while Mr. Collins was in Vancouver, his house and store caught on fire and burned down. He was covered with $750 fire insurance, so said that he would rebuild as soon as he could get material. The post office never reopened so was discontinued.

*****

St. Martin Hot Springs was considered to have the best water.

St. Martin married an Indian girl, Margaret who raised a family and out lived Mr. St. Martin Everyone loved Margaret.

Bill (Mort) Nickelson told this to the writer, "I was born at Wyeth, Oregon. My dad had a logging camp there. He logged with oxen, I was born in a log cabin--me and Abe Lincoln! ha, ha--but I never got to be president of the United States. At that time, old lady St. Martin (Margaret) was the owner of St. Martin Springs. She was the midwife for my mother at the time of my arrival. My Dad rowed across the river, at midnight, to Wind River, directly across from Wyeth, and brought her back to our home. She had eight children of her own, but she came and stayed with my mother when I was born. That was July 29, 1888. Thats quite a while ago - I don't remember

128

the time (chuckle). Dad was a friend of the St. Martins, and had known them for many years before.

After I had grown up to manhood, I used to go visit the St. Martins, and she would say, "You look pale, you must take a bath in my water." So I always did before leaving her.

*****

STABLER was named for Horace O. Stabler who was Supervisor of Columbia (now Gifford Pinchot National Forest from 1908 until 1913.

Post office was established May 26, 1915 with Mrs. Edythe Hutching the postmaster in her home. Mail was carried in horseback until the carrier, Ulrich Freeburg started with a horse and buggy and later used a small Reo truck, bringing in the mail once a week at first, then tri-weekly. Chris Fletch took over the carrying of the mail which was on snow shoes in winter time. April 2, 1918, Mrs. Pearl Cline with the office in her home; Oct. 6, 1919, Mrs. Ella Hoffman; Dec. 10, 1920, Mrs. Florence Blaisdell with the office in her home; Stabler mail was discontinued Dec. 30, 1933 and diverted to Carson.

*****

Wood Scows came in to this landing and a wood yard was kept in operation. Eary Settlers besides the Collins were J.R. McKeighans and Bill Bergmans.

The Collins Hot Springs came in use around 1900. W.J. Hosford in 1902 built a small bath house with five wooden tubs and also a store. In 1903 Charles T. Belcher developed the spring and secured a lease on the property, building a bath house with 16 porcelain tubs, because of the mineral action on iron.

He also built guest rooms. Steamboats stopped with paying customers so with brisk business, a larger store was built and a 96-room tub bath house and hotel were soon in operation. A barn with riding horses and trout for the nonriders. Guests arrived on every steamboat, wealthy business men often brought their office girls when their wives were not along.

The hot water was famous for its curing powers, attracting people from afar. Those that desired more than just being cured had a fine bar handy with the finest liquors.

The coming of the railroad soon put the steamboats out of business so the Hot Springs boom ended.

Shipherds Hot Springs Hotel near by.

Collins Hot Minerial Springs

COOK

In 1894, Charles A. Cook and Johan, his wife, homesteaded the site that now bears their name. Little is recorded about the stay of the Cook family except that there was a boat landing there. Later the property was sold to a man named Gerlinger. In 1908 it is known that Mr. Ellsworth, a Chenoweth merchant, had a saloon at Cook's Landing. In 1909, Mr. Gerlinger sold to Mr. and Mrs. O.A. Perry, who it is reported, had the first store there. Mr. Perry formed the Cook Investment Co., Inc., and platted the town site of 6 blocks and $53\frac{1}{2}$ lots. Heretofore it was necessary to go to Chenoweth or cross the river to Viento for mail. So the people of that area petitioned for a post office in January of 1909. Perry started a hotel known as the Mahoma Hotel Co.

In 1919 the Perrys sold their holdings to Miss Nancy Wallace who had the hotel finished before moving to Cook. She brought her many fine possessions to the hotel that was her home, including collector's items and her beautiful Oriental and Persian rugs, all to be lost when the hotel burned to the ground. "Miss Nan," as she was known, and her sister, Laura Wallace, then lived above the store that Laura operated until her health failed.

Minnie Fouts ran a confectionery store, and also operated a dance hall over the Jackson Garage.

The first post office to be established as the direct building of the S.P. & S and it was named for Charles Cook, purser on the steamer "D.S. Baker."

Dec. 24, 1908, Seymour Harris; Sept. 7, 1912, Miss Laura Wallace; July 20, 1932, Mrs. Edith Wilson; June 15, 1946, Mrs. Albert Girard.

*****

CHENOWITH

Post office established May 4, 1881, James Kimball with the office at Chenowith Landing; Feb. 13, 1883, David Ordway, with the Weidler & Ordway Lumber Co. had the office in the company store. Mail was brought each Saturday by horseback by an Indian, Joe Alleck, from Hood River to Mitchell Point on the south bank of the river opposite Chenowith Landing. Alleck rowed the mail sack across the river in a skiff to the landing and carried the mail on his back to the store.

Nov. 2, 1892, John Fisher. Fisher moved the office north to a log store at a site just east of the later office of Willard. Mail was brought in by Alleck, three times weekly. Around

1900, Fisher moved the office to a frame building on the old Chenowith Road.

Feb. 16, 1903, John Hill; discontinued Nov. 30, 1904 with mail to Underwood; re-established May 7, 1905, Miss Sadie Orser; Sadie married Clarence Cromwell and took the office to her home. July 24, 1906, Mrs. Anna Wise; Mar 9, 1908, Clifford Stipp, took the office to his home, a shack near the sawmill. Dec. 16, 1910, John Fisher with mail discontinued Nov. 30, 1928 with mail to Underwood.

HOMES
Post office established Oct. 31, 1910, Mrs. Hulda Homes, office discontinued Dec. 31, 1912, with mail to Cook. A part of the Homes' parlor was boxed in as an office. Mail came three times weekly by horse and buggy from Cook Patrons were settlers of the valley of the Little Salmon River and U.S.F.G. Guard Station.

DRANO
Post office established Nov. 1, 1894 by Charles Early and discontinued April 21, 1896, with mail to Chenowith. Office was in store of Oregon Lumber Co.

Before any mills were in this area, cord wood was the big industry. Thousands of cords of wood were loaded on the sailing wood scows for shipment to The Dalles.

It has been told that when the Bothwick and McClain mill closed its operation in winter time and moved their teams back to Oregon, that the river was frozen over and the oxen could not walk on the ice as the horses could with their caulked shoes, so the oxen were thrown and tied down on sleds and pulled across the ice to the south bank.

*****

WILLARD
Emil Willard, the oldest resident, realized the need for a post office as settlers were following the logging operations. He persuaded Ben Brown, a minister, to apply for the office. Mail was brought in with horse and buggy from Cook.

May 15, 1914, Benjamin Brown with the office in his home; Sept. 19, 1918, Eddie Howe; July 30, 1927, John Weigant; Sept. 10, 1928, Donald Stevenson; discontinued Jan. 15, 1945, with mail to Cook.

*****

DRANO LAKE

A nice bay on the north bank of the Columbia near Cook and not a lake as named. The railroad filled across the mouth of the bay caused it to appear as a lake. Rafts of logs are stored in Drano and taken out under the railroad bridge. Received its name from William Drano (French Billy) who settled here in early days

WHITE SALMON BLOCK HOUSE

(Mrs. E.P Roberts' dictation to her daughter, Charlotte Roberts)

"Came to White Salmon, Mar. 29th, 1862. Lived at Mr. Joslyn's until October when father bought land on which was located the old Block House. We moved into the Block House as the high water had washed away the only other dwelling. It was made of logs and was standing broadside to the river. The front door was very heavy, about 3 inches thick, the lock was very large and to make the door secure against battering rams, a large catch was fastened on the inside of the door."

The Joslyn home built here in 1853 was burned by the Indians in 1856.

Mr. and Mrs. Joslyn returned after awhile to White Salmon to build themselves a new home. They still were the only settlers there. After some time and still interested in The Dalles from their short stay there, they helped to establish the First Congregational Church at The Dalles, and were charter members of that society in the fall of 1859. Mr. Joslyn represented Skamania County in the Washington Territorial Assembly in the 1860's. In 1875 he sold his home in White Salmon and moved to Colorado

White Salmon sold for Bacon and Spuds
so George Gilmer told

George who was born at The Dalles in 1860, and his parents settled in Gilmer Valley in 1872. George says he saw the site of White Salmon purchased with a supply of potatoes and bacon.

He married a pioneer girl and they brought up 3 children with the nearest doctor at Hood River.

In 1860, two brothers, Neil and Girdon Palmer, settled on land between the Joslyn farm and the White Salmon River. In the early '60's, David Street settled 4 miles above the mouth of the river. Joslyn developed a truck garden farm which he sold in 1874 to the Suksdorf brothers, F.W. and Douglas.

*****

Uncle Sam did not care if the mail was delivered by pack horse, stage coach, canoe, snow shoes or foot leather, but he

Colorado Springs Col. July 25 1881

Friend Thompson
    I see that Mr Joslyn does not
feel at all like writing and if I should once begin
I fear your patience would be sadly tried to glean
a little of interest from much rubbish.
    It is so full of interest to me. Our
winter in Portland —— the winter of /52 + 53
the streets not yet cleared of stumps above
the Cong'l Church, indeed, many places below
were dangerous in the dark rainy nights
    The few warm friends that stood
by us in sickness and poverty. — The decision
to go to the Upper Columbia in March, and
the journey of three weeks so full of new experiences. A small steamer landed us at
the lower Cascades — No place of welcome there
But at the middle portage some bachelors
shared their log-cabin with us while the
men brought over the freight — and this
was very precious, our food and seed for
a year, the bedding and other necessaries
They tried to haul it in boats along shore
but the strong current around the points
whirled the boats, and the sail knocked two
men into the swift river.

and as a man came and reported my husband
drowned I ran for the river to meet him
barely escaped — I think the other man was
lost —   Then, the slow hauling over
the one horse rail road and the waiting at
the upper portage for a favorable wind, after
our effects were loaded on a flat boat
How opportune was the arrival of another
party going to the "upper country" to trade
with the Indians: taking the wife and child
along. They had many comforts that we
had not thought of — So their covered
wagon was our retreat in the storms That
so often delayed us   and our cook stove
on deck did service for all our meals
Potatoes for which we had paid $3.00 a bushel
and Flour at 16.00 per hundred # we enjoyed
but did not feel like wasting — Still when
a man came aboard who had nearly
drowned in Hood River, and had been without
food two days how gladly we supplied him.
          The Dalles was our destination but the
wind failing, we stopped for the night at
Chenoweth, walking over to town in the morning which consisted then of a few log houses
and tents and the barracks a mile away
I remember even now the exceeding beauty of
that morning.

but when the gentleman proposed that we
return down the river twenty miles as a more
favorable location for stock — I called to mind
the sunny valleys where we had rested
by the way and felt quite willing to escape
the Dalles winds which had fearfully rocked
the warehouse, driving sleep from our eyes
the previous night —

It can never be written the wild romance
of that isolated home on the bank of the Columbia
Only husband and myself and a little child
— hundreds of Indians, who fully intended to keep
that favorite spot for their own.

We asked the Lord day by day to be our
counsellor and help, and He stayed their wicked
plottings and overruled their many schemes
against us —— first their chiefs came in state
Representing three tribes, and claimed the land.
We traded fairly and openly with them paying each a
sack of flour, some sugar and tea and a blanket
So that afterwards they recognized our title
— and as one remarked "that first year
they told us what we might do," The next asked
" What we were going to do" and the next
" What they might do.

The first year small-pox broke out among them while they were in the back country. Their numbers were much thinned by Fall and they began to learn that they could buy or work for provisions and clothing, and thus self interest made them friendly

I think we learned to respect and trust each other, and in all those years when our life and property was in their hands, the Lord watched over us else had we labored in vain. We tried to raise high His standard and He honored the effort, though it was in weakness and much halting and I feel now and often then that the presence of the Lord was our defence and our shield

When the wicked rose up against us and boasted in their strength to crush out our life blood, then the Lord made their strength weakness and we lived and prospered. It is worth much to have so tested His word, though we bowed our heads at the time. I wish may be written not in our praise, but in praise of Him who sustained and helped us — Of our successes and our failures it is more becoming that others should write. There are many bright spots in our life's history; many blessed memories of dear friends at White Salmon, Hood River and the Dalles which will remain with us while life shall last. Yours sincerely

Mrs. E. S. Joslyn —

Klickitat River Valley history would not be complete without mention of one pioneer family.

Mr. & Mrs. Wols homesteaded a few miles up the Klickitat River back of Lyle. The crystal clear river ran through the farm. They not only raised hay, cattle, corn and first, but also a large family of 3 boys and 9 girls

One must know the family to appreciate the excitement to have 9 healthy sisters with only a few years between their ages. If there wasn't any excitement, the girls would soon cause it.

One sister while bringing home the cows to milk, grabbed a cows tail which ran for the barn with the girl hanging on. The cows flying legs upset a rattle snake and before the rattle snake could recoil to strike, Dot's flying bare foot had landed on it's head killing it.

This same sister dropped a harmless snake into another sister's shoe and it was not discovered until the foot slipped into the shoe and found the cold garden snake under her toes. Then there was a race to dodge flying shoes, rock and sticks.

Bringing home the cows, one sister told another sister, "Jump on old Pansy and ride over these sharp rocks." So the barefooted sister did climb upon Pansy, just as the other sister gave the cow a whack with a stick and she raced down the hill toward the barn with the rider bounced all over the boney back, and hanging on for dear life.

Five of the girls were hoeing corn in the hot Klickitat sun when they decided to have a swim in the crystal clear river. There was a nice swimming hole near the logging railroad and out of sight of the wagon road. They did not have bathing suits so hurried and took off their clothes and waded into the swimming hole just as the unexpected train whistled. Dot called to her sisters, "Hurry and get under water and they wont' know that we don't have bathing suits." So you can see that they were taking emergency action with so limited time to act.

did insist that it be delivered, regardless of the weather. When the driver arrived at the ferry or boat landing and found the river blocked with ice, it was up to him to secure his team or horse and tote the mail sack across the river.

When the Columbia River becomes ice bound, it isn't a smooth solid ice, it is small icebergs or chunks of ice that have come down the river and floated together and frozen between, so it is very rough ice, a series of ice mounds and hillocks. Often between these mounds are soft spots or mush ice. If one barged over this mass of ice without first testing it and finding a safe pathway could be disastrous, falling into a fissure with no escape from being sucked under by the current.

The mail carrier with his stage or horse was always the one who would need to find the safe pathway. On securing the team or horse, the driver would find a long pole and test the ice by sounding with the end of the pole ahead, if satisfied he might take the mail on a small sled with a rope tied around his waist. Then carrying the pole crosswise, he would start across. This way if he broke through a soft spot, he would only go in to his armpits as the ends of the pole would reach across the soft footing. If the ice proved solid, he might return for his team. The settlers and the Indians always waited for the mail man to find the safe passage first.

In 1890 the ice had stopped all steamboat transportation and a party of railroad survey men found themselves marooned at Lyle and wanting to get over to the Oregon shore to Rowena where they could get on the train to Portland. The mercury was below zero and had been for several days. Finally an old experienced ex-mail man offered to take them over a safe route for $5 and a quart of whiskey, which he was taken up on. When they handed him $7, he went and got a long pole and called, "Come on, let's get going." He was anxious to cross the river and get the whiskey from "Whiskey Bill" at Rowena. He found the river solid after a few tests, but to earn his money, he faked a few spots and led the tenderfoots around them.

Many early pioneers had taken part in some stirring events, before they found themselves permanently anchored in Klickitat County. Many had fought, on both sides, in some of the bloodiest Civil War battles.

One, whose varied experiences and adventures include nearly all the dangers and excitement of covered wagon days, was Harry Lamont, pioneer at Lyle. He was a rider on the original Pony Express. When the Overland Pony Express was discontinued in 1861, he became a commercial guide and Indian scout for covered wagon caravans. In this work he was in many skirmishes with

140

warring Redskins. In the '60's he was a rider on the Pony Express service, owned by Ben Holladay, stage coach contractor between Boise, Idaho and Portland, Oregon (The Dalles). His career as a Pony Express rider ended when he brought the last sack of Pony Express mail carried in Oregon, from Umatilla to The Dalles. After this he worked about Portland and Oregon City as a livery and stage barn hostler. In the '70's he enlisted in a Multnomah County (Portland) volunteer Indian fighting company. He was in active service during the Modoc war, 1872-73.

After the Indian wars, he drifted back to the Columbia River region. He lived about Cascade Locks until the early '90's, when he located on a homestead near Lyle, in Klickitat County, Washington. His place was on the north slope of the heights where the present inland highway begins to descend to the bottom of Big Klickitat River canyon.

*****

In the early summer of 1860 a determined faced youth, about 18, was in the Overland Pony Express headquarters office at St. Joseph, Missouri, applying for a job as a pony express rider. While making his desires known to a clerk behind a rough board counter, the lad did not notice that a big, red faced man seated in a dilapidated swivel chair in front of what was supposed to be a desk, was listening and eyeing him keenly. This man was attired in a creased and wrinkled business suit--offset by a battered stock stetson, flannel shirt and high heeled riding boots. He was superintendent of the Overland Pony Express company. Perhaps a boy with less self confidence would have been some-what flustered to have a sudden question popped at him when the big man suddenly said, "Ever do any ridin', kid?" The lad's reply was just as determined as his countenance looked. He calmly said, "Yes sir, I was the best race jockey at the county fair where my folks live in Indiana." When the big man spoke again, he was at the outside door of the office. He said, "Come on, kid! We'll go to the stables and I'll give you a tryout." At the barns a hostler saddled a large, but agile, big bay horse for the big man. The boy got a regulation Pony Express mount. There were no red tape rules for the test. As they started away, the big man said, "Now kid, you watch me and my hoss. You do everything we do and do it pronto."

The first maneuver was a quick stop, dismount and remount by the big rider. The boy followed suit. He was back in his saddle and riding along in step with the big bay. His effort, however, caused the only criticism made by the big man during

141

the tryout. The boy had held his bridle reins against his horse's neck. The big man said, "When you get off your hoss, kid, always throw the bridle reins over his head and let 'em drag on the ground. He will never leave you then." The balance of the tryout was a 10-mile cross country ride. It included fast gallops up hill and down, more quick stops and fast wheeling turns. Perhaps the boy did not know it, but on both up and down hill gallops, the big man watched his every move to see how he shifted weight in his saddle. The Pony Express riders who could cover a run in the shortest time did so because they knew how to give their mounts every advantage on every kind of terrain--hill, mountain, or plain. As they neared the stables the boy began to wonder what his examination marks would be. The big man said nothing about this, but asked a question that had nothing to do with horseback riding. "Know anything about guns, kid?" Again the boy replied with sincere candor, "No sir, I don't. My pa had an old muzzle loading shotgun, but he wouldn't let us boys use it. I guess he was afraid we would blow our heads off." Before the boy had finished, faint lines appeared on the granite-like surface of the big man's face. His friends would have perhaps said this was the nearest he ever came to smiling His answer conveyed information to the boy who wanted to be a Pony Express rider. It was, "Well, kid, you gotta know how to use a six gun and Winchester if you stick in the west. You can't fight Injuns with a jackknife and fishin' pole. I'll put you on as a hostler and see that you learn how to use guns." Instructions along this line were given by another hostler--an old Indian scout and plainsman.

Summer, fall and winter had passed. The boy was still a hostler. He again began to wonder if he would ever become a Pony Express rider. He had heard many glowing tales about wonders of the Oregon country. He had just about decided to strike out for himself, with some passing wagon train company when the superintendent's clerk came to the barns one day and said, "The boss wants you at the office, kid." When the boy arrived, the super conveyed a message in his customary terse, explosive speech; this time it was welcome news. "You're goin' out with the mail in the mornin', kid. I'll give you an order on the store for any new togs you want." Thus a ride began which eventually ended at Portland, Oregon, 2000 miles away-- after many startling adventures.

When asked to tell his most thrilling experience as a Pony Express rider, Harry Lamont said it occurred on July 12, 1861, when he rode into Rock Creek station, between St. Joe and Fort Kearney, Nebraska, and found no stock tender waiting with a fresh relay mount. Nor, was there any hot food or coffee awaiting him.

Rock Creek station, on a tributary of the American River, was established on public domain during first carrying of transcontinental mail with stage coaches. It was also on the main route of travel for wagon train immigrants from St. Joe to Fort Laramie, Wyoming. In 1859, David C. McCanles, disappointed Pike's Peak gold seeker, came back to Rock Creek and filed on a homestead there. He also built a toll bridge. Soon afterward, several other families took adjoining claims. Some of them were his relatives. McCanles was a north Carolinian, said to have a rather firey disposition. Stage company buildings and corrals were on his homestead claim. He at once made a demand for cash rent. Rather than pull up stakes, stage company executives agreed to pay him a stipulated montly rental. When Russell, Majors S. Waddell, owners of the Central Overland California & Pike's Peak Express Company, got into financial difficulties, rental payments became long over due.

The station was a relay change place for both stage coach and Pony Express horses. Horace Wellman, certified agent in charge, had a wife and two small children. The family lived in a building used jointly as a residence, express company office and store room for equipment.

It was a starlight night. After Harry Lamont looked around, he went to this building and found it barricaded. The agent's voice hailed him from inside the darkened interior to say, "You'll have to get your own horse, Harry, and go on with the mail. Dave McCanles and his gang tried to run us out of here this mornin'. We had a big fight and shot three of them, but the rest is liable to come back any minute." Harry could hear the agent's wife and children sobbing and crying, almost hysterically. He offered to stay and assist in defense of the station, but the agent ordered him to ride on with the mail. Harry's only retort was to pull in his riding belt a couple of notches before he started to a corral after a fresh horse. When he clattered across the toll bridge in a fast gallop, Winchester bullets, fired from brush along the bank below, whizzed about him in the cool night air. His horse shied, but he galloped on into the prairie darkness, toward Fort Kearney. He never knew if the shots were really aimed at him, or were merely a salute of protest over what had happened.

Many versions have been published about what happened on this fateful day in the annals of the Overland Pony Express, both with regard to cause of the trouble, and things that occurred. Some say it was a sideline civil war battle, with Wild Bill

143

Hickok representing the Union Army and the settlers led by Dave McCanles, fighting on the Confederate side. Others assert that the trouble was over alleged stealing of stage company horses by McCanles et all. One version ascribes the affair to personal animosity between Wild Bill Hickok and Dave McCanles, because of slighting personal remarks the latter had made about the contour of the former's mug. It is said this was carried so far as to nickname the young stock tender "duck bill". Perhaps the most authentic account states that a short time prior to the trouble, McCanles told agent Wellman that past due rent money must be paid before a certain date, or the station would have to be moved from his premises. It is said the agent told him he would go to St. Joe headquarters and get the money. This trip was made, but Wellman failed to get the money. On the morning after he returned, McCanles, with his nephew, James Wood, and a rancher named Gordon, are said to have called on agent Wellman and assertedly told him all settlers in the group had held a meeting and decided that the company and all employees must vacate his proptery at once, or force would be used to bring this about. Just as agent Wellman and McCanles were getting into a heated verbal controversy over the matter, it is claimed Wild Bill opened fire with a Winchester, killing McCanles instantly in the stage company office. This is said to have been followed by shooting the others who were outside. Other settlers, waiting in a nearby ranch house, came and got the bodies, but no further attempt was made to molest stage company employees. Instead, relatives of the slain men and other settlers appealed to the law. Officers came with murder warrants. Agent Wellman, Hickok and another stock tender named J.W. (Doc) Brink, were arrested and taken to Beatrice, Gage County, Nebraska, to stand trial. All pleaded not guilty. Juries in a Justice of the Peace court acquitted all--after hearing pleas of self defense.

Not long afterward Harry Lamont was sent to a run in the mountain wilds of Wyoming, between Fort Bridger and South Pass. It was here he, himself, became involved in a fight which terminated in his killing three men. His victims were Redskins bent on acquiring his scalp. He had just galloped into a relay change station for Pony Express horses only. It was located in a foothill mountain meadow near a bubbling spring. Again, he found no stock tender awaiting him with a fresh horse. He soon found out why. A lone stock tender was stretched out across the threshold in the doorway of a small cabin. Three Indian arrows were sticking in his body. One of them had pierced his heart.

The corpse was still warm. This indicated the murderers might still be lurking in the vicinity. Glancing inside, Harry Lamont noticed a Winchester was still in an antler horn gun rack. A belt filled with shining cartridges was hanging from an antler prong.

Remembering what the big, red faced superintendent had said to him: "You can't fight Injuns with -- --." He got the rifle and buckled on the cartridge belt. It was plain to him the stock tender had been surprised and shot down at close range. He reasoned the Indians had timed their attack to take place just prior to his arrival and that the stock tender had started out of his cabin in expectation of greeting a mail carrier. He then went to a corral where remount stock were held. The pole bars had been hastily pulled apart and tracks of five shod horses went out into the meadow. Behind were small hoof prints of three cayuse ponies. This checked with the three arrows in the stock tender's body. There had been three warriors in the attacking party. He found all the tracks circled around and disappeared in the direction he must take with the mail. With this knowledge, he faced the supreme test for a Pony Express rider. His horse was fairly fresh. He could gallop back to Fort Bridger and give the alarm. On the other hand, others were that the mail must always be carried forward--never on a back track. He had not heard of any Indians on the warpath and was inclined to appraise the affair as the work of independent raiders--probably hot-headed young bucks. He was puzzled that they had not waited and tried to ambush him also.

Suddenly it dawned on him why they had not done so. A few miles ahead, his way, a short cut Pony Express trail crossed a canyon hillside arroyo drain for a small stream. The bottom was covered with a tangle of thick brush. He reasoned the Indians would hide there close to the trail and try to shoot him.

He ran to his horse, still standing with dangling bridle reins, in front of the cabin. As if talking to his mount while he climbed in the saddle, he said, "We'll git them varmints." The canyon bottom was reached by a short, steep, zigzag, rocky stretch of trail. The rim was littered with patches of large boulders. When he reached sloping ground, leading up to the trail head, he concealed his horse in a clump of second growth forestry. Taking no chances, he crawled to cover of some protecting boulders as he neared the top. Looking around below, there was no sign of Indians or horses. He knew that around a bend, about one quarter of a mile away, there was a meadow shielded from his view by an intervening grove of cottonwoods. He felt sure the horses had been left on this meadow. He scanned the brush along the trail immediately underneath him for any sign of moving limb or twig, with no avail. He knew that Indians were patient when stalking a paleface. He was in a hurry. He wanted to get a fresh horse and go on with his mail sack. He was well hidden behind some boulders nature had placed in a manner that gave him a vantage point, where he could observe movements below without exposing himself. He decided to use daring strategy. Seizing a round stone, he tossed it over into the trail in a hope that the noise made would be mistaken for hoof beats of a horse. He had his Winchester poised through an opening between the boulders. As he let go of the stone, he trained the sights on a spot where he thought the redskins would most likely be. This trick worked. A plumed war bonnet bobbed up in the brush right under him. He pulled the trigger just about the same time. He knew by the way the bushes swayed and parted when the head disappeared that this Indian would not bother him any more.

He knew the Cheyenne Sioux were cavalry fighters and seldom left their steeds. He decided the two others would worm their way back under cover of the brush, to reach their ponies. To do this, they would have to cross an open space between their place of hiding and the cottonwo0d grove. He trained his rifle on the open space and waited. Again, he was rewarded. Two war-bonneted Indians arose together for a dash to safety. His second shot hit one of them. This Indian threw up his hands in spread eagle fashion and pitched forward--never to arise. The other gained cover again. It was now a question of wits. He ran for his horse musing to himself as he went. "That other varmint will get a horse and try and come around behind me. I'll have to head him off, and get him before he comes out of the canyon." He rode along under cover of the canyon rim until he came to an Indian trail from the back country. He left his horse again and concealed himself behind some rocks where this trail ascended from the meadow. He had guessed right. On the meadow was the company stock and three Indian ponies. The remaining warrior was nowhere in sight. Just as he began to ponder about his next move, he heard the clink of a horse shoe on the trail below. An Indian, riding one of the stolen horses, was just coming out of the brush toward him. This savage was naked except for a war bonnet and beaded buckskin breech-cloth. His face and body were smeared with hieroglyphic-like markings of red war paint. These formed a bordered space around his heart. Taking this for a bull's eye target, Harry Lamont said aloud to himself, "Here's where I fix him just like they did the stock tender." When the warrior fell off with a bullet through his heart, the horse turned and galloped back to join his mates. Harry was soon there and mounted a fresh horse to gallop away with his mail sack.

The 2000 mile run of the Overland Pony Express from St. Joseph, Mo., to Sacramento, Cal., was discontinued October 24, 1861, after the owners had sunk a fortune estimated at several hundred thousand dollars.

Harry Lamont found himself out of a job but did not cease his riding activity. Instead, he embarked on a venture of his own. It was becoming a commercial guide and Indian scout for immigrant wagon trains through hostile Indian country between Fort Kearney, Neb., and Fort Laramie in Wyoming. By this time the way was more defined and immigrants were making swifter progress across the plains. Harry got some fleet horses. When he reached Fort Laramie with a wagon train, he at once started back over short cut trails to obtain another job. In this way he escorted 12 trains across the plains during the summer of 1862.

When Harry learned that Ben Holladay planned to maintain auxiliary Pony Express mail service with his stage lines to Oregon, he applied for a job as a rider. This time no test was required. Ben Holladay had heard about him He advanced westward, run by run, to the land end of the Oregon Trail, The Dalles.

His homestead in Klickitat County was near an American country estate owned by Sir Thomas Balfour, British nobleman. Lord Balfour's son, known about the Lyle countryside as "Young Tom", once offered him a position as master of fox hands. The pay was good, but Harry declined. He did not fancy it would be fitting for an ex-Pony Express rider to don the liveried uniform required.

During the apple land boom days, when James J. Hill built his North Bank railroad along the Columbia, he sold his skyline homestead and moved to Lyle. He lived in a little cabin on the bluff in the old Balfour townsite. He was considerable of a jester and divided his time between entertaining new comers with tall yarns (baiting tenderfeet) and acting as handy man for Lyle citizens.

There were other jokers in Lyle and he often found himself on the receiving end. Also, his own jokes sometimes had an unfavorable rebound. An instance of this kind occurred at a time when he was janitor and porter in a general merchandise store owned by Mr. and Mrs. C.L. Howard. The store was located in the old townsite, south of the railroad track. The Howards had a home on the hillside in the new townsite. During the cool weather season, his duties required him to be at the store, building fires very early in the morning, to get the place warmed up before the owners came. It happened one morning just as Mrs. Howard was preparing breakfast, a tramp appeared at her kitchen door and asked that he be given work for something to eat. Mrs. Howard had no work, but she told the tramp she would give him breakfast and he could go to their store, where an old gentleman would find something for him to do in payment for the meal. After a meal of pancakes, ham and eggs and hot coffee, the tramp made a bee line for the store. When he conveyed her orders to Harry Lamont, the old timer was vexed in two ways. One, because a hobo was so dumb as to offer to work for a meal that had been duly panhandled. For the other, he con sidered Mrs. Howard's gesture a reflection on his work. He quickly conceived a solution in a form of a double barrled joke--for the benefit of both.

Heavy rainfall had created a miniature pond several inches deep in a depression hollow in front of the store. Handing the tramp an empty candy bucket, Harry said, "She wants the water dipped out of that pond out in front." The tramp went outside, shed his coat and was energetically dipping water and throwing it about when Mr. and Mrs. Howard came along. She was puzzled, as she stopped and said, "What in the world are you doing this for?" The tramp said, "That old guy in the store told me you wanted it done." Mrs. Howard reached for the pail as she said, "You have earned your breakfast. Give me that pail. I'm going inside and smash it over that old smart aleck's head." Harry was looking out a window. He could not hear what was said, but pantomime observations were enough for him. He went out the back door and fled to seclusion in his cabin, just as Mrs. Howard opened the front door. The store was without a janitor for a fortnight. It took Harry that long to muster up courage enough to go back to his job. Even then, he did not do so until Charlie Howard assured him the danger was over.

Harry Lamong died at Lyle, October 11, 1921. His grave is in the Balch cemetery, on a bench land bluff amidst surroundings that enchanted him most after his 2000 mile journey as a Pony Express rider.

DALLES PORT

This place has had many name changes since it was first seen by the white man, The Falls, and then in 1825, the French-Canadian Fur Traders called it 'La Grande Dalle', later the settlers called it Grand Dalles, Rockland, North Dalles and in later years, Dalles Fort.

John Nelson and Indian wife had a store there in 1872. One of their daughters married Captain Lars Jensen who ran an early ferry between The Dalles and Rockland. Capt. Jensen homesteaded some tillable land nearby and he hired an Indian named Tumula to build a rock fence around a meadow, after giving the Indian instructions about how the rock should be arranged. The foxy old buck, in turn, gave the instructions to his squaws who completed the fence.

*****

Fred Wilson who lived here many years and once operated the ferry here, told about the early cattle men swimming their cattle across the Columbia River just below here. They would drive the cattle into the river near Crates Point and swim them to an island in the center of the river--this island is now under water from the Bonneville Dam--after letting the cattle rest awhile on the island, they were driven into the river and forced to swim over to the north bank.

Some times it was necessary to have a man in a skiff with a gentle cow on a rope; he would row out pulling the cow and the others, with cowboys yelling behind them, would follow. The weaker ones sometimes didn't quite make it across the mile of water.

*****

Frank Sherried farmed here as early as 1875, raising fruit and dairy cows. His son Ralph operated a store here. Frank did much to bring in the first piped water to the dry area.

*****

COLUMBUS NOW MARYHILL

A wood yard was established at Columbus in charge of Hadley. The first settlers cut and hauled cord wood to the steamboat landing. The first price paid for a cord of wood was $10 delivered. However, it was soon cut to $8.

No timber grew on the hills alongside the Columbia so it was necessary to go beyond Goldendale for the wood, with a haul of 12 miles. The first settlers brought very few work horses with them, so most all the hauling was done with ox teams which because of their slowness, made two days necessary for the round trip. With five or six yoke to a wagon it was possible to haul five cords to a load. The cost of feeding oxen was simple, as they would be turned out at night to feed with good pasture everywhere, bunch grass was abundant and they loved it.

CASCADE LOCKS

The natives called the people here 'Wana pum', according to the old Indians, Lewis & Clark called them Wahclellahs, David Thompson in 1811 called them Weeyarkeek but he called the place the Great Shoots. Alexander Ross in 1811, in his writings, said the natives called themselves Cathleyacheyachs, and he referred to the swift water as the Cascades so this may be when the name came into common use.

The first settlers, the Attwells and the Chipmans, called it 'The Falls', a few years later when the portage road was in operation it was called 'Cascades', Oregon and also Wasco Landing and even Portageville, but the name Cascades held longest until the canal was built and the name changed to Cascade Locks. The locks are buried under backwater from Bonneville but the name remains Cascade Locks.

In April 1853, four adults and three small children were the only whites living here. Roger Attwell built a sawmill and a boat building yard and built the steamboat "Mary" for Mr. Bush this first year. We do not know how many more people settled here this year of 1853, but when the census was taken 7 years later there were 50 adults living here. The Ruckle portage road was hiring construction workers, the boat yard built the "Wasco" in 1854 for McFarland, the "Hassalo" for the Bradfords in 1857, and the "Idaho" for the O.S.N. in 1860. We know some workmen came across the river each morning to help build the boats.

These early pioneers did not complain about the inconveniences before the days of gas, electric lights or even kerosene, for artificial light was with a tallow candle and almost every family had a candle mold and made its own candles.

George Iman said, "Roger G. Attwell manufactured the first matches in the early '50's." Before this the old timers always had a piece of flint they could strike a spark with and sometimes get a fire going with dry material. Flint was used on the old flint-lock rifles to ignite the powder. Some smokers carried a piece of smoldering punk to light their pipes with.

Ivan J Donaldson, author of Fish Wheels on the Columbia, a persistent researcher for facts and know-how after much effort found and wrote, "I have found that one, Roger Attwell, made the old poisonous "Phosay Jaw" phosphorus-sulphur matches at Cascade Locks, Oregon, in the 1850's. Very few, if any steamboats in 1852, had power enough to penetrate the foot of the Cascade Rapids, therefore, the phosphorus and solvent were probably purchased in Portland and transported in saddle bags to the Cascades, where the blocks of matches were split and chemically treated."

Many old settlers wore 'buck skin' pants which would stand more wear than 50 of today's pants, but if they were not properly tanned and it rained, they would keep getting longer, and you would cut off a few inches; with more rain you would cut off still more; then when the sun came out they would shrink and the bottom of the legs would be up to your knees.

The houses were built of logs and roofed with split shakes, but window glass was available. Nearly all the cooking would be done in a large fireplace. Water was always carried from a creek. The early settlers found no roads so used Indian trails along the shore, or a boat on the river.

*****

EARLY DAYS AT CASCADE LOCKS
by Monty Attwell

"My father was a master carpenter and built boats and mills along the Columbia River until I was ten years old--that would be 1865. In that year Father started for Texas, Mother received letters from him each week for several months, and then the letters suddenly ceased, and from that day to this I have never heard, directly or indirectly, of or from my father. Conditions in Texas just at the close of the Civil War were unsettled and the probability is that my father was killed.

"Mother was left with four children. She supported the family by keeping travelers. Like most pioneer women, she was a good cook and a hard worker. In addition to keeping travelers, we boys worked on the place and raised cattle. In those days, just as today, you could pick up calves, particularly bull calves, at a very low price. We would let the young calf feed all it could from two cows. This would give it quick growth and the start in life needed to make it a large animal later. As a 4-year old steer, if its girth was 8 feet, it would bring $150 from a logging company. If it wasn't 8 feet around, you couldn't get over $25 for it. Loggers wanted unbroken steers and would pay $150 for large, strong steers of good stock.

"Our land claim was at the Upper Cascades, Oregon, which is now known as Cascade Locks. We had ample barn room and feed to put travelers' horses out of the weather. People usually started on horseback from Portland, stop overnight at Latourelle and the second night at our place, put up at Hood River the third night, and make The Dalles the next night. There were no roads, so all travel was on horseback over the trail, or by boat.

151

"In the spring big herds of cattle were driven from the Willamette Valley up the trail along the south bank of the Columbia to feed on the bunch grass east of the mountains. Sometimes these large herds would be made to swim across the Columbia just below The Dalles to the Shuster flats and then driven into Eastern Washington.

"We always aimed to have a few heifers on hand which we could usually swap for a cow with a young calf or heavy with calf as the herders didn't want to be bothered with young calves which could not keep up with the driven herd.

FIRST SAWMILL

"The mill was powered by a large overshot water wheel on Attwell Creek near Forest Lane and Pleasant Drive. When father built the mill in 1853, its main saw was what was called a 'sash' saw; this was before circular saws were used. This saw went up and down like a giant hand saw would in a giant's hand. When circular saws became available around 1860, he converted the saw to the improved saw which increased the mill's capacity.

"We brought logs to the mill with teams of oxen on skid roads. Loggers usually called the oxen 'bulls', although they were nearly always steers. Sometimes 5 or 6 yoke of oxen in a team. The yoke is made of wood and fits on the top of the oxen's necks against his shoulders, and has a bow that comes up under the neck, straddling the neck and pinning into the yoke, with two oxen to a yoke. When one speaks of a yoke of oxen, it is two oxen; six yoke would be twelve oxen.

"The skid road is first graded much like a wagon road. On this roadbed, every 7 or 8 feet, is a skid made from small trees. These skids are a foot or more in diameter, 8 feet long and laid crossways and buried into the road bed with only 5 or 6 inches remaining above the surface. The bark above the ground is taken off the skids. Heavy logs can be skidded over these skids with the oxen.

"The logs that are to be skidded over this road are barked on the 'ride' side. As soon as the tree is felled by the 'fallers' the 'barker' or 'sniper' strips the bark off the side of the log most likely that it will ride on. He has learned with experience which is the ride side of the log. He also snipes the end so that it will have a rounded tow end and will lift up on the skid as it comes to it. A 'grease monkey' or 'skid greaser' carries a pail of grease and slaps grease on each skid so the heavy logs will pull easier. The 'dogger' drives iron dogs into the log so

152

that when the teams are hooked to the logs, the log will ride on its 'ride' side.

"Some drivers yell at the oxen and can be heard a mile away, others command their teams with a mild command. My half brother Celly was one of the best drivers. He spoke softly to the oxen, the 'Hee' or the 'Haw' for direction to turn, but if need be, he wouldn't hesitate to prod an offender with the 'gord' stick

"Some professor might call it a 'goad' stick, but these loggers and bull drivers called it a 'gord' stick. It is a short stick like a billy club, with a sharp end, and is carried by the driver. It is used on an ox that becomes unruly; if a new ox attempts to run a horn into the driver, a jab on his nose will change his mind; or if an ox refuses to pull his share, a jab will bring him around Celly has been known to jump upon the back of a lazy oxen and walk down his back with 'calked' shoes (loggers' shoes with sharp spikes in them for jumping from log to log without slipping). An ox is like some humans, he wants to try something, he might lean in the yoke, run his tongue out like he was pulling and not be pulling a pound. Celly was wise to this shennanigan, and about this time he would land on the bull's back and walk down it; this was only needed once."

"These teams were used to pull the "Sadie B", a steamboat, around the rapids. Celly is on the far team of 6 yoke.

"The "Sadie B" was cut in two and one-half pulled at a time. Wheels were cut from a six-foot diameter, fir log; they were two feet in width. The axles were made of six-inch oak trees. Sometimes block and tackle were used going up hill, but on the level the two teams could pull the load. One mishap occurred when going down hill; one-inch ropes were used to snub the load by taking a few turns around trees. The snubbers were using green trees and the bark slipped and the snub lines could not hold the heavy steamboat, and it ran into the ox teams, hurting a few of them but not crippling any. When they got the boat above the rapids, it was put back together with four feet added in the middle.

"An oxen is an intelligent animal. They are driven without a bridle and reins as with a horse or mule, and take their orders by voice from the driver. He will tell them when to go and when to stop. He will tell them which way to turn. The best oxen are made from wild steers, a tame pet is worthless; he is not afraid of you and will not obey, but a wild steer fears you and he will make the best work animal.

"When you come out to the ox pen in the morning and they have finished eating, you hold up one end of the yoke and call the ox's name, King, Pat or Reverend, and that ox will come over and turn his head carefully so as not to touch you with a horn while you put on the yoke. Then you call his team mate and he does the same.

"You will need some help to get a wild steer yoked the first time, maybe blindfold him, then call old Job (from the Book of Job), and he is yoked up with the wild steer. You then take off the blindfold and get out of the way. The new steer will buck and snort and try to break loose, but big, old, powerful Job does what he wants to do and the new ox is dragged along. After a day or two, the new ox is broken to yoke and can soon be put to work.

"Oxen will respect the driver and will not intentionally hit him with a horn or step on him, but a stranger coming too close to a team might end up hurt.

"As an example, when I was feeding the oxen one morning, my brother John came into the pen all dressed in his Sunday suit and shiny shoes. I noticed an ox eyeing John so I told him to watch out and John replied, "They know me, I work with them every day." I told John, "But you are dressed different and he doesn't recognize you." At that instant the ox charged

John, who leap-frogged a stump with the ox only inches behind him. The ox was so close behind John and with his head down, hit the solid stump square. John went over the fence, the ox turned and went through the fence and the other excited oxen with him. I had to repair the fence and take the dog and round them up and bring them back.

"Quite often someone who had not worked with oxen would come by and stand alongside the skid road as the team approached and you would have to call to them to step back away from the road because one of the oxen might run a horn through a stranger. It might be a protective instinct rather than just meanness, as the water buffalo in India will do when a tiger attacks the human herder, these buffalo will charge the tiger and fight it off in protecting the herder."

*****

John Wilbur Attwell tells of early hunting.

"Deer were plentiful with so few settlers here in the 1870's and 1880's. Almost every homestead had a deer hound or two. I will mention one we had, we named her TOPSIE, and she was one of the best. When we needed meat, all we needed to do was walk out of the house with a gun and TOPSIE was ready. We would walk out to a fresh deer track and tell her to "Bring 'em out" and she would sniff the track with her keen nose. Like all good deer hounds, she would smell the sides of a bush that the deer brushed through; this would tell her which way the deer was going. A man will look at the track and tell, but a hound can not tell by looking at the track so must smell the brush along the trail. When she picked up the good scent, she let out the 'bay' or 'bawl' of the deer hound's tracking call and she was off. The deer would take off when this 'baying' became too close for comfort. Deer have learned from time far back that a wolf or any of the dog family can't track by scent in water, so with a river close by they head for the river. We could tell from the 'baying' about where the deer and hound would come to the river. Often several deer would come into the river together and if several of us were on the hunt, one of us would be in the right spot with a row boat. Monty was the smallest of us so we would have him in the boat and Celly and I would bring up the flanks.

"When the deer runs into the river, it will swim out a ways from shore and the dog or dogs. Monty would gently row the boat between the deer and the shore and slowly move toward the deer. The deer did not seem to fear the boat so would allow the boat to come right up to it. The man or boy in the boat would

155

then reach out and take the deer by the tail, never by an ear or horn, because you touch an ear and a front foot would come up like lightning and either hurt or break your arm. The front feet of a deer are fighting weapons, but by taking a grip on its tail and lifting slightly, its nose will go under water and in a moment you have a drowned deer to tow ashore.

"One time several deer came down on the beach and one decided against going into the water and ran by me. I had a small caliber gun and took a fast, unsure shot at it and it fell stone dead. When we skinned the hide off this deer, we never found a single hole in it anywhere, so we decided it dropped dead from fright. Several years later, this same thing happened again. but with more careful search we discovered that the bullet had entered the ear, lodging in the brain and leaving no mark.

"The persistence of a good deer hound is something. Once a coyote came a little too close to the barn and old TOPSIE took off after it. The foxy old coyote tried everything in the coyote book to shake old TOPSIE but couldn't do it. We could hear TOPSIE's baying for three days and three nights along the mountain back of now Cascade Locks. Sometimes high up on the mountain and later down near the river but continuous. On the third night the coyote tried one more scheme so he led her back to the barnyard, hoping she would stay this time, but she overtook him there and killed him. She had traveled so far in those seventy hours that her feet were sore and swollen and it was several days before she moved about again.

"In the 1860's, Celly and I had walked over to Wiley's which was about the east end of the present airport. We started home after dark but there was some moonlight. I remarked to Celly, "There is a deer alongside of us." Celly answered, "That is no deer, that is a cougar." It was sort of loping and it kept getting closer so we took off our coats and waved them and yelled at it. Wiley heard us so came toward us with a lantern and when he came close, the cougar left. He told us to take the lantern and he returned home. Celly had killed a cougar the day before so this may have been a son or mother of that one.

"Another time at Wiley's when several of us were sitting around the fireplace, Wiley's dogs made a fuss in his wood shed. Wiley went out to see what the fuss was about; he had a beef quartered and hung from the rafters. The dogs were barking at the workbench so Wiley took a quilting frame and poked under the bench and out came a cougar and the dogs took after it. Wiley came running in and yelled "Cougar!" Everyone grabbed a gun and ran after the barking dogs. I was a little slow in getting a good gun so took what was left, a single barreled shotgun.

The dogs had separated and I ended up at the river with one dog that had the cougar treed on a leaning dead tree over the water. I shot the cougar with the shotgun.

"Our first guns were muzzle-loading. You poured some powder into the barrel, then a little cloth wadding and then the ball or bullet, then you poured a little powder in the trough under the flint and it was necessary to keep your powder dry. When you took aim at a running deer, you had to follow the deer with the barrel of the gun, because after you pulled the trigger and the flint struck the file and put a light spark into the powder, it burned along the flume to the firing chamber before igniting the charge; this took a little time to get the shot off and the deer might be harder to hit.

"One time Monty ran out of wadding and bullets so he cut a piece off his overalls and left the ramrod in the gun for a bullet. He killed his deer and decided to ride the dead deer down the mountain. This was fine for a spell but it coasted so fast on the icy snow that he lost his gun and fell off himself a half mile later. He had to crawl back up the mountain to retrieve the gun.

"One time I was sneaking up on some ducks on a lake when just in front of me a cougar raised up as he was also looking for a duck dinner. I blasted him right in the face with the shotbun, only 20 feet away. We ate cougar instead of duck. A cougar has good flavored meat--but I never liked eating cat.

"Occasionally one would see a wolf, the grey timber wolves. One time while I was resting and had sat down alongside the trail

157

and without a gun, a large timber wolf came down the trail, and as I remained still, he never noticed me. As he came as near as I liked, I coughed and he turned and snapped his teeth as he departed.

"On a hunting trip alone on the mountain back of Cascade Locks, half way up the mountain, I ran into snow. I worked my way up a little higher. It takes four hours steady going to climb a mountain as steep as this mountain, so I worked my way alongside of the slope. I soon jumped a doe and a buck deer and they took off down the mountain, the doe was in the lead. As I watched them, a large cougar jumped from a leaning snag onto the buck. The buck shook him loose and again bounded down the hill. The deer were breaking through the crust on the snow but the cougar was not breaking through so had the advantage and overtook the deer several times but was unable to hang onto the buck. I hurried down hoping to get the cougar and when I passed the snag the cougar jumped from, I noticed that he had walked back and forth on that snag for several days, packing the snow down to solid ice. He must have had a long wait for something to come under him. I did not find the cougar or the deer after they got below the snow line.

"I remember the first repeating rifle I had seen. A newcomer came into town with a Henry rifle that would hold 7 cartridges. He wanted to hunt so I took him out. We jumped a doe with a buck 100 feet behind her; he shot seven times at the buck and killed the doe with the last shot 100 feet ahead of his target. None of us felt so bad with our trusty olde muzzle-loaders.

"About 1875, or just before any work was started on the canal, I was hauling wood to the steamboat landing. I had a yoke of oxen pulling the wagon and when I got about where the post office is now, it was in the morning and a little foggy. I saw what appeared to be a large dog ahead, and it was approaching my small dog which took off as the big dog sprang after it. I jumped off the wagon with my 'gord stick' and ran down near them My little dog had jumped off over the side of the road and the big dog turned out to be a cougar. I ran on back past what is the man-made Bridge of the Gods to a cabin The woman there told me that her husband was in the woods and had taken the rifle with him, but she gave me a shotgun, so I ran back to my wagon. When I got there the oxen were standing as I had left them, chewing their cuds, but my dog was barking into the brush shortly ahead. I went down there and found a large windfall log laying into the brush, so I crawled out on it on my hands and knees and when I came within six feet of the end, the cougar raised and snarled as I pulled the trigger. I was so close the gun powder burned its whiskers off. It was a large female cougar.

"One hard winter when the Indians living on our land grant were very hard up for food, Celly killed 33 deer that winter and gave them to the Indians.

"Sometimes in the summer we would see a few wild honey bees working in a spot of clover. We would sprinkle a little colored chalk on a few of them and then watch which way they flew and time them with a watch. Celly would do the timing; I think he said that they flew 300 feet a second and I fail to remember how long it took them to unload on reaching the hive. Celly was a sort of mountain man so he knew when the bee returned with the colored powder on her back, the direction and feet it would be to the bee tree. We would fall the tree and smoke the bees out and gather the honey.

"A mother bear had crawled into a hollow tree to sleep through the winter, and a bear is thinner than she will be in the spring They will suck their paws while hibernating and grow fat, sort of full of blubber, however, after they rampage around for scarce food in early spring they soon lose this soft fat. This mother bear had given birth to two small cubs and when it was time to come out, she was too fat for the hole. Some loggers felled the tree, killing the mother, so when they found the two little cubs, they gave one to me. I brought it home which didn't please Mother, but like all mothers, she gave in and let us keep it. I kept it penned and fed it. However, they grow fast and when it grew too large for its small pen, we made a collar for it and secured it to a post with a chain. It would climb up the post and sit on top and then pull up the chain and coil it on the post so that it wouldn't hang heavy on its neck. When we fed it, it would move a little way away from the food and coil the chain under it. Then it would wait patiently for a chicken to come sample the food and "Poof", it had a chicken for dinner and the food also. Mother finally gave it away to someone in Portland for a zoo.

"I must tell about an ox that had wandered away late in the fall. It was several weeks before we received word as to where he was. He had wandered just east of Shell Mountain when winter hit. I went after him and coming home around Shell Mountain, which slopes right into the river, and this was long before any roads were built along here, and when we reached the mountain slope it was covered with ice and no ox could walk around it. I had an axe with me so I chopped notches in the ice to step into and the old ox was so anxious to get home, he followed me and carefully stepped into each notch until we got across the slide; one misstep and he would have slid into the ice cold river. When we reached level ground, he followed me home with his nose almost in my rear pocket.

"I liked the old days better than the present days of the 1900's."

Business District of early Cascade Locks is shown in winter. Wind River Lumber Company commissary is large pillared building.

*****

In 1872 the legislature appropriated $50000 to build a wagon road from the mouth of the Sandy River to The Dalles. A road on paper but not completed for forty years.

June 23, 1874--Congress passed an Act authorizing a survey of the Cascades and The Dalles of the Columbia River for the purpose of ascertaining the practicability and cost of constructing canals and locks at these points.

1	Atwell, Mary	49	f	Pa.	farming
	*Charles	22	m	Ill.	miner
	*Marcellus	17	m	W.T.	wks on farm
	James	15	m	Ore.	wks on farm
	Wilbur	12	m	Ore.	
2	Throssel, Thomas	36	m	Eng.	farming
	Mary L.	22	f	Ore.	keeps house
	Hannah J.	1	f	Ore.	
3	Humphrey, Henry	48	m	Ohio	farmer
	Jane	30	f	B.C.	keeps house (Indian)
	Emily J.	12	f	W.T.	(breed)
	Towner, Ezra	44	m	Ohio	carpenter
4	Graham, David	37	m	Mo.	laborer
	Martha	19	f	Ore.	keeps house (Indian)
5	Burston, Magness	27	m	W.T.	farming (1/2 breed)
	James	8	f	W.T.	(1/4 breed)
	Margaret	10	f	W.T.	(1/4 breed)
	Gibson, William	87	m	Scot	farmer
	Nancy	67	f	B.C.	keeps house (breed)
	Lyon, John	55	m	B.C.	laborer (breed)
	John	28	m	B.C.	farmer (breed)
	Henry	20	m	B.C.	wks on farm (breed)
	Burston, William	32	m	B.C.	farm laborer (breed)
	Jenette	27	f	B.C.	keeps house (breed)

*These two listed under Atwell (Attwell) were sons of
Mrs. Attwell by her first husband, Williams. James Fremont
was known as Monty, John Wilbur was called Wilbur by his
mother.

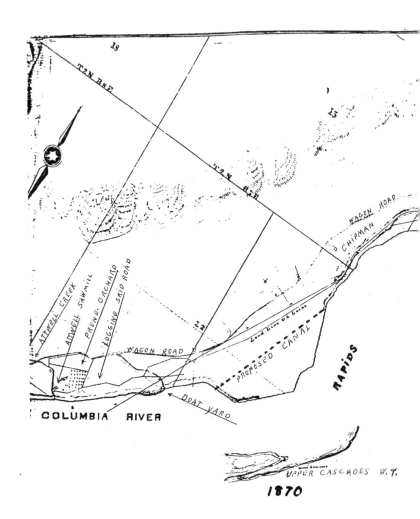

COLUMBIA RIVER

UPPER CASCADES W. T.

1870

BONNEVILLE, OREGON

Many of us often wonder why this place was named for Captain Bonneville who we doubt ever set foot on the spot.

Captain Bonneville's expedition was organized on military lines however he joined up with Wyeth on a planned joint fur trading expedition but later changed his plans and proceeded on his own account. His second season was marked by contention with representatives of the American Fur Company and the Rocky Mountain Men. He traveled on different extended journeys, sometimes hastened by suspicion that he was being shadowed by Blackfeet, or Crows. Christmas morning 1833 he left Portneuf river to visit the basin of the Columbia, and ascertain the prospects of trading there. He reached the Hudson's Bay Company post, Fort Nez Perce at Walla Walla Mar. 4, 1834. The Chief Factor there, while hospitable, made it plain the competing traders could not hope to get help from his compnay. All that Bonneville could get from him was some advice as to the safest direction to avoid hostile Indians. He returned east, reaching the Bear River settlements in August 1835

He was dismissed for overstaying his furlough and the war department files show that President Jackson restored Bonneville to the service. He was placed in command of the Army post at Fort Vancouver in 1853.

A railroad station a few miles west of Cascade Locks is called Bonneville. The dam across the Columbia River here bears his name and the Army Engineers at the north end of the dam, renamed the Cascades to North Bonneville, Washington.

Files of Columbia Gorge Post Offices show . . Bonneyville . . Multnomah County . . . Mar. 17, 1900.

* * * * * * * * * *

A short distance below Bonneville there used to be a sign board bearing the words, "Petrified Trees."

When the railroad contractors were building the railroad along the river bank at this point, they ran into a perfect forest of petrified wood. The logs and limbs were piled up by the cord alongside the new railroad. Much of wood has been carried away by collectors but some of the heavier logs still remain.

WASCO COUNTY ROAD BOOK

July 11, 1879--Lease award to Victor Trevitt for a 10-year permission to establish toll gate at most practical point with following rates; sheep and hogs .03 cents; horses, mules, asses or meat cattle .12 cents; person other than footman and not traveling in vehicle .30 cents; two wheel vehicle, loaded or unloaded 60 cents; four wheel vehicle loaded or unloaded $1.20. Trevitt agrees to complete road within 10 days and deposit surety bond of $2,000 to bind contract.

*****

HISTORY OF THE CASCADE STEAMBOAT LOCKS

The name "Cascades" was changed to Cascade Locks in 1878 when the government started the canal.

163

The first survey for a canal and locks around the rapids was made in pursuance of an Act of Congress on June 23, 1874.

The survey was made under the supervision of Major Michler in the fall of 1874. Robert A. Habersham, later Surveyor General of Oregon, was chief of the survey party and Capt. Allen Noyes, rodman. The map of the survey was sent to Brigadier General A.A. Humphries, the Chief of Engineers.

The Cascades consisted of a series of rapids with a fall of 37.3 feet in a distance of five and three-fourths miles.

The land for the construction of the canal was obtained from the Oregon Steam Navigation Company and the title vested in the United States in July, 1876.

The canal was to be 90 feet in width and 3,000 feet in length. One lock 521 feet, and the other 514 feet, the depth of water 8 feet, the lower lock to have a lift of 24 feet and to operate up to a 20 foot stage above extreme low water at the lower entrance of the canal. The upper lock is formed by the upper gates of the lower lock and a pair of guard gates so the canal can be used up to a 42 foot stage of water at the lower entrance.

Major Michler estimated the cost of the canal and locks and removal of rocks to be $700,000.

The bids were opened for the first proposal of contract October 1, 1878. The contract was awarded to Ball and Platt of New York, for $79,911.67. Contractor Ball arrived at the work with a force of men Oct. 21, 1878, and commenced the erection of buildings.

On January 4, 1879, Mr. Ball died at his residence on the ground. After his death, Mrs. Ball and the other partner carried on the work to completion of this contract Dec. 2, 1879.

A contract for removal of rock in the river between the site of the canal and the lower end of Bradford's Island was given David Chalmers and William Holmes of Portland, on Aug. 13, 1881. They removed 4527 cubic yards, receiving $3 per cu. yd. for exposed rock and $25 per cu. yd. for submerged rock, completing their contract on Feb. 22, 1882.

The work was carried on with day labor on several projects. While superintending the work of blasting operations at Umatilla Rock in Dec. 1882, Captain P.M. Price was struck by a flying piece of rock and his leg broken. Several Chinamen were later drowned when a boat sank returning them to shore from work blasting rocks in the river.

On March 10, 1887, an electrical set blast of eight holes was fired at noon. A piece of rock weighing about 150 pounds was thrown so that in descending, it fell through the roof of a house of Thomas Coyle, janitor on the government works, killing his little daughter Teressa, aged three years. The Coyle home was located at that time about where Mrs. Anders lived in 1932.

Sept. 15, 1892, proposals were invited for the completion of the work. A contract was awarded to J.G. and I.N. Day of San Francisco, the successful bidders.

A large amount of stone had been gathered by the government and most of it was cut and ready to be used, this was turned over to the contractors.

The completed locks were turned over to Capt. W.L. Fisk of the Corps of Army Engineers on Nov. 5, 1896, the contractors receiving $3,820,629.

OREGON STATE PORTAGE ROAD

The north bank portage road was called the 'Racket Road' because of the high prices being charged for the short portage. So the State of Oregon built a portage road around the rapids on the south bank to control prices. It was called the Oregon Portage and was in operation in 1881. The first year, 8,000 passengers and 10,000 tons of freight passed over this new portage.

The steamer "Regulator" built in The Dalles in 1891, 152 feet long, and of 508 tons, hauled freight from this upper terminal to The Dalles and the steamer "Dalles City", built in Portland, 142 feet long and of 402 tons, brought freight and passengers to the lower state railroad terminal from Portland.

When the locks were opened to navigation, the Oregon State Portage Railroad was taken up and the locomotives and cars sold.

*****

May 7, 1890, H.A. Leavens elected County Commissioner at The Dalles.

Oct. 9, 1888, J.F. Attwell, Supervisor of Road Dist. 1. "Wagon road bridges at Shell Rock, Herman Creek and Middle Landing are in unsafe condition and in need of immediate repair. We need to purchase lumber and spikes in the amount of $40.25."

Purchase approved by County Commissioners.

*****

At the opening of the locks, the following boats were lined up to pass through. The "Sadie B", "The Dalles City", "The Sarah Dixon" and the "Harvest Queen".

Many stories have been passed down by the pioneers who lived at the Cascade Locks at the time of construction.

"Hours were 6 A.M. to 6 P.M. and 12 hours a day. Times were very hard and one just about had to wait for one man to die before another man could get the job," John Attwell said. "I.N. Day was a hard man with his men and he continually walked over the project. One day he came up on a little Dutchman who had stopped to light his pipe and he told the little fellow, 'Pick up your tools and get to hell off this job.' The little old Dutchman was heart broken, but he started gathering up his tools (carpenter tools) and placed them in his tool chest. This took him some time and finally he put the chest on his shoulder and started for the gate. Here he ran into I.N. Day who called out to him, 'Where the hell are you going? Get back on the job,' so the little fellow returned to work.

"Another time I N. Day came aboard a rock scow and noticed a tall young fellow standing by the rail. I.N. walked up and grabbed the fellow but at the same instant found himself knocked overboard. I.N. crawled out of the water soaking wet and noticed the young fellow working so laughed and went on.

"Many Irishmen were working on the contract and many of them were doing laborer tasks. The boarding houses and hotels were all over-populated. An overworked cesspool would no longer contain the sewage so two Irishmen were sent over to clean it out. The Irish are always noted for their wit regardless of the work. A ladder was placed into the pit and Murphy was sent into the pit with a shovel to load a bucket which Pat above would pull up with a rope and dump. A curious, well dressed lady wondered what was going on so she walked over to the hole to look down. Murphy saw her there so he called up, 'Hey, Pat, send me lunch down in the next bucket.' The embarrassed lady had seen and heard enough; she did not wait to see if Pat did send the lunch down."

STEAMBOATS THAT RAN THE RAPIDS

All these boats ran the rapids during high water while rocks were buried under water. The water ran very fast at this time and the "Hassalo" was timed at a mile a minute.

"Nez Perce", "Shoshone" and the "Okanogan". June 2, 1882, the "Elvira" under Capt. McKenzie. July 6, 1882, the "Mountain Queen" under Capt. Troupe. May 26, 1888, the "Gold Dust" with Capt. Martneau at the wheel, the same day Capt. Troupe brought the "Hassalo" over the rapids, and on June 15, 1889, he brought the "Wasco" over and on June 18, 1890 he brought the "Harvest Queen" over. Capt. Martneau took the "D.S Baker" over June 26, 1893.

Captain Monty Attwell shoved several barges over the rapids in 1882, one weighing 1100 tons. The O.R. & N. wharfboat from The Dalles went over with drag chains behind to keep it headed in one direction; the chains caught on rocks and almost sank the barge.

After the locks were built, the "Bailey Gatzert" piloted by B. Short and Capt. Geer ran the rapids June 19, 1917 with 64 passengers and 64 tons of freight on board. The river was so high that the locks could not be operated. Charles Smith took the small towboat "Roxanna" over the rapids June 8, 1925.

While the Lewis & Clark World's Fair was on in Portland the summer of 1905, 1417 boats went through the Cascade Locks Steamboat Locks, carrying 133,070 passengers.

*****

This story received from The Dalles Library:

The work of building the locks and canal at the Cascades was a lengthy one. Work would progress from one Congressional appropriation to another. Of course the railroads did everything they could to block the work.

When it was finished, government engineers declared the locks and canal made up the finest piece of masonry work in the world. Some of the base rock underwater was obtained from boulders nearby, but the top rock was shipped by train from a gray granite quarry on the Snake River. It's the toughest granite that ever a chisel was put to. And now all of that fine stonework is submerged forever under water by the lake created with Bonneville Dam.

Normally the town of Cascade Locks had about 200 residents, but when Congress would put through an appropriation, new jobs would become available and there would be 800 to 900 men move in to work.

In the spring of 1888, the town was filled with newcomers when election time came along. Two candidates were running for county clerk. One of the candidates was Curd Cates, a merchant of Cascade Locks. A man from The Dalles was the other candidate.

Now not one man in 10 among the male adults of Cascade Locks had a right to vote, since most of the men were outsiders just arrived. But all hands took part in the voting.

The election was held in the back room of Major Alec O'Toole's saloon. O'Toole was a character if ever there was one. He stood behind his bar, wearing a silk plug hat and a cutaway coat with a white vest. An Irish man as his name indicates, he was extremely dignified in side whiskers. He claimed, among other things, to have ridden with the Immortal Six Hundred at Balaklava.

As was customary at many an election in those days, each candidate had a keg of beer in the voting booth. Each had a sign over it, urging the voters to "Help Yourself", and cast a vote for the man who had supplied the keg.

Before the day was over, while the other fellow wasn't there, Cates introduced free whiskey. This, of course, swung the feeling of the crowd over to Cates' side.

A.G. Hall, Justice of the Peace at Cascade Locks, presided at the election. He ordered that there should be no fighting in the voting booths. And so, when the fellows wanted to fight, they would go into the saloon and have it out. Major O'Toole would walk out from behind the bar to assume the duties of referee and he saw to it that the fellows fought fairly.

After a dozen or so fights and after all the free beverages had been consumed, the polls closed finally, after a good time had been enjoyed by everyone.

Of course Cates carried Cascade Locks strongly, but he lost out for the county clerkship because he was outvoted in The Dalles.

*****

COXEY'S ARMY

In 1894, Jacob Sechler, popularly known as "General" Coxey, led groups of unemployed, popularly called "Coxey's Army", to Washington, D.C., to gain Congressional attention for the unemployed. His army reached the Capitol on April 28, but an attempted demonstration led to his arrest.

A freight train was commanded in Portland and the railroad officials allowed them to take the train, and even furnished the train crew with relief engineers.

These hungry men without food aboard, would stop the train when passing farms and help themselves. They stopped at

Cascade Locks while the helpless residents watched as the demonstrators helped themselves, unload the smokehouses, root cellars or gardens, taking cabbages, potatoes, turnips, hams and bacon or anything to fill the empty stomachs.

The "army" was broken up and sent home, and Coxey released after a month in jail after being nominated for Congress from Ohio. He later ran for the Presidency of the U.S.

*****

BY SETH LEAVENS

in 1894 flood, the railway was washed out in many places. The old wagon road had washed out and grown over in many places. Gangs of people from Cascade Locks reconstructed the road and built bridges across creeks, good one over Eagle Creek. Road went up mountain side of Eagle Creek. I drove a 4-horse team with a wagon up this grade and wonder why I am still alive today. Very sharp turns. There was a bridge across Dead Man Creek (Ruckle). I was 16 years old at the time. From the Cascade Locks east my father graded the nearly impassable road. There was a deteriorated road east. My father had oxen and horses for grading roads and hauling wood to Government Works and people at the Cascade Locks. Also sold wood to the railroad. Collected $3 poll tax to build and maintain roads. Not much road because traffic went by steamboat or railroad. When the railroad washed out in 1894, it was hard to get provisions and food, so the road had to be fixed and some of it was still in existence when in 1915 the Columbia River Highway was constructed.

*****

MRS. ATHALIE LAGE WROTE:

When construction was begun on the locks, several enterprising persons opened businesses here. The town was variously called Upper Cascades, Whiskey Flat and sometimes Bagdad. It was at first located close to the river east of the present park site. The district where the town is now located was called Emmigrant Hill and few people lived there.

It was during the canal construction days that both the Catholic and the Protestant churches were built. The present Community Church was built in 1894. The guiding hand in its erection was a Mr. Haskins, who solicited contributions of money and labor from the stone cutters and workers. Mr. Haskins was a Methodist preacher and preached in the church for several years.

While work had been progressing on the canal, railroad interests were not idle, and in 1884 final connections were made with eastern railroads. Cascade Locks was no longer dependent

169

on the river for communication with the outside world, and it was evident that the steamboat era had ended.

Some of the names synonymous with the latter part of the 19th century were Bothwick, MacKinnon, Dyer, Cameron, Olin, Olson, Hull, and many others.

Two other developments occurred after the turn of the century to link the town with the outside world. In about 1920 the Columbia River Highway was finished and in 1927 the Bridge of the Gods was constructed. The town gradually moved back and the highway became "Main Street".

Some of the people who are remembered from this period are the Brolliars, Haggbloms, Sundstens, Leahys, Corvenishes, McDaineys, Granstroms, Ericksons, Pedersons, Lovels, Rosenbacks, Wigrens and Harrisons.

In 1930 the construction of Bonneville Dam gave stimulus for further growth. Housing became a severe problem and the town suffered all the growing pains of the typical boom town. Nearest town to the dam site on the Oregon side of the river, it had schools, churches, lights and water. The census in 1930 gave it a population of 250, but within the year it had grown to 1,500 people. But with the completion of the dam in 1937 another era ended. As the lake behind the dam filled with water, the rapids disappeared. It was now possible for ocean-going vessels to go up the river. The locks were abandoned and the gates were eventually taken out.

In 1934, the town suffered a severe setback. A Fourth of July celebration backfired when a skyrocket, thrown by a careless prankster, fell into a fireworks booth and started a conflagration which threatened to destroy the whole town. Much of the business section was burned, including several stores, the post office, I.O.O.F. hall and the Catholic Church. All have since been rebuilt with the exception of the Catholic Church.

In 1938 Cascade Locks became the first town to sell power from Bonneville Dam, but it was not without a struggle. When power became available from Bonneville Dam, the city voted to go into the power business.

*****   *****

EARLY WATER SUPPLY By Earl Henry
(Descendant of Patrick Henry, and grandson of Doc Leavens, tells of early water works.)

"Grandpa Hi had a private spring a pipeline that furnished several homes. This spring was fenced, good enough to keep out humans and farm animals Hi did not worry his head about other "natural" forms of life. Maybe he had a screen over the

170

intake.   If so, it had corroded away on this day of doom.   A small "water dog" (looks like a lizard) came down the water pipe and into the tea kettle.   It had to be poor sweet Grandma Pluma who prepared the tea for her guests and discovered the well bleached body of the mud-puppy after it was too late to avoid the tragedy.

"Still another water supply was from a spring down in a hole, near the shack of Frank Miles and his black consort, Hattie. They might have been married to each other, nobody cared 2 cents either way.   This spring furnished drinking water for the two schools.

"Dear old Grandma Pluma 'treated' my ear ache with her own 'receipt' by means of puffs of hot smoke from the stem of her dearly loved clay pipe.   The 'Smuck, smuck' of her lips on the stem of her beloved pipe is a memory I'll never live long enough to forget.   Even as early in our WEBFOOT CULTURE in the 1890's.   It is no longer 'lady-like" to smoke a pipe and not yet lady-like for them to smoke cigarettes. Men had switched or started to switch from pipe to cigarettes. They 'rolled their own' from Bull Durham, calling them 'cigareetes'.

"Every last one of the older, old settlers at the Locks was an incurable, un-rootable OUT-Law, proven by the fact that they had to be superloaded with guts or foolhardiness to get there, as they did on foot, horseback or aboard a Prairie Schooner, before the days of nice, comfortable choo-choo cars, chewing coal smoke; there was mighty little Human Vegetation amongst them.   There was a "prowl by night" wild animal blood, a-plenty, in a big percentage of the Cascades people.   When I was a kid, we saw no pistol-packers around.   The only shooting in my time was Old Man Gebhardt who blew out his wife's brains, then his own with a shotgun, right in a crowded neighborhood during the night.   Nobody heard it nor knew it happened until the bodies were found next day.   Nobody even tried to guess Why the old man did it.   "Just crazy," was all anybody had to say about it. There was no 'Officer of the Law' of any kind at the Locks. Booze flowed freely; working men of the town well known to everybody, could and did repose in the dirt along the 'street', out like a light until they chose to wake up and stagger home, or at least out of sight.   Couples drifted into town and out, assumed to be married but nobody worried their heads over the question.   Frequently one of these gals would become con-spicuously popular with men having no claim of any kind on her, giving the Town Gossips, male or female, a chance to invent and repeat giggles and gags about the deal.   It was always

171

assumed in such a case that it was merely another case of cheating wife, a thing that few people seemed to get worked up about.

"I heard a yarn involving some people I knew. The husband surprised his wife and her boy friend who jumped out of the window. The husband hurried to explain to the neighbors that he was sore as H--- because the dirty so-and-so had helped himself to almost a quart of whiskey."

*****

NOTED OUTLAW GETS SHAVE & HAIRCUT IN CASCADE LOCKS

The Columbia Gorge without telephones or banks at this period, lacked outlaw experience. This outlaw was here and gone before most people were aware. However, one of the greatest manunts of the Columbia River area took place in the summer of 1902. A notorious outlaw, Harry Tracy, wanted for murder, escaped from the Oregon Penitentiary with David Merrill, a brother-in-law and partner in crime. Sheriffs and possees searched throughout Oregon and Washington for nearly two months, being led astray by the cunning intelligence and bold resourcefulness of the outlaws.

Harry Tracy was born in 1871 in Kentucky. He stood about six feet tall, his thin, wiry frame made him look taller. The most intriguing of his physical characteristics, were his steel blue eyes. When he focused his icy glare upon an enemy, it was said by all who witnessed the event, that it sent chills up the spine of any man. The intensity of his stare probably fostered his reputation for being cold-hearted and cruel. This is not entirely true When it came to shootouts with lawmen, Tracy was a deadly shot, but he did not kill wantonly, and often spoke of never harming women and children.

Harry Tracy was a member of various bands of outlaws, including the most famous of all, the "Hole-in-the-Wall" Gang which also included such desperados as "Butch" Cassidy, "Black Jack" Ketchum, Kid Curry, and Harry Longbaugh, the "Sundance Kid". During this time he served two sentences in the Utah Penitentiary. Tracy also was wanted in Idaho, Montana, Colorado, and Utah. He was a murderer of men in all four states. Teaming up with David Merrill in California, Tracy moved to Portland, Oregon to continue his criminal activities. The pair set up a massive crime wave that soon had the city in virtual panic. They robbed stores, banks and even street cars in broad daylight with Tracy holding his two pistols on the terrified victims while Merrill cleaned them out of valuables.

172

Merrill was captured by two detectives while hiding in his bedroom, and a short time later Tracy was captured in a street ambush. After serving three years of their 20-year robbery sentences in the Oregon Penitentiary, they escaped on June 9, 1902. They obtained guns which had been planted by a former prisoner, and Tracy wasted no time in using them to kill two guards, and wound another

The alarm of the escaped prisoners soon spread quickly throughout Oregon. Governor Greer called out National Guard units from Salem and Woodburn, and Sheriff Durbin of Salem formed a large posse that included Guard Carson from Washington Penitentiary at Walla Walla, who was master of the only pack of hounds in the area.

With the posse on their trail, Tracy and Merrill moved north. Only their stops at farm houses for food and clothing served as clues to their direction. Northern Oregon was rough country-- forests, hills, gullies and creek bottoms--and the posse dwindled to twenty or thirty men. The hounds were constantly fooled by Tracy's method of backtracking. He would walk into an empty farmhouse or shack and walk back over the trail until he came to a swamp or creek, which he would follow a mile or so, completely eradicating the scent.

A stolen team of horses finally brought Tracy and Merrill to the Columbia River, where they forced two men to ferry them across in a rowboat. When they landed on the Washington side, Tracy promised to send the two men $50 as soon as he reached Seattle, "...for being so nice."

As soon as he learned of the convict's landing, Sheriff Marsh, who happened to be an ex-schoolmate of Merrill's in Vancouver, Washington where both men were raised, formed a posse along Fourth Plain Road. Under the cover of night, the escapees slipped through and continued their way north. Sheriff Marsh, in an effort to capture the outlaws, set up a posse in the Salmon Creek area of Clark County. Accidentally, one posse member was shot in the leg, and another man was wounded by Tracy near Tenny and Belts Bridge. After this, the posse lost the trail. Tracy and Merrill quickly passed through Ridgefield, Lewisville, LaCenter and Kelso. In Cowlitz County they were taking two horses from a farmer but when he pleaded with them that he was a poor working man needing the horses for farm work, they dismounted and ran off on foot.

Tracy appeared alone at the Capital City Oyster Co. in Olympia, where he forced Captain Clarke and his crew to take him to Seattle in the motor launch "M & S" that was moored at the dock. On the way across Puget Sound, Tracy passed time telling of his previous exploits, and explained the disappearance of David Merrill. Tracy thought Merrill a coward because he did not like to rob farmhouses for food and clothing. He preferred to sneak the items needed. He told Tracy he was dissatisfied with the life on the run and wanted to separate. Tracy refusing, challenged him to a duel. They were to take ten steps, turn and fire, but Tracy said, expecting treachery on Merrill's part, turned and fired on step eight, hitting Merrill in the back. He then finished him with two close-range shots.

As the launch passed McNeil Island Penitentiary, Tracy swore he would kill any guard he saw on the walls. Captain Clark talked him out of any such action by explaining he would lessen his chances of landing in Seattle unnoticed. Tracy settled for taking pot shots at seals, impressing his marksmanship to the crew. Near Tacoma, he expressed a fond desire to shoot the captain of the tug "Sea Foam" because he insisted on heading toward the launch. Tracy resisted when the tug turned away for good.

Captain Clarke landed at Meadow Point near Ballard, at Tracy's request, and here he took ashore a young man as a hostage, a young man named Scott, whom he had taken a liking to on the trip up from Olympia He told Scott he was not afraid of any man or group of men, and no man could take him from the front. Scott was soon released and news of Tracy's arrival in Seattle soon spread throughout the entire area.

Outside Bothell, north of Seattle, a small posse surrounded a cabin near the railroad tracks. The men of the posse were trying to find cover, when suddenly from behind a stump, Tracy fired his deadly Winchester. In a period of two or three minutes, two men were wounded, one mortally, another was killed, Tracy jumped into brush and disappeared.

Next, Tracy appeared at the home of Mrs. Van Horn on the southwest corner of Woodland Park, Seattle, and demanded a meal. A delivery boy came to the back door, and when Mrs. Van Horn answered the door she told the boy to inform the King County Sheriff of the outlaw's presence at her house. When Tracy left the house with two hired men as shields, the men demanded Tracy to surrender. Tracy's answer was to shoot the men between the eyes with the Winchester he had concealed behind his legs. Later Tracy ate breakfast at the Fisher farm north of Green Lake. He then went back to Meadow Point and commandeered a Japanese fishing boat, ordered the Captain to take him to Bainbridge Island. Here he stopped at Johnson's farm for food and clothing. He took Johnson's rowboat and had the hired man, John Anderson, row him to West Seattle. The posse caught up with the outlaw at Gerrells' farm near Renton. A jeweler on his way home from work spoiled the ambush by yelling at the house, "Is that Tracy in there?" Tracy immediately jumped out a window and ran into thick undergrowth, sprinkling cayenne pepper on the ground to destroy the dog's effectiveness. Rumors placed Tracy in Oregon, Kanasket near Tacoma, north Seattle, Canada and Wyoming.

The next heard about him was east of Vancouver. Mrs. Stoggill told, "Tracy came to our farm after dark and asked if he could sleep in the barn. My father told him it would be alright if he didn't smoke in the hay Early the next morning he came to the kitchen door to thank us and mother invited him in for breakfast. It was then that we learned that he was Tracy. He was polite and courteous and thanked us for breakfast before he left. When we picked up the breakfast dishes from the table, we found a $5 gold piece under his plate. We were quite excited so we told our neighbors."

A Clark County Sheriff's Deputy had a narrow escape from Tracy's gun; it wounded his horse in the flank. Sheriff Bill Sappington retired the horse on the Blackwood ranch in Sunnyside, and it recovered. The author rode the horse in 1910 on the ranch. The deep scar had healed but still showed where the bad wound had been just between the ribs and the hind quarter.

Tracy came up to the Cascades and there he asked Ed Cook, a fish wheel operator, to take him across the river. Ed told Walt Attwell, "Tracy asked me to take him across the river.

Cascade Locks at time Tracy came through.

Knowing who it was, I decided I had better comply. We went down to my rowboat and I put the oars into the oarlocks and he sat in the stern. When we reached the Oregon shore, he said, 'Let me have your purse.' I handed it to him and he opened it and saw the $20 gold piece I had in it. He reached into his own pocket and took a dollar from it, dropped it into my purse, and handed it back to me with the $20 still in it."

He then walked up to Cascade Locks and stopped at the local barber shop. "I am Tracy and I want a hair cut and a shave." When he sat in the chair and noticed how nervous the barber was, his hand came out from under the apron and laid a six shooter on his lap and he said, "For every drop of blood you draw from me, I will take a quart out of you." It is said the barber was doing some trembling, but he never drew that drop of blood.

Tracy then went on up the river east of the Cascade Mountains, into a country that his wide experience should have kept him out of. Wide open spaces where everyone knew a stranger and every rancher for miles, and every man had a gun and knew how to use it.

On his travels eastward, Tracy stopped at the Eddy farm near Fellows for provisions. He let a young man named Goldfinch leave the farm as he pleaded urgent business. Tracy was relaxed and felt so good that he helped with the labor on a new barn the Eddys were building. While he was working, a posse surrounded the farm, told of Tracy's whereabouts by Goldfinch.

One of the men approached the farm to affirm Tracy's existence. Tracy grabbed his Winchester and a pistol and ran for the cover of a gulley. The posse that had been lying in ambush, opened fire. Tracy was running for better shelter behind a rock when his luck ran out. In the middle of a wheat field a bullet struck him in the leg, severing an artery. While dragging himself to the rock another bullet pierced his thigh. He kept up the gun duel for a while, but not wanting to deliver himself into the hands of the posse, he realized the hopelessness of the situation and accepted his fate with the same coolness that had brought him that far. He placed his thumb on the trigger of his pistol, since he was too weak from the loss of blood to use his trigger finger, and shot himself in the head just above the left eye.

The posse, with local physician, Dr. E C. Lanter, took the body into the town of Davenport where crowds had gathered to see the infamous outlaw in death By the time his body had traveled the distance of the main street, his clothes had been stripped to ribbons by greedy souvenir hunters. Those that did not get clothing were satisfied with locks of hair, chopped off with hacks of pocket knives. Naked, and bald, he was nailed into

176

a cheap coffin. Before the lid was closed, vitriol was poured onto his face to prevent people from stealing his body to put on exhibition. A number of people demanded to see Tracy's Winchester. C.A. Straub, who was in charge of the body, produced it for the crowd

Sheriff Cudihee was waiting in Davenport to recognize and claim the body. He was reported so overcome with emotion that he could not restrain his tears.

Tracy's coffin was paraded throughout the streets of Seattle and Portland where more relic hunters whittled splinters off the sides. Finally he was returned to the Oregon Penitentiary where he was buried next to David Merrill, his brother-in-law

So ended the life of one of the most notorious outlaws of the Old West. Harry Tracy is part of that period of American History that has been distorted and aggrandized by the passing of time, and it is fitting that the final chapter of his life took place in the Northwest, where also the frontier ended.

POWER PLANT--CASCADE LOCKS

The Young family, founders and builders of the first power plant in Cascade Locks, are descendants of Brigham Young, their great-great-grandfather being a brother of Brigham.

Before coming to Cascade Locks in 1904, the Young family lived in Baker City, Oregon and were owners and operators of a power plant near Haines.

A farmer's irrigation dam broke, flooding out the plant. Before leaving Baker City, Goodwin Young, the older of the two brothers, met and married Florence Carter, a Chicago girl who had come west with her father, a mining engineer. Shortly afterward, the whole family, including their father, John C. Young, moved to Cascade Locks, locating east of town on what formerly was known as the Field's ranch and which is now the site of the Cascade Lumber Co.

John C. Young, the father, later became the postmaster of Portland, Oregon.

Not long after arriving in Cascade Locks, Scott and Goodwin Young made plans to build a power plant on Herman Creek where they had acquired considerable property.

They cut a trail 2 miles up hill on Herman Creek, then had to carry most of the material up to the site on their backs. The generator was taken in on skids, by block and tackle.

When the plant was completed, it was called the Columbia River Light and Power Co. Power was furnished to part of the surrounding territory and Cascade Locks, while the Wind River Lumber Company of Cascade Locks served the remainder.

When the mill closed down for repairs for a period of six months, the Columbia River Light & Power Co. took over the service for the entire community, including the necessary lights for the mill. About 1914 the Youngs bought out the mill interest, thus serving the whole community permanently.

John Young tells an amusing incident: One day a man teacher came to inspect the plant, seating himself on one of the bunks used by the help who slept in the power plant near the generators. He wondered "how the men managed to sleep through the noise of the power plant" when soon he was nodding and fell sound asleep himself.

Operating a plant in those days posed problems in more ways than one. About 1914, during the fall salmon run, there were so many fish coming up Herman Creek to spawn, that the nozzles became clogged with salmon, necessitating the closing of the plant while the nozzles were removed and cleaned. Later when larger nozzles had been installed, it was not unusual to hear the "swoosh" of the salmon as they went right on through the nozzles.

The severe winters of those days presented other hazards to the plant. One winter, the running water in the flume froze solid. Again the plant had to be closed while men chopped the ice and removed it from the flume.

Whenever an unusually severe winter occurred after that, the plant was closed before the freezing could take place, thus avoiding the trouble and cost previously encountered.

The freezing of the running water was caused by the forming of ice around the nail heads in the wooden flume, building up from the bottom, and eventually freezing in a solid mass.

The Youngs built a tie mill on Bear Springs Flat on Herman Creek, floating ties about 2 miles down a flume to the old county road. The ties were hauled to Cascade Locks on a wagon, then loaded on a railroad car.

About 1917, the Youngs received financial backing to build another plant, this was the plant near the Columbia River Highway.

John Young, Goodwin's son, who was about 10 years old at that time, had the job of crawling inside the hydraulic pipe to hold the rivets in place while they were being riveted by the workmen.

Sam Samson's Skamania Light and Power Co. plant on Rock Creek near Stevenson had washed out so the Youngs merged with that company. It was at about this time that the Columbia River Highway was started, and Kern and Kibbee, Contractors, moved to Cascade Locks and set up a rock crusher. This placed an extra heavy load on the power plant. Having no governor as yet, John Young was again put to work, this time to help all summer long acting as a governor on the generator by lifting a lever whenever a heavy load came on the line.

1921--The Highway was blocked by huge snow drifts for at least 6 weeks. The river was frozen so the stern-wheelers could not make it up the river for several weeks. The railroad was closed by the severe weather. At this time, the power line which fed Stevenson and the Washington side of the river (crossing approximately where the Bridge of the Gods now stands) became loaded with ice to about 6 inches in diameter.

The Youngs, Goodwin, Scott and John had come down to inspect the line, while standing on the bank of the Oregon side the lines broke and plunged into the river. There was no power at this time. Goodwin Young immediately went to the telegraph station and ordered a new cable from Portland. The trains were not running due to the severe weather, so the cable came up by boat. However, when Mr. Young went to the canal at Cascade Locks to get the cable, it was buried under 85 tons of mail. The boat took the mail to The Dalles for unloading and brought the cable back on its next trip down.

*Herman Creek was originally Harman Creek. James H. Harman took a donation land claim through which the creek ran, selling part of the claim to Bolivar B. Bishop in 1867.

*****

THE BRIDGE OF THE GODS

1926 the Union Bridge Co. builds a steel bridge across the Columbia River where the Indian legends tell of the natural bridge 'Tahmahnaw' crossing the river before the mountain gods shook it down.

When work started, 3,000 people attended the colorful ceremony. Indian Chief is Speaker.

Martin Spedis, Klickitat chief, and one of the last aged men of the once powerful tribe, spoke in his aboriginal tongue, his son Dave Spedis, interpreting. The chief declared, not as a fable but as Indian fact, that some 300 years ago a bridge, the work of the Great Spirit, joined the north and the south banks of Wauna, as the Columbia was known to the Indians.

The chief recalled that his forefathers and the forefathers of other tribes from near and far, from east and west and everywhere were accustomed to gather there at Indian villages, located on either bank of the river.

179

The popular paleface conception of the Red man's early life is one of constant warfare and friction among the different tribes, a conception well based on extant knowledge, but the Bridge of the Gods, that mighty link in the Cascades seems to have been instrumental in breaking down tribal friction. It was a highway of peace and apparently brought about something akin to cooperative planning among the chiefs of older times.

The two Indians were accompanied by Susie, Ellen and Ida Spedis, squaws of the tribe who came down from Wasco County for the celebration, followed the address with a song.

George Rauch, the chairman of the celebration, followed with an address. "My friends, we all meet together where once Indian villages used to be on both sides of the river. Then Indians came here from east and west and every point. Like today with the big highway built here so people can travel roads from east and west to here. About 300 years ago the Bridge of the Gods crossed the river and people walked over many years. When bridge falls, no place to cross; now comes back so everybody can go over as it used to be.

"My friends, I can be happy. I'll be walking over myself like old people used to walk across the natural Bridge of the Gods. Explorations of the wilderness on the north bank of the Columbia have disclosed well-marked trails leading to the very brink of the precipice supposed to have been the abutment of the natural Bridge of the Gods. This new man made bridge will create a union of the people on both sides of the river."

*****

PORT OF CASCADE LOCKS BUYS THE BRIDGE

The 45 year old bridge was purchased for $892,500 in 1961 from Columbia River Toll Bridge Co. The sale was financed entirely with revenue bonds which will be retired from tolls collected from the users of the crossing.

SHELL ROCK

There was a post office here before 1878--when it was moved across the river to Collin's Landing Aug. 19, 1878. There isn't much evidence of a settlement being here to warrant a post office, but there could have been. No road or trail went around Shell Mountain, but some old history says a ferry was operated around the mountain for ferrying cattle and horses as there were trails to it on both sides.

Augustus Granzback had a "Eating House"
J.W. Allen homesteaded in 1866, was an Engineer.
J.W. Tompson homesteaded in 1866, built sawmill.
Marion Vanderpool was listed as a 'Miller'.
Joseph Jones as 'Sail maker' was also a teacher.

Walter Attwell says, "In early history don't forget 'Hans Wicks, The Brollier family, Old man Frazell, Charlie Steward, Dug Crates who ran the water company, Dr. Candina with his razor strap made of human leather from the back of patient· who did not quite make it, The Harpans, Justin, Benson who raised cattle up around Herman Creek, the Conlins who lived near Herman Creek, Eunice Blackwood a first school teacher and Erma Benson and early school teacher who married Mr. Pennock who was office man for the Wind River Lumber Co. Charlie Olene who caught many a salmon and could take his small boat into the swift water of the rapids where other dared not go. Mable Barrett, Al Meyer the colorful barber who was a natural animal trainer, Jack Hendricks, Capt. Nelson, Phil Lahey, Joe Douthit, O'Connors who worked on the Canal; Storey and Keeler owners of the mill, the Washburns, Clif Haycock, Hi Leavens and his daughter Ada and grandsons, Earl & Clive Bruce and the Ash family and Mr. Black. Also the old time Woodard family.

1935 Cascade Locks becomes a city.

Capt. Charles Nelson	*Mayor*
W.L. Carlson	*Recorder*
Vera Sprague	*Treasurer*

Carl Epping, Silva Porras, Ed D. Clodfatter, Max Millsap, Julius Carlson, Mae Silva Alderman

The large sand island in the Columbia River near Cascade Locks was noted seineing ground

181

Pot fish traps were used in many places

Warren and other cannerys used fish wheels for catching salmon.

Picture taken of salmon in Warren's cannery at Warrendale, Oregon

VIENTO

Viento is a Spanish word meaning "wind" and this could be a very fitting word as across the river is "Wind Mountain" so named for the strong winds that gave it its name.

A post office was established here Jan. 24, 1896 until May 31, 1919.

The Oregon Lumber Co. had two mills up the Little White Salmon River and flumed lumber down to the Columbia River near Cook. The rough lumber was towed across the Columbia to Viento where the lumber company had a planing mill. Here the lumber was loaded onto the railway. The lumber company operated a ferry for its own accommodation between Viento and Cook for around 15 years.

WYETH

Was named for the explorer Nathaniel Wyeth, after the railroad came through. A railroad tie pickling plant operated here while the railroad was being built. The post office was established April 18, 1903 and discontinued Dec. 15, 1936.

STARVATION CREEK AND THE TRAIN

(courtesy of Ruth Guppy)

Driving down the highway in the January sunshine is a far cry from the winter of 1884-85, when winter grabbed the Columbia gorge and shook it from end to end from Dec. 10 well into January.

Thereon hangs the well-authenticated tale of how Starvation Creek, west of Viento, got its name. The facts were dug out with much research in Portland, Hood River, and The Dalles by Mrs. Bob Moller for a term history paper several years ago. We thank her for their use.

Dec. 6, 1884--Cleveland's election had just been confirmed in Oregon newspapers. At The Dalles, the Umatilla House boasted the longest bar on the coast. A paper there commented on the "delightfully spring-like weather".

Dec. 10--It began to snow hard. The wind in the gorge was a snarling hound and for three weeks the constant snow and wind were to compound miseries along the Columbia at zero temperatures.

Dec. 18--Trains halted at The Dalles by snow-clogged tracks to Portland were combined to make a run for it. There were two Northern Pacific, two Short Line and two Oregon Railroad and Navigation trains in all, with 148 passengers and crew members aboard. A train in those days consisted of the engine and nine small foot cars, running at a top speed of 25 mph.

The engines pushed to Hood River, following a clear track opened by a snow-plough. Two miles below Viento, rounding a point, the combined train hit a slide estimated at 20 to 25 feet deep.

Fortunately, passengers had eaten a meal before boarding the train at The Dalles, and most of them had packed an evening meal. The 40 emigrants in special cars had a place to cook and the equivalent of one meal left. The baggage car, it was found, contained three cases of oysters, two quarters of beef, one mutton and 50 to 75 jackrabbits.

Men passengers and crew shovelled, but another slide almost reburied the engines.

Dec. 19--Shovelling behind the stalled train allowed it to back a quarter-mile onto a trestle, out of reach of slides Word was sent on foot to Hood River, from where provisions came by sled.

According to one passenger's diary, they consisted of "...biscuits, one hog who had the misfortune of being in Hood River at the time...The food was disgusting."

Another plough and nine locomotives left The Dalles to help. The crew had to shovel at each drift, taking all day to reach Hood River. Making good time over the trestles west of here, the engineer in the front locomotive saw the warning signal on the marooned train loom through the blizzard. He jammed on the emergency brakes and halted. An engine behind was not able to stop so quickly and the resulting pile-up sent all of the following engines off the track.

Dec. 20--All relief engines were either wrecked or out of fuel and there were that many more mouths to feed. Coal gave out on the stalled train and wood had to be gathered from under the snow for stoves in the cars. Available meat was distributed to the passengers, who dug away the snow along the track and made fires to cook it. J.A. Soesby of Hood River walked back to town to arrange for food to be brought in.

Dec. 21--The first party arrived with cooked food, which was frozen when it reached the train. Groups of Hood River men were to make the trip every day for the next ten days.

Dec. 22--Food was getting low in Hood River, too. All able-bodied men left the train to walk to Portland, their feet tied in towels and sacks.

Dec. 25--(Christmas Day)--From Cascade Locks 12 men packed in the Christmas banquet: bacon, beans, canned fruits, pickles and coffee. From the west, 1,000 Portland men were hacking at the slide with picks and shovels.

Dec. 26--The train was able to back up to Viento. The adventure was costing the railroad $5,000 a day.

Jan 1--A 900-foot snow slide was reported behind the train at Mitchell point.

Jan. 2--Weather cleared some and the train moved forward to Bonneville.

Jan 6--"Chinooking" had opened the tracks somewhat. The last barrier at Oneonta gorge was broken through.

Jan. 7--The snowbound train reached Portland, after a trip from The Dalles which had taken three weeks. A passenger who kept a diary wrote:

"These daily jottings...will interest some while they teach others how much can be endured when a cracker is a blessing and a potato is a luxury; when the snow in the Cascade Mountains is 45 feet deep; when there is nothing warm among a hundred passengers except human sympathy, and nothing light but hope and a tallow candle."

*****

It was amazing that no one starved, died or was lost during those miserable three weeks. Today a tumbling 186-foot water-fall, a small creek running into the Columbia and a little state park nestle in a curve alongside the fast highway, a monument to a heroic struggle against winter in the gorge and aptly named "Starvation Creek".

*****

4 R 1910

It encourages Hood Riverophiles to know that so many show a genuine interest in our early history, such as the train incident at Starvation Creek. There are many dramatic stories in this area which can be told, and some which are best left at rest.

*****

As late as 1910, with people from the east having come in a wave of enthusiasm since 1905, Hood River was still a raw western village. There were no sidewalks, and the road to Pine Grove was by buggy over the old east side grade. The route to The Dalles was worse, dodging as it did through the back hills to Mosier and beyond. Imagine how it appeared to young brides fresh from the comparitive sophistication of the east!

*****

185

1	LANG, Julius E.	37	m	Prussia	farmer
	Rosa	37	f	Bavaria	keeps house
	MILLER, Anna	13	f	Iowa	
	Augusta	10	f	Iowa	
	Anna	8	f	Iowa	
	Albert	6	m	Ore.	
2	NEAL, Jesse	32	m	Mo.	farmer
	Lucy A.	33	f	N.Y.	keeps house
	Flora J.	10	f	Ore.	
	Jesse F.	2	m	Ore.	
3	NEAL, Peter	55	m	Tenn.	manufacturer
	Mahla	49	f	Tenn.	Keeps house
	Peter	14	m	Ore.	
	William	12	m	Ore.	
	James	9	m	Ore.	
4	TURNER, David A.	33	m	Mo.	farmer
	Mandy J.	19	f	Ore.	keeps house
	William	3	m	Ore.	
5	HOGAN, Marcus	36	m	Tenn.	farm laborer
6	NEAL, Martin	27	m	Mo.	farmer
	Margaret J.	16	f	Ohio	keeps house
7	MC KAY, Jackson C.	52	m	Ky.	manufacturer
8	PAYTON, James	37	m	Ohio	laborer
9	O'DELL, William	36	m	Tenn.	farmer
	Diona	22	f	Ore.	keeps house
	Milton	6	m	Ore.	
	James A.	5	m	Ore.	
	Emma	3	f	Ore.	
	Charles P.	2	m	Ore.	
10	FIELDS, Reuben	33	m	mo.	wks in saw mill
11	HUNTLEY, John	39	m	Ohio	laborer
12	DIVER, Daves	49	m	Va.	farmer
	Parthena	50	f	Va.	keeps house
	John O.	27	m	Va.	farming
	William	20	m	Mo.	farming
	Joel D.	23	m	Mo.	farming
	Wilheim M.	14	f	Iowa	keeps house
13	STANLEY, John	39	m	N.Y.	farmer
	Nancy	33	f	Ind.	keeps house

HOOD RIVER PRECINCT

14	HAY, William B.	39	m	Scotland	farming

15	ROBERTS, George P.	56		Tenn.	farmer
	Mary	30	f	Calif.	keeps house (Ind.)
	Laura	5	f	Ore.	(Indian breed)
	Cora	4	f	Ore.	"
	Lod	2	f	Ore.	"

16	MARDEN, John M.	41	m	Dist. of C.	farmer
	Hattie A.	28	f	Ill.	keeps house
	Virginia	9/12	f	Ore	Oct.
	REED, Benjamin	24	m	Ill.	farm laborer

17	STILWELL, William B.	44	m	N.Y.	farmer

18	BENSON, James M.	41	m	N.Y.	farmer
	Margaret	34	f	N.Y.	keeps house
	Frank	10	m	Ore.	school
	James C.	8	m	Ore.	
	Mary Bell	1	f	Ore.	
	DORNING, David R.	30	m	Scotland	teaching school

19	NYE, Michael	49	m	Pa.	farmer
	Harriet	42	f	S.C.	keeps house
	Covillard, Frank	8	m	Calif	
	CRAWFORD, Reuben	43	m	Mo.	farm labore (blk)
	Vina	35	f	Mo.	domestic "
	Harriet	8	f	Mo.	"
	William	6	m	Mo.	"
	Cupid	4	m	Mo.	"
	Susie	2	f	Calif.	"
	Frances	2/12	f	Ore.	April "
	JONES, Charles	23	m	Prussia	farm laborer

20	COE, Mary W.	67	f	N.Y.	farming
	Charles	36	m	N.Y.	farming
	Eugene F.	34	m	N.Y.	stock raising
	Roxa	22	f	Mo.	keeps house
	Henry C.	25	m	N.Y.	farming
	Mary E.	17	f	Iowa	keeps house
	LYSLE, John F.	7	m	Ore.	

21	WARD William	45	m	Ohio	farmer
	Hannah	43	f	Ohio	keeps house
	Joseph W.	18	m	Ohio	wks on farm
	Herman	14	m	Ohio	wks on farm
	John C.	10	m	Ore.	school
	Samuel P.	7	m	W.T.	
	Victor	3	m	Ore.	
	ANDREWS, Horall(?)	40	m	N.Y.	farm laborer

22	BALDWIN, Stephen	39	m	Mass.	farming
	TIEMAN, Henry	38	m	Denmark	farming

23	CORUM, Harrison	56	m	Ky.	farmer

WILLIAM JENKINS AND FAMILY
(Hood River News, June 1947)

William Jenkins came with Nathaniel Coe to this valley in June 1854. He claimed the land abandoned by Dr. Farnsworth, on which a good house had been built in 1852.

Mrs. Jenkins, accompanied by her brother, James Benson, reached her new home in November; they were both warmly welcomed in the little community, and Mrs. Coe rejoiced in the fact that she was not the only woman in the country. Early in its existence the pioneer community made provision for a school, land was donated by Mr. Jenkins and a building about fourteen by twenty feet in size, erected thereon.

Mr. and Mrs. Jenkins had two children, a boy and a girl.

A.C. Phelps lived on the west side of the valley and made oak kegs, which he shipped to The Dalles where they were used to hold whiskey, and carried on the backs of mules to the mines.

On the morning of May 14, 1864, Mr. Phelps requested Mr. Jenkins to help him transfer his load of kegs to the river steamer. The river boat would not land and the transfer was made by using a small sloop belonging to Henry Coe; James Laughlin, The Dalles, who was visiting Henry Coe, went with Mr. Phelps.

Walter Jenkins accompanied his father. He had been told to sit down several times but persisted in standing up. A sudden shift of the boom knocked him into the river; his father sprang after him and caught him as he came up, and called for help. James Laughlin threw off his coat, seized a keg and went to the rescue. He was a strong swimmer but was probably seized with cramps, for before reaching Mr. Jenkins, he abandoned the keg and turned towards the shore and soon afterwards sank. Mr. Jenkins, with his child in his arms, was still struggling in the water, and before Mr. Phelps could bring his boat around, the icy waters had closed over them.

*****

NATHAN S. BENSON AND FAMILY
(Data furnished by Bell Benson Maheur & Coe Records)

Nathan S. Benson came to Dog River in June 1854, in company with Nathaniel Coe and William Jenkins. He located a homestead on the east side of the river; it is now known as the "Button Farm".

Only a few years since, the little house which Nathan Benson built in 1854 was torn down to make room for Mr. Button's modern residence. During the summer of 1854, Nathaniel Coe and his two sons, Charles and Eugene, Wm. Jenkins and Nathan Benson were the only white inhabitants in the valley. Mrs. Coe and Henry joined them in September and Mrs. Jenkins and James Benson in November, and these were the only settlers until after the close of the Indian War in 1856.

Their daughter Florence was born in Dec. 1859, and was one of Hood River's first babies. Walter Jenkins was probably the first.

Mrs. Martha Benson was, if not the first, the second post-master in the valley. Claims for that honor are made for both W. Stillwell and Mrs. Benson but dates are not obtainable.

*****

JAMES M. BENSON AND FAMILY
(Data furnished by Mrs. Bell Benson Maheur)

James M. Benson was born in Lodi, Seneca country, New York, June 12, 1828. He arrived in Dog River, November 1854, coming with his sister, Mrs. Jenkins, from New York. Nathan Benson, an older brother, and William Jenkins, a brother-in-law, had located in this new settlement in June 1854 and already had comfortable houses built and other improvements on the way. James Benson took a homestead on Indian Creek and built a log cabin. He and Mr. Jenkins began raising stock, the bunch grass of the valley providing excellent feed.

Nathan Benson went to New York in the fall of 1858 and returned, bringing with him a wife, Mrs. Martha Benson. They were accompanied to this coast by the fiancee of James Benson, Miss Margaret Williamson. She was a native of Schenectady, New York, born in 1834.

The party came by way of the Isthmus to San Francisco, then took a steamer to Portland but were wrecked off the coast near the mouth of the Umpqua River. They reached Portland, November 30, after a voyage of 19 days from San Francisco. James M. Benson and Miss Williamson were married the same evening L.W. Coe and H.P. Isaacs were witnesses and Judge Strong performed the ceremony.

The Benson families came up the Columbia River the next day and the women began their pioneering among the lonesome pines of the Columbia Gorge. A little Indian village was located on Indian Creek when James Benson took his claim, and the Indians had continued to live there.

During the summer they were away hunting, fishing and gathering berries but when winter came, that was their home. The arrival of Mrs. James Benson caused considerable excitement among the Indian women who crowded around the house and peeped in the windows trying to get a glimpse of her. She was

189

a handsome woman and they were full of admiration and greatly pleased to be noticed by her.

On January 1st, 1859, Mr. and Mrs. S.B. Ives, Mr. and Mrs. Nathan Benson, Mr. and Mrs. James Benson were guests at a New Year's dinner given by the Coes. James Benson improved his little cabin by filling the cracks with mortar and covering the walls with house lining.

Their first visitors to take dinner with them were H.P. Isaacs and Mr. and Mrs. Cornelius McFarland of The Dalles. The tablecloth was made from four flour sacks.

On February 22, 1860, they were made glad by the arrival of a son, Francis Coe Benson, who was born in the little log cabin on Indian Creek.

William Jenkins and James Benson were partners in the stock business; early in the winter of 1861-62 they took their stock to the Powder River mines, selling all but one cow. As most of the stock east of the Cascade Mountains perished that winter, they were fortunate in disposing of their holdings early in the season.

On May 24, 1862, another son, James C. Benson was born. On May 5, 1869, a daughter, Mary Bell Benson was born at the home on Indian Creek.

In 1871 the family sold their home on Indian Creek and moved to Five Mile Creek near The Dalles where they bought a farm. The children grew up on the farm at Five Mile Creek, and the youngest son celebrated his twenty-first anniversary on May 24, 1883, with a birthday party.

On November 28, 1888, the daughter, Mary Bell Benson was married to Harry Maheur Rev. A. Brongeest officiated. They moved to Eight Mile Creek where they made their home.

James C. Benson was married to Fannie Wilerson of Portland January 1, 1896.

*****

HOOD RIVER TOWN

The town site as originally platted and laid out by H.C. and E.F Coe, consisted of four blocks near the railroad station on the donation land claim of Nathaniel Coe. To everyone who would agree to erect a building immediately, the land was given. To those who wished to purchase for future use, from $50 to $75 was asked

A prohibitory whiskey clause was inserted in each deed. Other plats were added later, and when the brothers divided the property Mr. E.F. Coe disposed of his half and abandoned the whiskey clause

John Parker erected the first building in July, 1881; T.J. Hosford erected the Mt. Hood Hotel in August, G.M. Champlin erected building in September in which he moved his stock of merchandise from the building in use on Dr W.I. Adam's farm. E.L. Smith

190

purchased an entire block, erected a two-story building and moved his merchandise from Frankton to the new town. The town continued to grow until it covered the entire donation land claim of Nathaniel Coe. To the south it reached the Parkhurst tract, which consisted of forty acres, bought from the state by the widow of Dr. Parkhurst. It lies south of the east half of the Coe claim and extends to Indian Creek. Oscar Stranahan had homesteaded land south of the west half of the Coe claim and just west of the Parkhurst tract. The demand for lots brought "Stranahan's First Addition" and later "Stranahan's Second Addition" to Hood River.

All this land is located on the Heights and May Street is near its northern boundary. On the west the town overflowed 13th Street, the eastern line of Paradise farm. This land was first claimed by Dr. Farnsworth in 1852; it was abandoned by him and claimed by Wm. Jenkins in 1854. It was sold by the widow of Wm. Jenkins in 1869 to Mitchell and Nye, who sold it to W.P. Watson in 1870. He sold it to Dr. Adams in 1876. Lyman Smith Avenue bounds it on the south.

*****

In early days, Odell, Oregon district included all the area east of Hood River. Settlers began coming to this valley closely on the heels of Oregon's admission to the Union on Feb. 14, 1859. As early as 1844, Peter Neal and Jerome Winchell came to look over the valley. They became its first settlers in 1860. In the following year two young men came up from California. Dave Turner homesteading in what is now Pine Grove, and William Squire Odell locating in the district which now bears his name. The Dave Divers family came here in 1864

*****

PINE GRO√E by Mrs. Riddle Lage

The first settlers in the area were the David Turners, who arrived in 1861. Coming with them were the Neal, Corum and Odell families, all from California. In 1864 Jerome Winchell arrived and staked a claim. This claim included the Fike place; Jerome married Neal's daughter Julia in 1865; their son Virgil was born in a log house and had the distinction of being the first white child born in the Pine Grove Community. In 1872, F.M. Jackson arrived, followed by Hans Lage and E.L. Smith in 1876. 1879 saw

191

the families of Peter Mohr, Wm. Webster Foss, Chris Dethman and Dave Divers.

In the spring of 1879, neighbors were few and far between and three fathers decided to get their families together for religious services. These three were F.M. Jackson, a Methodist; Hans Lage, a Lutheran, and D A. Turner, Methodist. They met at the Lage home and this was the beginning of the community Sunday school. Those present the first Sunday were Mr. and Mrs. F.M. Jackson and children, Lillian and William, John, Mattie and Mabry; Miss Delia Thurman, a sister of Mrs. Jackson; Mr. and Mrs. D.A. Turner and children, Warren, Roswell, Mace and Lucella; Mr. and Mrs. Hans Lage and children, Mets, Emma, Henry, Laura and Ben.

The first school building was built on the Lentz Butte, halfway between the Odell and Pine Grove school houses of today. Students walked to and from school, the distance being so great that Hans Lage offered land to build a school in the Pine Grove area. When surveyed it was found that this land was on the Feak place, now owned by Martin Dragseth. A one-room log structure was built on this location in 1887. It was named Pine Grove, for the grove trees in which it was built.

Pioneers bragged of the healthful air of the valley, and it was said that, "Pine Grove was so healthy that they had to shoot a man to start the cemetery." However, the earliest marked grave in the cemetery is that of one of the Neal girls who was buried here in 1863. The Pine Grove Cemetery is often referred to as "God's Acre."

*****

FERRYS by Eph Winans

There was a ferry operating across the Columbia when I came to Hood River in 1886. It was operated by Captain Stanley who operated from Koberg's beach to Bingen.

Ferry boating in those days was primitive. Stanley used a barge and a sail boat; the barge to haul stock and wagons and the sail boat for passengers. He died shortly after I came here and was succeeded by Gordon Palmer, who in turn was followed by Captain R.O. Evans who ran the ferry for 10 or 12 years. For a while Evans used the sail boat as prime power, but later took on a small gasoline powered boat to be used when there was no wind. It took 20 minutes, more or less, to cross under sail.

Evans sold out to J.R. Rankin, who operated the ferry service for another 10 or 12 years, and then sold to Commodore Dean. Later Dean sold out to a young fellow named Otis Treiber. Homer Van Allen was the last one to operate the ferry until the interstate bridge was built in 1925.

192

There was another ferry in operation from Underwood to Hood River, run by Captain Amos Underwood. He too used sail boats for power. Underwood's son-in-law, Captain Harry Olson, later brought in a small steam tug boat.

The Rowena ferry was started before 1900 by Andy Pearson--he ban Swede like Captain Olson. He had both sail and gasoline powered ferries.

GEORGE GINNE-DEE-AH

Indian George had a nice piece of ground on the Yakima Reservation and the Indian agent sold the acreage for $1,200.

Both banks here wanted to handle the money as guardians. The money was placed in the Butler & Co. Bank. Since George was unable to read or write, he had to sign his checks with his thumb print. Henderson, an attorney, was chosen to manage George's business. When George wanted a little money, usually five or ten cents, he would take a blank check to Henderson to have it filled out for the five or ten cents and then plant his thumb print on it and take it to the bank and cash it.

*****

Hood River Valley was still a raw and primitive land when I came here in the 1880's. There was little in the way of commercial fruit production here then. Most of the valley was in virgin timber. It wasn't until around 1893 that E.L. Smith set out around 30 acres of apples on his place on Dethman Ridge, a ranch he called "Beulah Land". About the same time Sears and Porter set out around five acres of commercial orchard on the East side, less than a mile south of Panorama Point, as I recall. The favorite apple then was the Spitzenberg.

Logging was a leading endeavor in Hood River Valley as in other areas of the Columbia River Gorge. A great productive area was just being scratched so lightly by mankind.

Life those days was pretty tough. And the men were tough, too, whether honest or on the shady side. They were hardened to a wild life and they made the most of it with what they had.

Why, in those early days you did not dare let a calf or colt graze all night. If you did, a cougar was bound to get your animal. My brother, W.R. Winans, had a pig in a pen about 100 yards from the house, well before the turn of the century, and one day while he and his family were at dinner they heard the old sow squealing. My brother ran out with a rifle, and what do you think he saw? A big bear had the sow in its paws and was eating her alive!

MRS. ENGLISH TELLS COUGAR YARN

Mrs. Dolly English, a grand young girl who was born here in the valley in the 1870's, can tell you what it was like.

"We had plenty of cougars in the old days," she says. "If i weren't for our hound dogs, I'm sure that the cougars would have eaten up we children."

"Davis Divers, my grandfather, had a blacksmith shop where the Dittbenner store is now on the river road. One day in the early 1870's a cougar prowled in the shop while my grandfather was hard at work. Grandfather's back was to the door and he never heard the cougar until "whang"--the cougar jumped on his back!

"Grandfather squirmed away and laid to the cougar with his blacksmith hammer, left and right. The cougar proved no match for grandfather, who escaped with some bad scratches.

"In our fishery above The Dalles back in the early 1890's, we employed a carpenter by the name of Z.T. Jones. He was a rough, crooked Nova Scotian who worked on a wheel. He worked for us for awhile and then decided to quit in the summer of 1893, for a new enterprise.

"He bought 25 or 30 head of hogs and built a pen alongside of Harrick's cannery in The Dalles Harrick, as you recall, was the man who bought those hundreds of head of horses from young Kamiaken and canned horse meat for the French Army. Kamiaken got the horses by promising the Indians a Chinook wind (which he knew about through a telegraph message sent to him in Yakima from Portland).

"Well, this fellow Z.T. Jones had the intention of fattening his hogs on the fish heads among the refuse from Harrick's cannery. Of course the hogs there added to the infernal stench already coming from the cannery, and the people living and working in The Dalles were anything but happy.

"The city marshal (I forget whether it was John Crate or Bert Thurston) came down one day and said to our former employee: "Now, listen here, Jones, you'll have to move those hog pens. You are stinking the town out."

"Jones readily agreed to move. But, by the next week, the stench was still there and the marshal came down and said: "I thought I told you to move those hogs?"

"I did move 'em," returned Jones.

"But all he had done was to build another pen alongside the one already built and had then moved his hogs over a few feet. So, he says to the marshal: 'What are you going to do about it? I obeyed orders'.

"All the marshal said was: "I'll be d....d!" And he let it go at that.

194

"Later on Jones talked a butcher in The Dalles into buying all the hogs. Soon some of the hogs were butchered and hung up for sale. But the flavor of the fish and pork didn't go together. The butcher finally moved the hogs out to Dufur and there the animals were fed on grain for three months by which time they had lost their spicy fish flavor."

Mosier   Census 1870

1	McClure,	William	52	m	Tenn.	farmer
		Amelia	48	f	Ky.	keeps house
		Thomas J.	23	m	Mo.	farmer
		William T.	20	m	Mo.	wks on farm
		James	74	m	Ky.	farmer (was in war of 1812)
2	Easterbrook James		33	m	R.I.	farmer
3	Parodi, Barhalow		42	m	Italy	farmer
4	Pitney, Abigah		20	m	Ore.	wks on farm
5	Clary, John		30	m	Ireland	farmer
		Mary	21	f	Ore.	keeps house
		John D.	3	m	Ore.	
		Mary E.	1	f	Ore.	
6	Schidaman, Christian		55	m	Hanover	wks on farm
7	Lawley, Lewis W.		39	m	Ala.	farmer
8	Miles, James		45	m	Va.	farmer
		Nancy	40	f	Ohio	keeps house
		Alminia	15	f	Iowa	
		Viola	14	f	Iowa	
		Douglas	12	m	Iowa	
		John	10	m	Iowa	
9	Graham, Francis		22	m	Mo.	wks on farm
		Sarah F.	18	f	Ore.	keeps house
10						
10	Jones, Henry		43	m	Ohio	wks on farm
11	Smith, George H.		29	m	Mo.	wks on farm
		Eliza	38	f	Eng.	keeps house
12	Lawernce, Nicholas		35	m	Ill.	farmer

195

13	Mosier,	Jonah H.	49	m	Pa.	farmer
		Martha J.	30	f	Ky.	keeps house
		Emily	18	f	Mo.	
		Mary	15	f	Ore.	
		Josephine	13	f	Ore.	school
		Benjamin	11	m	Ore.	school

1918

In order to supply the quartermaster department with several thousand gallons of vinegar, the total output of the Hood River Vinegar Co. . . . for the next 30 days has been commandeered by the government.

*****

MOSIER

Jonah H. Mosier (original spelling Mozer), youngest of six children, was born March 10, 1821, in Pennsylvania. He married Miss Jane Rollins in 1846 at Paradise, Clay County, Miss. He and his family joined an emigrant train heading for Oregon, arriving in The Dalles in the fall of 1852. At that time only two buildings were in evidence with tents comprising the rest of the town.

Building materials apparently were as hard to obtain then as now, for history tells us Mr. Mosier, seeing the great need for lumber, cast about for a location for a mill site. In 1854 a sawmill was erected 16 miles west of The Dalles on a stream tributary to the Columbia. Thus the present won and that tributary dervied their names from the founder of the mill and became known as Mosier Creek and Mosier Landing during the steamboat days.

Three times the mill was washed away by spring freshets, the last time being about 1858. By then Mr. Mosier had become discouraged with his bad luck and quit the lumber business.

After going out of the lumber business, Mr. and Mrs. Mosier took up a 320 acre land donation claim. The death of Mrs. Mosier followed in 1865, leaving him seven young children. The following year while on a cattle buying trip to the Willamette Valley, he

196

married a young widow with three children. To this union two more children were born, making an even dozen to help populate the valley of Mosier.

Following the death of Jonah Mosier in 1894, his son, Jefferson N. Mosier, bought out the interests of the other heirs and the present town of Mosier was platted.

The first school in the valley was a one-room affair built by Jonah Mosier next to their dwelling and George James Ryan was hired as the first teacher, a position he held for the next 14 years. This was in 1864. The school term in those days was from January 1 to December 31 with half a day off on Saturdays. The Fourth of July and Christmas were recognized as the only full holidays. In the latter years of this school, Mandy McClure and the three Bradshaw children living in Washington Territory, attended this school by rowing across the Columbia morning and evening.

The next school, and the first public one in the valley, was held in a homesteader's cabin one half mile northeast of the present home of T.M. Morgansen. This school was for a three-month term, taught by Miss Cordelia Therman in 1874. About the same type of school was held in a one-room log cabin on the Mosier homestead about $1\frac{1}{2}$ miles east of town. It was taught by the Rev. Garrison of Hood River. This was also a three-month term and 12 pupils were in attendance.

The first schoolhouse was built of logs. A one-room building built about 1884, it was approximately $1\frac{1}{2}$ miles east of Mosier (or where Mosier now stands). Miss Julia Meyers was the first teacher in this building. Some of the children walked as far as seven miles.

The first regular church meetings were held by William Mitchell of The Dalles. His first meetings were held in the woods about one-half mile southeast of where the Marsh family now lives. This was about 1880. In the fall the services were moved to the McClure home. The next summer the services were also held out of doors. Church was held in a log cabin on the Milner place four miles east of town until the log school was built.

J.J. Lynch was the first railroad agent after the road came here in 1882. He put up a building across the track from the depot and thus the first store came to Mosier. Mr. Lynch was also the first postmaster of Mosier.

The first white people to come to Mosier Valley to live was the Jonah Mosier family in 1854. The next family to arrive was the Marshall family. They took up a donation land claim where the C.D.M. ranch is now located. The next to arrive was the Bradshaw family. They lived on the Marshall place now in the possession of Mosier (or, to keep the records straight, in the possession of Mr.

Mosier at that time). Then a Mr. Smith and wife moved up on Mosier Creek near the Fisher place and operated a sawmill. Little is known of these three families except they were living here in 1868.

The W.C. McClure family came here in 1866 and took up a homestead $3\frac{1}{2}$ miles east of Mosier. Mr. McClure was a stock raiser. James Milner arrived in 1867 and took up a homestead to the east of Mosier, now owned by Mr. and Mrs. T.M. Morgansen.

A family by the name of Reynolds moved onto the Mosier place after the Bradshaw family had moved away. Next to arrive in the valley was John Marden, who resided on the Middleswart place, now owned by William McClure, descendant of W.C. McClure. Next came Mr. Schiedeman, who lived on the same place after Marden moved away. Thompson was the next to move onto the same place.

The Bills family moved into the valley, first living on the Mosier place, then taking up a homestead five miles east of Mosier, now known as Hog Canyon. The Dunsmore family, descendants of the Bills, are still living in the valley. Lakden Lamb arrived in 1877 and took up the place now owned by J.O. Beldin.

The Amos Root family arrived in 1878 and bought a place three miles east of Mosier. The place is still owned by Mr. Root's heirs. Howard Root is on the place at present. Joe Stranby first lived on the place later owned by the J.W. Wilcox family and now owned by Bessie and Frank Marsh.

A Mrs. Blakney arrived about 1869 and purchased the place later to be known as Mayer Park, but better known today as the lookout on the top of Rowena Loops. All these pioneers arrived before the completion of the railroad in 1882. The first death to occur in the valley was Dick Marshall. He was buried under a large oak tree by the lake on the old Marshall place.

Before the coming of the railroad, water transportation was used as well as team and wagon. The Dalles was the closest postoffice, which was about 16 miles by the old state road, so in the fall of the year the pioneers would buy their food supplies to last till the roads were open in the spring.

The first commercial fruit orchard to be planted for dry farming was set out by Amos Root. Jefferson N Mosier, son of Jonah Mosier, built his family home in 1904. This house is now owned and occupied by Mrs Ethel Bruce.

Post office was established Jan. 1, 1884.

THE DALLES
The Indian name WASCO was a word for basin and was named for a basin the solid rock with a spring coming up in the basin. Wasco Pum is Wasco People in their language. The mission called the spring 'Mission Spring'.

1	MC CLURE, William	52	m	Tenn.	farmer
	Amelia	48	f	Ky.	keeps house
	Thomas J.	23	m	Mo.	farmer
	William T.	20	m	Mo.	wks on farm
	James	74	m	Ky.	farmer (war 1812)
2	EASTERBROOK, James	33	m	R.I.	farmer
3	PARODI, Barhelow	42	m	Italy	farmer
4	PITNEY, Abigale	20	m	Ore.	farm laborer
5	CLARY, John	30	m	Ireland	farmer
	Mary	21	f	Ore.	keeps house
	John D.	3	m	Ore.	
	Mary E.	1	f	Ore.	
6	SCHIDAMAN, Christian	55	m	Hanover	farm laboer
7.	LAWLEY, Lewis W.	39	m	Ala.	farmer
8	MILES, James	45	m	Va.	farmer
	Nancy	40	f	Ohio	keeps house
	Alminia	15	f	Iowa	
	Viola	14	f	Iowa	
	Fouglas	12	m	Iowa	
	John	10	m	Iowa	
9	GRAHAM, Francis	22	m	Mo.	farm laborer
	Sarah F.	18	f	Ore.	keeps house
10	JONES, Henry	43	m	Ohio	farm laborer
11	SMITH George H.	29	m	Mo.	farm laborer
	Eliza	38	f	England	keeps house
12	LAWRENCE, Nicholas J.	35	m	Ill.	farmer
13	MOSIER, Jonah H.	49	m	Pa.	farmer
	Martha J.	30	f	Ky.	keeps house
	Emily	18	f	Mo.	
	Mary	15	f	Ore.	
	Josephine E.	13	f	Ore.	school
	Benjamin F.	11	m	Ore.	school
	Jefferson	9	m	Ore.	
	Lydia	6	f	Ore.	
	Effie	2	f	Ore.	
	Kate	1	f	Ore.	
	LEWIS, James	12	m	Ore.	
	Emma	9	f	Ore.	
	Ida	8	f	Ore.	
	RYAN, George J.	65	m	Ireland	school teacher

The name Dalles is from the French word dalle, meaning flag-stone; the narrows here ran through flag-stone.

Harbor Rock or Witness Rock at the mouth of Mill Creek just west of the olde Umatilla House on the sand beach, where for years the ferry boat landed. It was the reference for all government surveys in the early days. The U.S. Geological survey started here in 1850.

The neighborhood of Mill Creek was called Quenett by the Indians, which was a word for Salmon trout Lewis and Clark camped at the mouth of this stream on October 25, 26 and 27, 1805, and recorded the form Que-nett in their journal.

Celilo may have come from the name of the Indian tribe Si-le-lah who lived near the falls. The Indians used a throat guttural sound in their native tongue, that was difficult for the white man to plainly say, so many of these names were recorded a little off-key.

The Celilo Falls were submerged under backwater of The Dalles Dam, March 16, 1957.

The Dalles was the end of the Oregon Trail, the longest road in human history. The first settlers could go no further with their ox teams and wagon, here they built rafts or hired flat sail boats or take their wagons and supplies down the river and drove their stock over the Indian trails to Vancouver or the Willamette Valley.

In the days of the bateau, before roads came in to being along the Columbia, this area east was known as "The Narrows" and from here west, as "The Gorge".

When the name Dalles became the used name until about 1860 when "the" was used as an attachment, "The Dalles", and as the place grew into more aristocracy after 1860 the "The" was capitalized and known as "The Dalles".

M.N. Cashing established a post office here in 1853, then called Dalles.

In the 1870's one would leave Portland on board a steamer at 4 or 5 in the A.M., have breakfast on board for 25 cents and arrive at the Lower Cascades around 11 A.M. The little portage train would be waiting. The passengers during good weather would walk ashore as it required some time to wheel the freight up the incline on hand trucks to the railroad freight car.

The small locomotive whistled and the passengers climbed aboard the elegant, light colored passenger coach and then the train moved the 6 miles to the Upper Cascades. There everything was unloaded and put aboard the middle river boat while the passengers waited. Some spent their time walking around and looking at the rapids, some went to the Bush Hotel for a drink and lunch. Whatever they did, they had an hour or two to kill before the boat whistled to come aboard. It would be evening before the boat whistled for The Dalles.

Here one must find a place to spend the night. The choice, the Cosmopolitan Hotel or the Umatilla House. If you were lucky you might share the room with a stranger. One hundred and twenty-three rooms and two baths. This was O.K. because bath tubs were rarities, an 1880 survey showed that 5 out of 6 dwellings in American cities had no bath tubs. There were no bathing facilities in the White House until Jackson became president.

Times were changing fast. The Gettysberg address contains 266 words; The Ten Commandments, 297 words; The Declaration of Independence, 300 words; O.P.S. order to reduce the price of cabbage contains 26,911 words.

In 1900 an ad read: "I X L Restaurant where you can get as good a meal for 15 cents as you will have to pay 25 cents for elsewhere."

Two promoters settled in The Dalles and were running ads in eastern papers selling stock in developments at Grand Dalles. Their dishonest ads showed a large shoe factory and other developments at the barren Grand Dalles. A woman who had bitten on these ads and had invested several thousands of dollars, came west to see what she had invested her money in. When she saw that nothing had been built, she went into the harness shop and purchased a black-snake whip and walked into the shyster's place of business with the whip and they both ran out into the street with her whipping them. The streets were lined with cowboys and teamsters cheering the lady on and keeping the shysters from getting away from her. She whipped them out of town and they were never seen again.

In 1862 The Dalles to Celilo portage was in operation and The Dalles to Grand Dalles ferry was in operation, a sort of a sailing barge that was propelled by 8 Indian oarsmen when the wind failed to blow.

Company Hollow received its name when J.C. Ainsworth and the O.S.N. completed the portage road, passengers were hauled by teams to the portage and the company's horses were pastured in the hollow.

Dillon was a railway station near Celilo and was named for an army officer, Captain T.H. Dillon.

The Indian name for the Deschutes was Towahnahiooks, the French fur traders called it 'Riviere des Chutes'. In 1852, Olney established a ferry at the mouth of the Deschutes. Edward Craig said he paid $1 for 12 corn seeds.

1879 a big fire started while filling lamps at the Pioneer Hotel and burned much of the business of The Dalles. Monty Attwell engineer on the railroad told of pushing several car loads of burning wool down the incline into the river to quench their fire. Damage to the town was estimated at $200,000.

The Dalles started becoming of age, large wheat and cattle ranches to the south, Seufert's salmon cannery and the transcontinental railroad, it soon deserved the capital "The" before Dalles. It now has fine historical museums and library and a nice business district.

CHENOWETH CREEK

Justin Chenoweth arrived at the Dalles in 1849 and settled at the west edge of Chenoweth Creek. He contracted to carry the mail from the Cascades to the Dalles and return by sail boat.

ROWENA

A post office was established here in 1911 until 1916. Rowena Dell...between Rowena and Mosier was first known as Hog Canyon. Hogs had been allowed to run wild in the canyon living on acorns and rattlesnakes or anything they could find for a number of years.

1902 YACOLT FIRE

Several stories have been told of how this great fire started; one that lightning set the first fire, but others tell that it was a man or boy started. An old settler says that two young boys at Bonneville started the holocaust while trying to burn out a yellow jackets nest; another old timer says that it was a steamboat crew that was loading wood aboard for fuel near Eagle Creek. Yellow Jackets with a nest close to the wood pile, considered it their wood, or at least their territory, so they set their stingers into several of the workers, who in turn started a fire around the hostile nest hoping to burn them out. The grass and brush was dry and the fire soon got out of hand with a stiff wind behind it.

The fire swept into the timber covered mountain, destroying everything in its path, creating disaster at Bridal Veil. Racing to the top of the mountains back of Cascade Locks, the terrific drafts caused by the great heat, uprooted burning trees, hurling them a thousand feet into the air, carrying them across the Columbia and starting fires on the north bank in Washington.

Frank Richards told, "The 1902 Yacolt Burn Fire burned around north of Stevenson. It was so smokey around the Richards' place that we had to take blankets down to the creek and wet them, take sticks and make like tents of wet blankets, and then crawl under them so we could breathe."

Phoebe Lindsay Yoe tells, "We were living at Cascade Locks and my parents decided to take us to The Dalles on a steamboat. The boat crew had to keep pumps running and spray water over the steamboat while going up the center of the river as burning limbs and wood were falling down on the steamer."

There were no telephones in this area and the air was so full of smoke that you couldn't see the sun, so no one knew just how far the fire had reached. The skies were so darkened with the heavy smoke that the chickens went to roost at noon. Ashes fell like snow flakes, only they were hot and light. Many homesteaders were wiped out, leaving their homes and racing to streams, immersing in the water. The fire would race up a mountain and jump across a canyon, trapping wild animals and people alike. The forest in the fire's path was virgin timber with trees 500 years old and 6 feet in diameter and often 200 feet high.

One can not picture the tremendous damage done by a forest fire of this caliber unless you were there. The heat is so great that green giant fir trees will explode as if blasted apart with dynamite from the sudden steam pressure built up inside the carcass and with loud reports like gunfire. The wind draft is so great from the tremendous heat that burning trees will be carried upward several hundred feet above the mountain tops, rock mountains will have their faces molten. Deer, as fast as they are, can not outrun this kind of fire.

Families loaded wagons and started leaving many areas, soon hearing the roar of the fire overtaking them, they hastily turned the horses loose and ran to the nearest creek and covered themselves with wet blankets. A creek bed was the only place left to go, the creek often had worn a small canyon for its creek bed, and often alder or willows grew along its banks and they remained green the year around and did not readily burn from falling embers. Some might get a little sleep while others stayed awake, but all had sore eyes from the smoke.

Thirty-eight bodies were found in Lewis River alone; up Wind River pitiful evidence was found among the ashes of fallen timber blocking the only road, nine charred bodies along with harness buckles, iron from wagons attested the fate of the unlucky party.

One half million acres of timber ravaged by the fire. The holocaust was first called the Yacolt-Cispus Burn but now known as the Yacolt Burn. It is said, "Besides destroying water sheds, that the timber loss has amounted to $10 million each year in timber production."

Natural Resources now have taken action to prevent future great fires. Ken Herman, Bill Baxter, Frank Murphy and others with crews of honor camp's prisoners have fallen snags. The Larch Mountain crews have fallen 19,200 snags and the Washougal crews,

21,135 snags, planted 3,608,875 young trees by the end of 1967. They have built fire roads zig-zagging through the Yacolt Burn area and are still continuing this good work while also rehabilitating prisoners into a better way of life.